The Palace or the Poorhouse:

The American House as a Cultural Symbol

The Palace or the Poorhouse:

The American House as a Cultural Symbol

by Jan Cohn

THE MICHIGAN STATE UNIVERSITY PRESS

East Lansing

Copyright © 1979

Jan Cohn

Library of Congress Catalog Card Number: 79-0130

ISBN: 0-87013-211-3

★
 ★
 ★
 ★
  ★
   ★

Manufactured in the United States of America

We can't put it all on the conditions; we must put some of the blame on character. But conditions *make* character; and people are greedy and foolish, and wish to have and to shine, because having and shining are held up to them by civilization as the chief good of life . . . [we] go moiling and toiling on to the palace or the poor-house. We can't help it.

William Dean Howells
A Hazard of New Fortunes

Contents

Preface

A number of years ago, a random assortment of books I was reading to prepare for my classes fell together into a suggestive trio: *The Rise of Silas Lapham, The Great Gatsby,* and *Absalom, Absalom!* In all three novels, the protagonist's house was developed as a controlling symbol. The symbol, too, seemed to have a similar force for each of the authors, representing the false values and ideals foolishly and sometimes fatally pursued by Lapham, Gatsby, and Thomas Sutpen. These parallels intrigued me; I thought about houses in other American novels— in Hawthorne and James, in Edith Wharton and Willa Cather. I reread some Cooper, I reconsidered the Naturalists. The house kept reappearing, but now other symbolic values became apparent, emphasizing the ideal of home, of the family homestead, the simple cottage. In addition to the anti-materialist message of my original threesome, I also found a sentimental separation of the house from concepts of economic success and social position.

After a number of months, I became curious about conceptions of the house outside fiction. I began reading a wide assortment of American materials. I went through histories and autobiographies, travel literature and letters. I examined studies of American architecture, scholarly and popular, as well as lavishly illustrated volumes of "notable," "famous," "historic," houses. The monthly magazines, too, carried essays on houses, average houses, excessive houses, vulgar houses. It seemed at last that every notable, famous, or historic American had made statements about the house in America, from Abraham Lincoln to Emily Post, from P. T. Barnum to Herbert Hoover.

What I had discovered in this reading was a set of assumptions and ideals about the house in America parallel to, but richer

than, what the novelists had suggested. The house appeared, as it
had in fiction, as the emblem of false materialism; it appeared,
as well, as the emblem of family and security. But other values
were also discoverable, conflicting and confusing values. What
some called materialism, others labeled the American Dream.
For them a fine house signalled the success a man had earned
with industry and preserved with thrift. By extension, a town, a
city, even a nation, with many fine houses was demonstrably a
town or a city or a nation with industrious and thrifty citizens.
Industrious citizens in good houses, furthermore, were property
owners, and by the latter half of the nineteenth century a good
many Americans, alarmed by urban violence and radical politics,
saw in the property-owning house-holder the bulwark of American society.

It was not long before our family trips were routed to include
visits to famous houses, houses celebrated for their age, for their
architectural beauty, for their historic association, for the men
who lived in them. For the long miles between notable houses,
we turned to not-so-notable houses; for cities less fortunate,
architecturally, than Boston or Philadelphia, and towns where
no presidents or poets were born, frequently boast an "old" house,
or perhaps a replica of an original settler's cabin. A tourist may
wander across the country from Mount Vernon and Monticello,
to the house where Jesse James was shot, to the mansion of a
sugar magnate in San Francisco. The fascination that brings
Americans to the Mark Twain house in Hartford and the Eisen-
hower home in Abilene is compounded of curiosity and nostalgia.
In London or Paris, a simple plaque on the wall of a building
announces the birthplace or residence of some famous personage.
But in America, the emotional juncture of architecture and
biography demands the enshrining of the house. In fact, in cases
where no house stands to satisfy the historic and sentimental
need, reconstructions are not uncommon. One can, for example,
visit an authentic replica of the birthplace of George Washington,
although that house was destroyed two centuries ago and no
records exist to tell us what it looked like.

Nostalgia and the attempt to define a national history have
created more house-shrines in America than in any other country
in the world. But nostalgia and sentimental history themselves
conflict with progress in the complex symbolism of the American

house. In the eighteenth century, wealthier sons of wealthy fathers replaced mansions and manor houses with something better, newer, larger. When log cabins first became the typical housing of the frontier settlement, personal and public pride demanded that they be replaced as soon as possible with "permanent" houses—better, newer, larger. And in the growing cities, each generation saw the fashionable set abandon their homes and move further east, or west, or uptown, to build their own better and newer and larger houses. As new architectural styles were introduced throughout the nineteenth century, each promoted as more suited to the life of American society, houses in outworn styles lost their attraction and fell into disfavor—until they were rediscovered. Seen through the eyes of nostalgia, they became evidence of a lost America, more innocent, more moral, more genteel.

It is the thesis of this study that the house has been, and continues to be, the dominant symbol for American culture. The complexities and the contradictions inherent in the symbol are the complexities and contradictions inherent in American culture. Therefore, to examine what Americans have said about houses, their own and those of other men, is to examine what Americans have said about their culture. In the writings of politicians and reformers, anarchists and feminists, sentimental novelists and social utopians, hucksters and poets, the American house appears and reappears, a potent and flexible resource available for the needs of each.

In the writing of this book, I have moved far from my original focus on the American novel; in the development and the enrichment of the house symbol, novelists have been no more than participants in a general cultural process. I have also moved far from my own professional field of American literature, never unaware of the special dangers of foreign territory. I have tried to read all the materials I have found, therefore, in two ways: as if they were all "literature," to be scrutinized for subleties of rhetoric and shades of tone; and as if they were all "documents," equally valid records of the history of cultural ideas.

Finally, I must add the obvious—that no such study would pretend to being definitive. The house is pervasive in American writing and the examples I cite by no means exhaust our cultural repertory of observations and evaluations, celebrations and lamentations, promises and threats. The interested reader will, I hope, discover or recall examples of his own.

I am grateful to the National Endowment for the Humanities for providing me the Fellowship under which this book was completed.

The Background: 1607-1850

Chapter One

The House in Colonial America

*Being thus passed the vast ocean, and a sea of
troubles before in their preparation . . . they had
now no friends to wellcome them, nor inns to
entertaine or refresh their weatherbeaten bodys,
no houses or much less townes to repaire too,
to seeke for succoure.*
    William Bradford, *Of Plymouth Plantation*

When settlements were first underway and plantations initially
undertaken at Jamestown and Plymouth and Boston, the planters
and adventurers confronted "a hidious and desolate wildernes,
ful of wild beasts & willd men."[1] With housing non-existent and
shelter a desperate necessity, the settlers pitched tents, threw
up hasty shelters on the model of English huts, even burrowed
into the hillsides. More substantial protection from the weather,
from wild animals, and Indian attacks came soon after; accounts
of the earliest settlements speak of the building of houses among
the first and most pressing work that fell to the colonists.

A number of the earliest accounts of settlement mention the
urgent need to erect shelters. Edward Johnson, for example, describes the hardships the colonists faced in Concord, Massachusetts.

> . . . after they have thus found out a place of aboad, they burrow
> themselves into the Earth for their first shelter under some Hill-side,
> casting the Earth aloft upon Timer; they make a smoaky fire against
> the Earth at the highest side, and thus these poore servants of
> Christ provide shelter for themselves, their Wives and their little
> ones, keeping off the short showers from the Lodgings, but the
> long raines penetrate through, to their great disturbance in the
> night season: yet in these poore Wigwams they sing Psalmes, pray
> and praise their God, till they can provide them houses, which
> ordinarily was not wont to be with many till the Earth, by the
> Lords blessing, brought forth Bread to feed them, their Wives and
> little ones. . . .[2]

Elsewhere, shelter was altogether lacking. John Smith wrote of Virginia in 1607 that while the planters were awaiting their first supplies from England, they were sickly and dying, for "Our drink was water; our lodging, castles in the air."[3] Even when fairly substantial houses were first built, some settlers, those with limited means, remained in temporary shelters. John Winthrop, in a Journal entry for February 10, 1631, commented on the death and disease rate among the ill-housed. "The poorer sort of people (who lay long in tents, etc.) were much afflected with the scurvy, and many died, especially at Boston and Charles-town. . . ."[4]

The entry from Winthrop's Journal confounds two elements in American mythology. For one thing, the Journal entry conflicts with a popular belief in egalitarian communities of settlers, particularly in the North. Another problem centers around the log cabin. Despite H. R. Shurtleff's major study, *The Log Cabin Myth* (1939), Americans continue to imagine the earliest English settlers cutting down trees and piling the trunks up to create picturesque log cabins. But the English settlers were totally ignorant of log-cabin construction. Furthermore, the skills necessary to build frame houses in the traditional medieval style the colonists were familiar with were not skills in the repertory of every settler. In new settlements, carpenters were in great demand; occasional sources noted the necessity to fix carpenters' wages which had responded to the laws of supply and demand.

> It was ordered, that carpenters, joyners, bricklayers, sawers, and thatchers shall not take above 2s a day, nor any man shall giue more vnder paine of xs to taker and giver and that sawers shall not take aboue 4s 6d the hundred for boards, att 6 scoote to the hundred, if they haue their wood felled and squared for them, and not aboue 5s 6d if they fell and square their wood themselues.[5]

Accounts of early American settlements frequently offered specific information about housing. A good number of substantial houses was a sign of progress, promising the success of a town or village. Not all forms of shelter, however, deserved to be called "houses," for the vocabulary of seventeenth century Englishmen reserved that term for a framed dwelling built in the English fashion. A bit later the term was emended to an "English," "fair," or "framed" house, as the unmodified noun began to take on a more generalized meaning. The simpler and less permanent shelters the colonists erected at first were called "huts," "cabins," "cottages," "booths," or from the Indians, "wigwams."[6] When a writer attempted to describe an American town for an English audience in the seventeenth or eighteenth century, the differentiation in terms was significant.

> The town of *Savannah* was laid out, and began to be built, in which are now 142 Houses, and good habitable Huts.

> . . . [in] the Town of *Ebeneezer,* which thrives very much . . . there are very good Houses built for each of the Minesters, and an Orphan-House; and they have partly framed Houses and partly Huts, neatly built, and formed into regular streets. . . .[7]

An often-quoted passage from Johnson's *Wonder-Working Providence* dramatizes the distinction between houses and other cruder forms of habitation.

> Further, the Lord hath been pleased to turn all the wigwams, huts, and hovels the English dwelt in at their first coming, in to orderly, fair, and well-built houses, well furnished many of them, together with Orchards filled with goodly fruit trees, and gardens with variety of flowers. . . .[8]

Although the meanest huts and hovels might mark the beginning of society's encroachment on the wilderness, true houses meant much more than this; structures that took time and effort to erect signified permanence. They represented, furthermore, a decisive grip on the land, a solid entrenchment in the continent.

Houses were a proof of civilization; conversely, poor shelters were an index to colonial failure. Malcontents who published pamphlets attacking the colonies pointed to the inadequacy of housing in the settlements. One defense against these attacks took the form of an admission of the rough and unprepossessing shelters of the early settlements, but turned the writer's scorn on the foolish expectations of the denigrators. What could these men have expected in a wilderness, asked William Wood in 1633.

> I have myself heard some say, that they heard it was a rich land, a brave country; but when they came there, they could see nothing

but a few canvass booths and old houses, supposing at the first to
have found walled towns, fortifications, and corn-fields, as if towns
could have built themselves, without the husbandry of man. These
men, missing their expectations, returned home and railed against
the country.[9]

Other writers chose to assert colonial success by the number of
dwellings in a settlement. Edward Johnson, for example, presented a tally for Charlestown, Massachusetts, in 1631: "it hath
a large Market-place near the water side built round with
Houses, comly and faire, forth of which there issues two streetes
orderly built with some very faire Houses, beautified with pleasant Gardens and Orchards, the whole Towne consists in its
extent of about 150 dwelling Houses."[10]
Contention over the success or failure of the plantations on
the southern coast gave rise to a number of these defenses. The
difficulties of the first years of the Jamestown settlement received
a good deal of publicity in England, and a number of the historical narratives written by Captain John Smith defended the
Virginia settlements and Jamestown particularly against charges
of hopeless failure. Like William Wood, Smith castigated those
critics whose expectations were fanciful, as "Being for the most
part of such tender educations and small experience in martiall
accidents: because they found not English cities, not such faire
houses, nor at their own wishes any of the accustomed dainties,
with feather beds and downe pillowes. . . . For the country was
to them a miserie, a ruine, a death, a hell. . . ." Smith asserted
that, although there had been dissension and difficulty in the
first months of the settlement, three months of industry in 1609
had brought about marked changes: "we made 3 or 4 Last of
pitch, and tarre, and sope ashes; produced a triall of glasse; made
a well in the forte of excellent sweete water, which teill then was
wanting; built some 20 houses; recouered our church. . . ."[11]
While most writers managed their defenses of the early settlements by counting the dwellings, one colonist chose instead to
describe the American house. John Hammon, in his praise of
Virginia and Maryland—*Leah and Rachel . . . the Two Fruitfull
Sisters* (1656)—did not boast of any one grand house, but talked
instead of the ordinary house, the typical house. He is the first
to find a special quality in what might, two hundred years later,
be sentimentally described as "cottage architecture."

Pleasant in their building, which although for the most part they are but one story besides the loft, and built of wood, yet contrived so delightful, that your ordinary houses in England are not so handsome, for usually the rooms are large, daubed and whitelimed, glazed and flowered, and if not glazed windows, shutters which are made very pretty and convenient.[12]

In this description from the middle of the seventeenth century, the ordinary, average house with its "convenient" and "delightful" qualities began to assume a special connection with the progress of civilization in America.

As the earliest settlers erected houses to answer their urgent need for shelter and as writers produced pamphlets and histories to justify and praise the experiments in colonization occurrring on the eastern coast, one vitally significant value began to attach itself to the house in America: the house came to stand as a real and visible index of community success. In the development of American culture, the house would become more and more representative of individual success, but this was not the case at the very first. In fact, scattered pieces of evidence reveal strong disapproval for individuals who built houses of any pretension whatever; such houses wasted precious time and labor on personal aggrandizement rather than on communal progress.

Early difficulties in the settlement of Jamestown illustrate the unpopularity of such architectural excess. John Smith collected materials from a number of different writers on the Jamestown settlement and included them in his own published works. In both *The Proceedings of the English Colonie in Virginia* and *The Generall Historie of Virginia, New England, and the Summer Isles*, Captain Smith cited the special evidence of his own masterful role in bringing the settlement from disorder and lethargy to order and industry. Having been set to the management of all "things abroad", Smith, "by his owne example, good words, and faire promises, set some to mow, others to bind thatch; some to build houses, others to thatch them; himself alwaies bearing the greatest taske for his own share: So that, in short time, he provided them lodgings, neglecting any for himself." The untiring and selfless labor attributed to John Smith was made more distinctive by contrast with the behavior of Ratcliffe, "thier sillie President that had riotously consumed the store; and to fulfill his follies, [set] about building him an vnnecessarie pallas in the woodes. . . ." In an election in 1608, Smith replaced Ratcliffe as president: "Now the building of Ratcliffes pallas staide, as a thing needlesse: the church was repaired, the storehouse, re-couered: [and] building prepared for the supply we expected."[13] Not only did the "pallas" emblemize the folly of Ratcliffe, but the forced abandonment of its construction brought harmony and diligence to the community, which now set about the building of useful structures.

A quarter of a century later, a similar struggle between John Winthrop and Thomas Dudley, the deputy governor of the Massachusetts Bay Colony, illustrates again the presumption that excessive refinements in a man's house went hand in hand with unethical or immoral behavior. A protracted quarrel between Winthrop and Dudley finally led to a meeting of the leaders of the Colony in May, 1632. According to Winthrop's Journal the set of charges against Dudley turned at one point to the question of his house.

> Upon this there arose another question, about [Dudley's] house. The governor [Winthrop] having formerly told him, that he did not well to bestow such cost about wainscotting and adorning his house, in the beginning of a plantation, both in regard of the necessity of public charges, and for example, etc., his answer now was, that it was for the warmth of his house, and the charge was but little, being but clapboards nailed to the wall in the form of a wainscott.[14]

The problem was not, however, simply one of ostentation; as in the case of Smith and Ratcliffe, there were implications that such overreaching was attempted at the expense of the community. The question of the wainscotting arose in oblique relation to the central issue at hand, that of Dudley's "usury" in selling poor men seven and a half bushels of corn against ten bushels in repayment at the time of harvest.

The colonists at Plymouth had hoped to avoid problems arising from individual successes and failures by establishing a temporary system of communal ownership in the "conditions" set for the new plantation. The settlers established a system of stocks and a plan for seven years of community labor and investment, after which time "the capitall & profits, viz. the houses, lands, goods and chatles, be equally devided between the adventurers and planters. . . . ." The Plymouth plan was not, however, accepted without considerable debate. Not only did men anticipate enjoying the personal profits of their individual labor, but a considerable body of contemporary political theory asserted that the security of a society lay in the private wealth, particularly in the permanent, well-built houses, of its citizens. The planters and adventurers of Plymouth, therefore, resisted the program of seven years of communal endeavor on grounds of political stability as well as by arguing that such a system would operate like charity and thereby discourage hard work.

To answer these charges and to alleviate this discontent, Robart Cushman wrote a letter to the settlers explaining that the projected system would not be a means of "giving almes, but [of] furnishing a store house; no one shall be porer than another for 7. years, and if any be rich, none can be pore." In response to the argument of societal stability, Cushman acknowledged the current theory that, "This will hinder the building of good and faire houses, contrarie to the advise of pollitiks," but he insisted that the colonists' strength had for the present to lie in their mobility. ". . . our purpose is to build for the presente such houses as, if neede be, we may with little greefe set a fire, and rune away by the lights; our riches shall not be in pompe, but in strenght. . . ." More to the point, Cushman's own political and social theories saw in fine houses the potential debilitation of a society. "You may see it amongst the best pollitiks, that a comonwele is readier to ebe than to flow, when once fine houses and gay cloaths come up."

Cushman had no doubt that the officials of the plantation could themselves prevent the construction of fine, permanent houses, but he asked instead that the citizens cooperate in the spirit of the venture. "The Government may prevente excess in building. . . . But if it be by all men beforehand resolved on, to build mean houses, the Governor laboure is spared." If desire to overreach one's neighbor was so strong that one could not be "contente his neighbour shall have as good a house, fare, means, &c. as him selfe," then such a man was not capable of living in society and was "fitter to live alone, then in any societie, either civill or religious."[15] By the "conditions" of Plymouth Plantation, therefore, strong sanctions were established against personal aggrandizement, most egregiously displayed in "fine houses and gay cloaths."

In 1623 in Plymouth, the arrival of the *Anna* with some sixty more settlers brought up again the issue of housing. Among the passengers were some of means, who wanted to build estates for themselves.

> Those that came on their perticuler looked for greater matters than they found or could attain unto, aboute building great houses, and such pleasant situations for them, as them selves had fancied; as if they would be great men & rich, all of a sudaine; but they proved castls in the aire.

The problem was settled according to the original terms of the plantation; it was agreed that the colony would allot these new men simple "competente places for habitation within the towne."[16]

A general desire to restrict excesses in house-building occasionally extended to the criticism of an entire settlement. When New Haven was founded in 1636 by an unusually wealthy body of men, the settlers were reproached for having exceeded the limits of simplicity in houses. They had "laid out too much of their stocks and estates in building of fair and stately houses, wherein they at first outdid the rest of the country."[17] According to Isham and Brown who made a careful study of Connecticut houses in 1900, exceptionally fine houses were built in New Haven. Some of these houses were not only quite large and relatively costly, but a few were unique for New England. Isham and Brown mention four homes which fall into the category of "manor houses" in the English sense of the term.[18]

For all the emphasis placed on the necessity of community effort in the very first years of a settlement, and for all the careful division of labor and of reward for which one can find evidence in the documents of Plymouth and Jamestown, it was early discovered that men worked with greater speed, energy, and efficiency if they were set to labor at building their own houses and working on their own fields, rather than if each were set some specific task to accomplish for the community as a whole, such as binding thatch or cutting timber. Different plantations and colonies were, of course, established under different philosophical, political, and economic premises, ranging from the initial Utopian communality of the Plymouth colonists to the economic individualism of some settlements on the southern coast. Nevertheless, records from several colonies, established under different theories or for different purposes, disclose conditions in which it became necessary to substitute individual labor and private property for communal. Of such conditions, the most general was the failure of the settlers to exhibit sufficient diligence.

Indeed, sloth must often have appeared as the principal of the seven deadly sins in some colonies. *The New Life of Virginea* (1612) depicted the decay of the Jamestown settlement but ascribed to the numbers of "irregular persons" who had augmented the population the situation in which "in a few months, Ambition, sloth and idleness had devoured the fruits of former labours, planting and sowing were cleane given over, the houses decaied. . . ."[19] John Smith, quoting from the material of Master Hamor, also described the condition of Jamestown in 1611, when ". . . most of the companie were at their daily and vsual works, bowling in the streets. . . ." But at the arrival of Sir Thomas Dale, all were set to work, "repayring their houses ready to fall on their heads. . . ."[20]

A more efficient enemy of sloth than Sir Thomas Dale was discovered in private property: a piece of land and the rights of inheritance. In *Leah and Rachel*, John Hammon, attributed the bad times at the outset of the Jamestown settlement to the numerous unsavory types who were sent to Virginia as well as to the fact that the men were overworked, underfed, and deprived of any system for redress of grievances. Then Hammon went on to explain how the situation was improved. The distribution of property induced a sudden new industriousness.

> . . . the bondage was taken off, the people set free, and had lands assigned to each of them to live of themselves, and enjoy the benefits of their own industry; men then began to call what they laboured for their own, they fell to making themselves convenient housing to dwell in, to plant corn for their food. . . .[21]

Robert Beverley, in his history of Virginia (1705), also explained the recovery of the Jamestown settlement in terms that underscore the efficacy of property.

> Then also they apportion'd and laid out Lands in several allotments, viz. to the Company in several places, to the Governour, to a

College, to *Glebes,* and to several particular Persons; many new Settlements were made in James and York Rivers. The People now knew their own property, and having the Encouragement of Working for their own Advantage, many became very industrious, and began to vie with one another, in Planting, Building, and other Improvements.[22]

Even in Plymouth, where the leaders had made the most explicit attempt to establish a society at least temporarily communal, it was necessary to introduce private property. Bradford reported that a dispute over the planting of corn was resolved in favor of private fields; "the Governor (with the advise of the cheefest amongst them) gave way that they should set corne every man for his own perticuler. . . ." There was, however, a compromise arrived at; for while private fields were assigned, the leaders "made no devission for inheritance" and the parcels of land given each family for planting were seen as "only for present use." Bradford emphasized the success of the scheme of private lands, "for it made all hands very industrious," and even the women "wente willingly into the feild . . . whom to have compelled would have bene thought great tiranie and oppression." This evidence of the power of private property gave Bradford the opportunity to castigate those philosophers who had seen in communal goods and labor the basis of a more perfect society.

> The experience that was had in this common course and condition, tried sundrie years, and that amongst godly and sober men, may well evince the vanitie of the conceite of Platos & other ancients, applauded by some of later time; —that the taking away of propertie, and bringing in communitie a comone wealth, would make them happy and flourishing; as if they were wiser than God. For this comunitie (so farr as it was) was found to breed much confusion & discontent, and retard much employment that would have been to their benefite and comforte.

He concluded piously, "Let none objecte this is men's corruption. . . . I answer, seeing all men have this corruption in them, God in his wisdome saw another course fiter for them."[23]

A less philosophical version of the affairs of the Plymouth colony appears in *Mourt's Relation* (1622), which noted simply the efficiency brought to their efforts by permitting each man to work himself on his own house: "After the proportion formerly alloted, wee agreed that every man should build his owne house, thinking by that course, men would make more hast then working in common. . . ."[24]

While the colonists and planters were erecting their first homes, the chroniclers of the earliest English settlements in America paid, after all, scant attention to the houses in themselves. Nevertheless, evidence from the seventeenth century serves to establish for us the attitudes toward houses that prevailed in the first decades of settlement. Initially, shelter was a matter of basic necessity. Subsequently, several concepts emerged with significant force. For one thing, early American writers consistently saw houses as signs of collective rather than individual success. A substantial number of good dwellings, especially of "fair houses," proved the vitality of a settlement. This vitality, furthermore, was ennervated by the construction of inordinately fine houses so that seventeenth century documents reveal fairly strong sanctions against personal aggrandizement expressed in excessively large or refined private houses. On the other hand, as the colonists discovered that energy in house building, as in the clearing and planting of land, was increased by the reward of private property, individual effort and personal rewards took precedence over community effort and communal rewards. By making the houses and the labor that went into them the responsibility and the property of one man and his family, colonial leaders discovered the most effective incentive to industry.

Obviously, a value-system was developing that held the seeds of an essential paradox. If houses were to be individually built and owned, then the sanctions against excesses in private houses would be seriously weakened. Furthermore, the evaluation of progress in relation to shelter would be confused by two sets of standards. By one index, a community made up of modest, but decent houses, reflected the success of that community. By another measure, a few unusually fine houses, built in emulation of English manor houses were proof of colonial progress. Clearly, behind these two standards lay distinctly different concepts about America.

It was only a brief period before wealthy planters and traders began to erect houses that signaled their personal economic achievement. But while the colonies first struggled for a foothold on the American seaboard, the values that would attach themselves to the American house were only beginning to be faintly discernable. Whether the house could remain long as an index of the success of a colony or whether new concepts of property in a mercantile society would alter the meaning of the house were questions not then posited. In the first decades of the American life, the houses of a settlement were clearly comprehended as a proud sign of the progress of civilization, the kind of civilization summed up by Cotton Mather at the end of the century: "Never was any plantation brought unto such a considerableness, in a space of time so inconsiderable! an *howling wilderness* in a few years became a *pleasant land,* accommodated with the *necessaries*—yea, and the *convenience* of human life . . ."[25]

Like the seventeenth century boosters and apologists who preceded them, eighteenth century writers continued to tally the houses in a community; now, however, they laid more emphasis on the quality of the buildings. For example, in his history of Virginia (1705), Robert Beverley took care to describe the architecture of Williamsburg, the new capital. Not only were the College and the Capital the "most magnificent of any in *America,*" but "The Private Buildings are of late very much improved."

> . . . several Gentlemen there, having built themselves large Brick Houses of many Rooms on a Floor, and several Stories high, as also some Stone-Houses: but they don't covet to make them lofty, having extent enough of Ground to build upon; an now and then they are visited by high Winds, which wou'd incommode a towring Fabrick. They always contrive to have large Rooms, that they may be cool in Summer. Of late they have made their Stories much higher than formerly, and within they adorn their Apartments with rich Furniture.[26]

Furthermore, while fine houses received praise, meaner dwellings frequently provoked disdain. In 1733, William Byrd wrote of the town of Edenton, "There may be forty or fifty houses, most of them small and built without expense. A citizen, here," he added, "is counted extravagant if he has ambition enough to aspire to a brick chimney." It was not only Edenton that offended Byrd;

country houses as well were remarked for their insufficiency. On his journey through Virginia and Carolina to establish the "dividing line," Byrd came across a number of poor and filthy dwellings.

> In less that a mile from thence we had the pleasure to discover a house, though a very poor one, the habitation of our friend Nat on Major Mumford's plantation. As agreeable a sight as a house was, we chose our tent to lie in as much the cleanlier lodging.
>
> About two miles more brought us to our worthy friend Captain Embry's habitation, where we found the housekeeping much better than the house. In that the noble Captain is not very curious, his castle containing of one dirty room with a dragging door to it that will neither open nor shut.
>
> It was dark before we could reach the mouth of the river, where our wayward stars directed us to a miserable cottage. . . . For want of our tent, we were obliged to shelter ourselves in this wretched hovel, where we were almost devoured by vermin of various kinds.[27]

That the master of "Westover" should have felt contempt for these shabby and verminous houses is not remarkable, but that his contempt should have been leveled as well at their owners is worth investigating. The poor men living in these hovels, according to Byrd, lacked not only ambition, but the necessary virtues of diligence and thrift as well. For example, Byrd once visited Cornelius Keith. He wrote twice about this visit, in *The History of the Dividing Line* and in *The Secret History*. In the latter, he described the dwelling and noted a minor act of charity he had performed;

> . . . Meanwell and I made a visit to Cornelius Keith, who lived rather in a pen than a house with his wife and six children. I never beheld such a scene of poverty in this happy part of the world. The hovel they lay in had no roof to cover these wretches from the injuries of the weather, but when it rained or was colder than ordinary the whole family took refuge in a fodder sack. The poor man had raised a kind of house, but for want of nails it remained uncovered. I gave him a note on Major Mumford for nails for that purpose and so made a whole family happy at a very small expense.

However, in *The History of the Dividing Line*, Byrd turned ironic; Keith was the victim of his own laziness, unwilling, it

appeared, even to turn for support to his useful trade, the
setting up of quernstones.

> However, 'twas almost worth while to be as poor as this man was, to
> be as perfectly contented. All his wants proceeded from indolence
> and not from misfortune. He had good land, as well as good health
> and good limbs to work it and, besides, had a trade very useful to
> all the inhabitants round about.[28]

Byrd saw poverty as the mark of indolence and prosperity as
the badge of diligence. This logic worked equally for individuals
and for communities. The unambitious citizens of Edenton could
be contrasted with the population of Norfolk as they were represented by their houses.

> The streets are straight and adorned with several good houses,
> which increase every day.

> The two cardinal virtues that make a place thrive, industry and
> frugality, are seen here in perfection; and so long as they can
> banish luxury and idleness the town will remain in a happy and
> flourishing condition.[29]

The theme struck here by Byrd depended on a premise basic to
American thought: hard work and thrift bring material reward.
As a man's house was the most tangible of rewards, it became
as well the singular evidence of his diligence and frugality.
Conversely, a wretched house was a shameful symbol, proof of
indolence or reckless waste, of a life misspent. Furthermore, as
America was conceived as the land where diligence and thrift
did not go unrewarded, where debt, in the words of Timothy
Dwight, was "an event necessary only from sickness or decrepti-
tude,"[30] a man's obvious personal failure, his wretched house,
was an assault on the American ideal.

How closely a man's house had come to represent his economic situation and, hence, his personal value, may be inferred
from the contemporaneous diaries of Samuel Sewall and Cotton
Mather. Sewall, at the age of forty, had achieved wealth and
reputation. Well-married, to the daughter of the rich merchant
John Hull, and successful in his own right, Sewall determined
to build himself a house. In his diary for January 25, 1691-1692,
he wrote that he had "asked Mr. Willard at Mr. Eyre's whether

the Times would allow one to build a house." Sewall must have welcomed Mr. Willard's reply: "I wonder that you have contented your selvs so long without one. . . ."[31] The career of a Samuel Sewall deserved a house; the individual had earned it, and the young colony would be adorned with another tangible symbol of progress.

While Samuel Sewall built and inhabited his house, Cotton Mather evaluated and reevaluated the one his congregation afforded him. In Mather's diary, woven into the long passages that assess the state of his spirit, are recurrent references to houses, enforcing the strong connection between the house one lived in and the wordly success one had achieved. Several references to houses in Mather's diaries occur in those passages in which he counted his blessings, spiritual and material. In a typical entry, he gave thanks first for the confession of his "horrid *Sins*" and then considered the "more *special Mercies* of Heaven," listing as number VI, "My Salary, and the comfortable Provision made for mee, in my Habitation, above what many other and better Servants of God enjoy." In 1700, a catalogue of "ANSWERS OF PRAYERS" included his satisfactions "in a grown and a great *Salary*, and a comfortable *Habitation*." But in 1710, when Cotton Mather's relative prosperity and material ease gave way to financial difficulties, his diary entries turned once more to housing, touching again on the comparison between his house and those of other men. Now, however, Mather looked enviously at the homes of others and, castigating his own bitterness, he set himself a series of projects for his moral betterment. Such projects were established to suppress and rebuke "The first and least Ebullition of an *envious Thought* at the Prosperity of others. . . ." and Mather cited several specific methods toward this end.

Thirdly, When I am sitting with my Friends in their Houses, and walking the Streets where I may see some of their most visible Possessions, I would employ the Ejaculations of my Mind, unto the blessed God, in as real and sincere Acknowledgements of His granting this Prosperity unto them, and with as true a Pleasure of Soul at the Prospect, as if it were *all my own*. Yea, and I obtain a Liesure to walk about the Place; and go round about the Neighbourhood, and tell the Smiles of God upon it, and mark well their Enjoyments, and consider their Consolations, and upon each of

them gett my Soul raised into those Dispositions of Joy, which I
ought to have, when I see the *Goodness* of the blessed God shining
forth in so obliging a Manner; with Supplications of my Neighbours,
that they may bring forth much of the Fruit, by which He may be
glorified.[32]

Cotton Mather may or may not be convincing in his struggle
against envy at the prosperity of his fellows, but he does reveal
clearly the sense that a man's prosperity was indicated by his
"most visible possessions," visible, that is, to one "walking the
Streets" and going "round the Neighbourhood." Further, the
properous houses he saw were not only the sign of an individual's
material success, but were as well the indication of God's
blessing, of the fruitfulness of His colony. But societal progress
could be cold comfort to a poor clergyman saddled with debt.
By the early eighteenth century the signs of wealth had come to
delineate clearly the growing chasm between rich and poor.

In a diary entry for 1721, Mather lamented, "I do not own a
Foot of Land in all the World."[33] Land had certainly been, and
continued to be, a basic source of wealth in colonial America.
But during Mather's life the laws of most of the colonies were
altered in such a way as to indicate the increased social and
material significance of personal, rather than real, property. As
early as 1691, the qualifications for voting in Massachusetts
were altered so as to extend the franchise to landless men who
owned personal property worth fifty pounds in sterling. By 1704
similar laws were enacted in New Hampshire, Connecticut, New
York, Pennsylvania, Maryland, and South Carolina. In New
Jersey, the vote was granted not only to those who possessed
either fifty acres of land or fifty pounds worth of personal property, but even to those men whose property consisted of no
more than three acres and a house in a borough.[34] While Virginia's laws continued to enfranchise only the free-holder, the
other colonies took cognizance of a new kind of wealth.

The development of a significant body of wealthy, landless
men was to have an important bearing on the history of the house
in America. Their city mansions, unlike the manor houses standing on vast holdings of hereditary land, were not part of an old
tradition. A city mansion was the bold symbol of its owner's
wealth, not, like the plantation house of Virginia, a seal and
ornament on the land. On these plantations, land itself was property, the land constituted the wealth of the owner; the great

house elegantly capped that property. As Vincent Scully has said in reference to Jefferson's Monticello, this house "is about a man owning the earth."[35]

But for the man whose wealth came from trade or speculation, the plot of land on which his mansion stood did not represent the earth. The city lot, even while it remained ample enough to support a garden and a small orchard, was not property in the traditional sense. What was required of that land was merely that it lie in the fashionable section of town and that it be large enough to hold the splendid house that stood upon it. The house alone made apparent, and tangible, the material wealth of its owner. So negligible was the land that, as cities became more crowded and fashion changed location, the house could be sold along with the inconsequential land on which it stood. A wealthy merchant might, of course, own land other than the meager piece on which his city mansion was situated. Country houses were built on more commodious properties, but here again the land was the foil for the house. Also, land was an exceptionally valuable commodity for speculation, but whether such land consisted of large tracts in frontier areas or of much smaller urban properties, its value was realizable in its sale. It was not "the earth;" it was a cash commodity. Where the land itself was no longer the basis for a man's wealth, where a moneyed aristocracy came into existence without hereditary land holdings, the house itself took on a new meaning as the singular, most visible expression of the economic standing of its owner.

Before the middle of the eighteenth century, a substantial number of luxurious houses had been built in America. As wealth began to be accumulated, men turned to the construction of fine homes in the cities and on country estates. A pattern began to emerge for self-made Americans; after the acquisition of a considerable fortune abetted customarily, by marriage to a wealthy or at least aristocratic wife, a successful man built a house that fairly aggressively signalled his success. Frequently, second-generation money was expended in the construction of a finer house. Of course, in the south and in New York state, especially fine mansions were inherited and maintained, but even in those areas where a landed aristocracy existed, the inherited house was sometimes not the first built by the family wealth, but the second.

Thomas Hancock (1703-1764) erected his mansion on the

foundation of a mercantile fortune. Hancock was the son of a poor minister, and at thirteen was apprenticed to a Boston bookseller and bookbinder. At twenty Hancock had his own bookshop and soon after moved into paper manufacturing and the exporting of codfish, whale oil, potash, and logwood. He progressed from supplying the fishing fleet with rum and molasses to the control of his own fleet of fishing boats. When, in 1730, he married Lydia Henchman, the daughter of his former master, the scale of his business ventures enlarged dramatically. He acquired the contract for supplying the British forces in Nova Scotia, an achievement apparently owed to the use of his already considerable fortune in the oiling of crown officials. His fleet of fishing boats was turned to new purposes as well, primarily the smuggling of tea and paper. When the British determined to relocate the Acadians from Nova Scotia to the south, Hancock's seventeen sloops were rented for the purpose. His wealth, including what he had inherited from the Henchman family, was modestly figured at £70,000 when he died suddenly of apoplexy, leaving his fortune to his famous nephew John.[36]

Thomas Hancock's house was one of the grandest in Boston. It consisted of two wings flanking a central structure that itself measured fifty-six by thirty-eight feet. The drawing room had dimensions of seventeen feet by twenty-five. There was even a ballroom.[37] Hancock apparently enjoyed his mansion, taking pride in its size and splendor as well as in its location on newly-fashionable Beacon Hill. He proudly dated the first letter written from his new home, "At my house in Beacon Street, Boston ye 22nd Mar. 1739-40," and noted in a subsequent letter that "we live pretty comfortable here now, on Beacon Hill."[38] Like other significant houses, the Hancock mansion received some public attention shortly after the Revolution, during John Hancock's occupancy. The *Massachusetts Magazine* featured an illustration of the house in a 1789 issue, with the comment that "The respected character who now enjoys this earthly paradise, inherited it from his worthy uncle, the Hon. Thomas Hancock, Esq. who selected the spot and completed the buildings, evincing a superiority of judgment and taste. . . ."[39]

John Singleton Copley (1738-1815), was another poor Bostonian who made money, bought land on Beacon Hill, and set about building himself a house. In 1736, Copley's parents had emigrated from Ireland to Boston, where his mother operated a tobacco shop on Long Wharf. Subsequently widowed, she remarried a merchant named Pelham. Copley himself married well, a Mayflower descendant with some money, and he was earning about three hundred guineas a year from his portraits by the late 1760's. When he bought a piece of land on Beacon Hill, it was still an undeveloped area, and Copley paid about $3,000. After moving to England, Copley sold his land to a Boston syndicate for $14,000, but Copley determined that he had been swindled, and a long and complicated law suit followed.[40]

But in 1771, while his house was under construction, Copley had thoughts only for its up-to-the-minute elegance. Traveling in New York, he saw a new architectural feature he wished added to his home; he wrote to one of his Pelham relatives who was supervising the construction in Copley's absence, "Should I not add Wings, I shall add a peazer when I return, which is much practiced here, and is very beautiful and convenient." Pelham was forced to confess his bewilderment; "I don't comprehend what you mean by a peazer." Copley responded with diagrams and a long description in his next letter.

> You say you dont know what I mean by a Peaza. I will tell you than. it is exactly such a thing as the cover over the pump in your Yard, suppose no enclosure for the Poultry their, and 3 or 4 Posts added to support the front of the Roof, a good floor at bottom, and from post to post a Chinese enclosure about three feet high. these posts are Scantlings of 6 by 4 Diameter, the Broad side to the front, with only a little moulding round the top in a neat plain manner. some have collumns but very few, and the top is generally Plastered, but I think if the top was sealed with neat plained Boards I should like it as well. these Peazas are so cool in Sumer and in Winter break off the storms so much that I think I should not be able to like an house without. . . .[41]

Some fine eighteenth century houses in New England were built with older money, two significant ones by the descendants of John Vassall (1625-1688). Vassall, whom the *Dictionary of American Biography* lists as a "colonial entrepreneur," came to the colonies following his father, William, who settled in America; his uncle Samuel, remaining in England, developed a prosperous trade with the colonies and was a patentee of large land tracts. John settled first in Massachusetts, in Roxbury and then in Scituate. By 1664 he had become a surveyor general in Carolina; still later he moved his operations to the West Indies. One of John's descendants, Leonard Vassall, coming to Massachusetts from the West Indies where he had been a successful sugar planter, built a country house in 1730-1731, in what is now Quincy. Another descendant, Major John Vassall, built a fine mansion in Cambridge in 1759. No family could have done better in the ancestral dwelling line; although the tory Vassalls left America at the time of the Revolution, they left behind them not only the Cambridge mansion known now as the Longfellow House (where George Washington had his headquarters for a period), but also the "Old House," in Quincy, the 150 year old residence of the Adams family, and thus the home of two presidents.

The Cambridge mansion has been the subject of many essays, literary and historical and architectural. The rambling home of the Adams family has received somewhat less attention. However, in 1818, a British traveler published *A Narrative of a Journey of 5000 Miles*; Henry Bradshaw Fearon had been sent to America by a group of thirty-nine English families to discover a suitable place for them to emigrate to and to inform them generally about conditions in America. In Quincy, Fearon visited John Adams, then 84, and discovered in the simplicity of the former president's house a symbol of republican virtue.

> The establishment of this political patriarch, consists of a house two stories high, containing, I believe, eight rooms. . . . How great is the contrast between this individual—a man of knowledge and information—without pomp, parade, or vitious and expensive establishments, as compared with the costly trappings, the depraved characters, and the profligate expenditure of _____ House, and _____[42]

In the nineteenth century, it was the simplicity along with the mellow tones of age that set Henry Adams to brooding on his boyhood and comparing the "magnificence of his grandfather Brook's house in Pearl Street or South Street" to the Quincy house. He had to confess that while "The President's place at Quincy was the larger and older and far the most interesting of the two," even as a boy he had "felt at once its inferiority in fashion. It showed plainly enough its want of wealth. It smacked of colonial age, but not of Boston style or plush curtains." No drawbacks, of course, but positive pleasures for Henry Adams, who "was born an eighteenth-century child," for "The old house at Quincy was eighteenth century."[43]

John and Abigail Adams had few pretensions and notoriously simple tastes. While an Englishman like Fearon, disgruntled at royal profligacy, might find the Adams' home a symbol for republican simplicity, and a subtle-minded historian like Henry Adams could discover in the house a personal antidote against the poisonous values of modernity and progress, most great eighteenth century houses were built, and observed, with an eye for splendor. The desire for splendor, in fact, urged men to replace the family home of one generation with one that was newer, larger, and more splendid. The Derby family of Salem exemplifies the saga of merchant shipping and, in its rise and fall, illustrates the hard lesson of over-extension in house-building. The family began its rise to fortune with Richard Derby (1712-1783), who went to sea early and by twenty-four was captain of his own ship, the *Ranger*. From captain to ship-owner, Derby made a fortune in the triangle trade, prospered as well as a merchant, built Derby Wharf in Salem, and constructed a dignified brick mansion for his family. His son, Elias Hasket Derby (1739-1799), employed the family fleet for privateering during the Revolution, and subsequently sent his ships to St. Petersburg, around the Cape of Good Hope, and to the Orient; his vessels were the first to reach Canton. Having amassed an enormous fortune, in 1791 he commissioned Bulfinch to build him a new house, the finest in Salem. In the third generation, however, the family declined. Quarrels occurred over money and their "reduced income did not suffice to maintain the Derby mansion...."[44]

In the south as well as the north, a younger generation replaced the older manor houses of their fathers with homes of new architectural grandeur. Thus, the "Westopher" (1690) of William Byrd the first was supplanted by the "Westover" (c. 1730) of his son, William Byrd. Between 1725 and 1760, a good number of the now-famous plantation houses of Virginia were constructed, among them "Tuckahoe," "Rosewell," "Stratford," "Westover," "Apthill," "Carter's Grove," "Gunston Hall," and

"Mount Airy." The fortunes that built these manors were founded in vast land holdings, but they were often considerably supplemented from other sources. Trade with the Indians, tobacco factoring, and ventures in mining were profitable, as were certain colonial offices, particularly those associated with granting lands. Robert "King" Carter (1663-1732), twice an agent for the Proprietor of the Northern Neck in Virginia, noted that "One great perquisite of this estate is the granting away the lands that are untaken up."[45]

When Carter died his estate consisted of 300,000 acres of land, along with 1,000 slaves and £10,000 in personal property. He had himself inherited a considerable fortune, and his heirs, intermarried with other great Virginia families, constituted an aristocracy of wealth and social position. The *Dictionary of American Biography* notes that Carter's children "married into the first families of the colony, and, as a result of a fortunate blending of superior strains, Carter had an unusual number of distinguished descendants," including two presidents, six Virginia governors, and Robert E. Lee.

Many of these descendants established their own grand houses, some with "King" Carter's financial assistance. His own home, "Corotoman," burned in 1729 and he probably did not rebuild it; nonetheless, he or members of his family remained occupied with the construction of manor houses. One of Carter's daughters married Benjamin Harrison who built her a new home, "Berkeley," which Carter may have partially financed. He also helped one of his sons in the construction of "Nomini Hall." Another daughter married Mann Page I (1691-1730) who built "Rosewell" (begun 1725), a mansion said to have had a front footage of 232 feet, and to contain some thirty-two rooms. Page died before the house was finished, leaving the completion to his wife and son; so vast was the conception of the house, however, and so large the expense, that the heirs were forced to sell off some land to pay the costs of construction.[46]

The great Virginia manors were typically built by men of the second or third generation, who inherited large tracts of land, and realized considerable fortunes either from land alone, or more customarily, from other ventures and investments as well. Further consolidation of land, wealth, and social position came about from the marriages between the sons and daughters of the great families. Although laws of entail kept the great plantations intact, some families owned several large holdings and were able to establish a number of their sons on large acreages, where they constructed their own manor houses. William Randolph (1651-1711), for example, came to Virginia in 1663, acquired a great deal of land, married a daughter of Henry Isham, and was able to establish all seven of his sons on plantations of their own. His descendants were the builders of such fine homes as "Tuckahoe," "Tazewell Hall," "Curles," and "Bremo." Marriages between Randolph's children and other important Virginia families produced another group of famous descendants, Jefferson, Lee, and John Marshall among them.

Manorial living and aristocratic intermarriage were not confined to the Tidewater, however; New York state's Dutch landholders operated in the same way. Olaff Stevenzen Van Cortlandt (1600-1684) is representative of the self-made millionaire. Probably born in the Netherlands, he came to New Amsterdam in 1638, by 1640 was appointed commissioner of cargoes, and by 1641 had begun to purchase land. His rise in importance was signalled by the public offices he held: mayor from 1655 to 1661, and again from 1662 to 1663, later alderman. At his death Van Cortlandt was rated the fourth richest man in the colony, but it was his children who realized fully the promise of the father's success. In 1697, his son Stephanus received the royal patent for Van Cortlandt Manor, comprising 87,713 acres. He married the daughter of Philip P. Schuyler, and his sister married Jeremias Van Rennselaer; thus, the Van Cortlandts were allied with two of the most powerful families in the colony. Stephanus built Van Cortlandt Manor House, a fort-like building little used as a home until it was remodeled in the middle of the eighteenth century by his grandson, Pierre, the Lieutenant Governor of New York.

Frederick Philipse (1626-1702) came to New Amsterdam in 1647. The *Dictionary of American Biography* claims that he made his money in trade and in the manufacture of wampum. Sabine's *Biographical Sketches of Loyalists of the American Revolution*, setting the date of his emigration at 1658, asserts that Philipse brought "money, plate, and jewels, with the design of settling upon and improving large estates which he had purchased on the Hudson River."[47] In any case, Philipse began his major land acquisition when he bought a section of the Yonkers plantation; he eventually acquired two patents, one to Philipsburg, 159 square miles, the other to Fredericksburg, 240 square miles. He consolidated his position by two wise marriages, the first to the widow of a wealthy merchant, de Vriew, the second to another widow, the former Catharine Van Cortlandt. Beside the town house he owned in New York city, Philipse built a manor hall in Yonkers and "Castle Philipse" near Sleepy Hollow.

The Schuyler family, however, waited four generations before the great mansion, "The Pastures" (1762), was built by General Philip Schuyler. The first American Schuyler, Philip Pieterse, came from Amsterdam to Albany and, prospering, married Margarite van Slichtenhorst, whose father served as the resident proprietor of Rensselaerwick. Schuyler's son Peter married into the Van Rensselaer family proper, and he formed the Saratoga patent out of his considerable land-holdings. Peter Schuyler's wife, Maria Van Rensselaer, was both commodity and status-symbol. Widowed twice, she married as her third husband Robert Livingston (1654-1728), who came to Albany in 1674, starting out there as the town clerk. Eventually his lands included 160,000 acres in Dutchess and Columbia counties; his lands were "erected to a manor" in 1686, and in 1699 he built his manor house. Although the possession of a manor and the symbol of a manor house were usually effective weapons against public criticism, Livingston's rise to riches elicited the following comment from Governor Fletcher in 1696: "[Livingston] has made a considerable fortune . . . , never disbursing six pence but with the expectation of twelve pence, his beginning being a little Book keeper, he has screwed himself into one of the most considerable estates in the province . . . he had rather be called knave Livingston than poor Livingston."[48]

For the most part, however, the great mansions and the fortunes that built them were accorded a good deal of respect, at least publicly. Although these houses represented individual economic success and were constructed for the pomp and pleasure of individual families, commentators nevertheless attempted to celebrate them as milestones in the progress of American civilization. In a mid-eighteenth century poem about the marvels of Charleston, for example, Charles Woodmason altogether forgot his ethical message in his enthusiasm for the splendor exhibited in the mansions of Drayton and Middleton.

> What! tho' a second Carthage here we raise,
> A late attempt, the work of modern days,
> Here Drayton's seat and Middleton's is found,
> Delightful villas! be they long renown'd.[49]

But splendor raised problems, for some Americans did not take Carthage as an appropriate model. When Josiah Quincy visited Charleston in 1773, he dined at the magnificent home of Miles Brewton. In his diary Quincy described some of the particular beauties of the house and went on to assess Charlestonian culture and ethics.

> State, magnificence, and ostentation, the natural attendants of riches, are conspicuous among this people; the number and subjection of their slaves tend this way. Cards, dice, the bottle, and horses engross prodigious portions of their time and attention: the gentlemen (planters and merchants) are mostly men of the turf and gamesters. Political inquiries and philosophical disquisitions are too laborious for them: they have no great passion for to shine and blaze in the forum or a senate.[50]

For Quincy, Charlestonian magnificence was the splendor of a society at once decadent and incapable of intellectual achievement.

The relationship between great wealth and intellectual culture posed a serious problem for Americans. Those conversations in the drawing rooms of the rich, were they frivolous or profound? Josiah Quincy missed gravity and depth at the dinner table of Miles Brewton, but sixty years later a descendant of New York's Robert Livingston could insist to Tocqueville that the little attention paid to "intellectual questions" in America was due not to the excess of riches, but to the breaking up of family estates and the consequent demise of a privileged, moneyed class. "When I was young," he reminisced, "I remember the country peopled by rich landowners who lived on their estates as the English *gentry* do, and who used their minds, and had too a sense of tradition in their thoughts and manners. . . ." With the Revolution came the end of the laws of primogeniture and entail. For Livingston, the laws "making shares equal" had forced the division of large fortunes and consequently "our former standards and conceptions have been lost. . . ."[51]

The prejudices of Livingston are as obvious as those of Josiah

Quincy, and for both the problem of intellectual excellence only disguises the real issue. At the bottom, the problem was excess; indeed, the first crucial question about great houses in America was the question of limits. A fine house was both socially commendable and personally desirable, but at what point did the manor or mansion exceed those undefined limits which marked the boundary between the fine and the pretentious, between the elegant and the overly luxurious? These boundaries were never drawn; nevertheless, individual examples of architectural excess were noted and they were criticized. The criticism, of course, was personal, directed at the man whose house transgressed the limits, but the grounds for the attack were a peculiarly American blend of ethics and nationalism. For Josiah Quincy such houses represented a culture whose luxury ennervated political genius. For Charles Bulfinch, himself the architect of dozens of mansions, they were simply unAmerican. Bulfinch commented that the marble palace of the Philadelphia millionaire, William Bingham, was "in a stile which would be esteemed splendid even in the most luxurious part of Europe. . . ." and in Bulfinch's opinion it was "far *too* rich for *any* man in this country."[52]

Such criticism presupposed a national ceiling on magnificence, but each such criticism remained idiosyncratic, for no yardstick was invented to measure the discretions of opulence. As shabby houses reflected not only the individual sloth of the owner, but could, in the aggregate, reveal the indolence and profligacy of a whole community, so overly magnificent houses could represent a threat to the wholesome social body, and to the extent that houses in the aggregate reflected the values of a community, the taint of excess, like the pallor of poverty, failed to flatter the healthy communal countenance. Unlike Europeans, Americans have never chosen to build behind high walls; our houses have faced the street and, if houses are private property, they have always been everybody's business.

Chapter Two

The American House in the Early Republic

The mere sentiment of home, with its thousand associations, has, like a strong anchor, saved many a man from shipwreck in the storms of life. . . . For this reason, the condition of the family home—in this country where every man may have a home—should be raised, till it shall symbolize the best character and pursuits, and the dearest affections and enjoyments of social life.

A. J. Downing,
The Architecture of Country Houses (1850)

. . . the greatest possible stumbling blocks in the path of human happiness and improvement, are these heaps of brick and stone, consolidated with mortar, or hewn timber, fastened together with spike-nails, which men painfully contrive for their own torment, and call them house and home.

Nathaniel Hawthorne,
The House of the Seven Gables (1851)

In the first few decades of the Republic, the American house became a significant metaphor for American culture. The cultural values connected to the house in the early nineteenth century were inherited from the seventeenth and eighteenth centuries, but now they were articulated more frequently and more self-consciously. As American culture began to grow more complex, the metaphoric house assumed a more complex burden of meaning. In fact, the American house came to carry different meanings for men of different persuasions. Variety of meaning, however, did not inhibit the vitality of the symbol. By 1850, the metaphor of the house was sufficiently complex and vital to be adopted and manipulated in the work of major writers, including Hawthorne and Thoreau, Rufus Griswold and A. J. Downing. For each of these men the house had symbolic value, but for each the symbol, and the values, differed.

A great deal more was written about the American house after 1800 than in the Colonial period. Some of the same points of view persisted, but new aspects colored all of them. Thus, domestic architecture continued to represent national progress, but now frontier life set a new architectural pattern for progress. The log cabin appeared, a temporary dwelling but one establishing the first inroads of civilization. As in earlier periods, towns were evaluated in terms of the quality of their houses, a good number of substantial houses continuing to advertise the same virtues of thrift and industry that had marked eighteenth century comments. But cities like Boston, with areas of small and poor homes, posed new problems in evaluation, for these shabby areas were valuable as evidence of American history. Large and opulent houses continued to receive attention, but now a new factor was introduced. Style emerged as a new issue to be debated in essays about American homes. Mansions and villas were constructed in the Greek style, then in the Gothic. Some of the new rich, however, preferred the more exotic Tuscan, Egyptian, and even Moorish designs. Underlying the fascination with style and the debates that raged over their relative values was the desire to discover or to create an American architecture.

Finally, in the first part of the nineteenth century specific house-types began to appear in the popular imagination; the brick mansion, the country villa, the simple cottage, and the log cabin assumed particularized metaphoric significance. The values associated with each house-type were imperfectly defined in this period, preparing for the more generally accepted values, and the stereotypes, of the decades to follow. The early years of the Republic were, in general, a period of increased fascination with and concern about the American house, but a period before the codification of American attitudes.

During these years, serious writers, men with European reputations, began to discuss houses in their works; not all "local color," these houses took on a representative, if not yet a symbolic, force in the works of Washington Irving and James Fenimore Cooper. Cooper's *Notions of the Americans* (1828) treated domestic architecture in two contexts, describing well-known national figures like Washington and Jay and also depicting the typical house of the New Yorker or the overall effect of the domestic architecture of Philadelphia. New American periodicals, too, began to print material on houses; some featured a monthly illustration and description of a gentleman's house, while others presented general essays on the state of domestic architecture. This material frequently had a nationalistic impetus, demonstrating American success and sophistication by the presentation of American houses.

Some magazines regularly featured an engraving of a house with a brief encomium on the facing page. Large and luxurious houses were evidence of American taste and prosperity. Smaller houses, on the other hand, demonstrated the national admiration for unaffected simplicity. In such terms, the *New York Magazine* described, and defended, the long farm house, unornamented and without claims on any architectural school, of Henry Livingston, Esq. of Poughkeepsie, "the mansion is far from being magnificent . . . no artificial fountains sprinkle the parterres, no statues or pagodas are seen in the gardens, nor any extraordinary effort of expense exhibited. . . ." The house, nevertheless, took good advantage of the beauty of its natural site, as the editors more or less apologized.[1] Another attractive but architecturally unimportant house, the "Seat of Samuel Meredith, Esquire" near Philadelphia, was commended for its simplicity: "It is large and commodious . . . of brick, erected in a plain but neat style, and makes a handsome appearance." More important, Mr. Meredith, who used his property for experimenting with silk-worm breeding, could be praised for an activity which "reflects great credit to the enterprising spirit, and patriotism. . . ."[2]

Nevertheless, the opportunity to feature a more imposing house drew forth a more expansive prose style, suggesting delight and a general sense of relief in being freed from circumspect defensiveness. In 1792, the *Massachusetts Magazine* carried a fold-out page with an engraving of the "Seat of Hon. Moses Gill" in Worcester County, Massachusetts. The mansion boasted columns two stories high, double pairs of chimneys, and a symmetrical facade. The *Massachusetts Magazine* made no little matter of that fold-out engraving: "At a considerable expense we have procured the view of the elegant building and perspective which embellishes the front of our magazine for the present month." Such a house, and the illustration that promoted it, had not only architectural, but patriotic, significance, "In doing this we were actuated not only by a wish to gratify our customers, but by a laudable ambition to do honour to our own country and our own state." Since in 1766, only twenty-six years earlier, the Gill estate had been a perfect wilderness, the progress of America's civilization was here emblemized in one of America's houses; the editors boasted that "Foreigners must have a high idea of the rapid progress of improvement in America. . . ."[3]

Magazines also occasionally printed poems addressed to particular houses. The Barrell mansion (1792-1793) near Boston, designed by Bulfinch, was the subject of the following lines, suggesting that the larger the house the more florid the rhetorical style.

> A good sight in sooth it is, to stand
> On Boston's banks, where western breezes play,
> To note the green round hills or level land
> That skirts the surface blue of Cambridge bay.
> One house there is midst groves of poplars gay,
> To know whose owner, strangers oft desire;
> When Phoebus downward winds his westering way
> To see its windows look like crimson fire;
> Whose that conspicuous roof they then enquire?[4]

The Barrell mansion was indeed an imposing structure, although the roof was in no way its most conspicuous feature. Bulfinch had designed the house with some of the newest architectural ornaments, including an oval drawing room and a "flying staircase." Contemporaries who remarked about the house were impressed by its size. One viewer noted that Barrell had "gratified his love for show by building a finer house and laying out larger gardens and pleasure grounds." Another more generously asserted that the mansion, when completed, "will be infinitely the most elegant dwelling house ever yet built in New England."[5]

Barrell's house was the subject of more than one poem. In 1794, the *Massachusetts Magazine* printed, "Reflections: *On viewing the Seat of* Jos. Barrell, *Esq.*" The poet, however, did not intend simply to praise the house; instead he chose to develop a social theme. The mansion, standing on soil where the Revolution had been fought, was first likened to a baronial castle and, absurdly, labelled as "venerable."

> Where once the breastwork marked the scenes of blood,
> When freedom's sons inclosed the haughty foe,
> Rearing its head majestic from afar
> The venerable seat of *Barrell* stands.
> Like some strong English castle much it seems,
> When the great Barons of the feudal times
> Had num'rous vassals waiting their command,
> And each rais'd armies in his own domain.

The poet then compared ancient forms of noble hospitality and generosity to modern selfishness; today only the poor and those of the "middle ranks" welcome "the faint and weary traveller . . . to the lowly cell." In the modern world where "The rich support the rich, but grind the poor," the poet pleaded with Barrell to bring back the virtues of the past.

> But thou, whose stately castle overlooks
> The briny wave to Boston's crowded shores . . .
> Be thou excepted from the common herd
> Of selfish, full blown opulence and pride.
> Love thou the virtues that once deign'd to dwell
> In ancient years, beneath a roof like thine.
> And in despite of modern wond'ring eyes,
> Bring back old fashion'd customs to our view,
> The lib'ral train of virtues that adorn'd
> The former ages of the English realm.[6]

"BLANDULUS," as the poet called himself, made no direct attack on the opulent house or on the wealth that produced it; instead he called for a kind of medieval stewardship from those "blest with plenty by a bounteous God." Other writers, however, did take issue, not with the ostentatious display of riches in any particular house, but with architectural ostentation in general. In a 1789 essay in the *Massachusetts Magazine*, for example, while the writer advanced the customary connection between architectural improvement and societal progress, he placed a limit on improvement in houses, a limit, though a vague one, on excessive luxury. The essay cited the movement of mankind from the cave to the house as a part of the "natural progress of the works of men . . ." travelling along the route toward civilization "from rudeness to convenience, from convenience to elegance, and from elegance to nicety." Elegance represented the acceptable limits; nicety was excessive. The article closed with the warning "The passage is very short from elegance to luxury. Ionick and Corinthian columns are soon succeeded by gilt cornices, inlaid floors, and petty ornaments, which shew rather the wealth than the taste of the possessors."[7]

One difficulty in exhibiting architectural taste rather than vulgar wealth lay in the uncertain and changing canons of taste. Yesterday's Ionic columns are today's inlaid floors. Since the early eighteenth century English pattern books had laid down the articles of taste, instructing the merchants and planters of the colonies in matters of style and elegance, but when political events made English styles, in architecture as well as in the other arts, unpopular, a search began for an American style, one suited to the characteristics and the aspirations of the new nation. Such an American architecture, could it be discovered or invented, would solve the problem of taste by establishing a standard that satisfied both nationalistic and aesthetic needs.

The issue of style had not been paramount in earlier comments on American houses, which had changed from their first medieval form to what we know as Colonial style, according to the dictates of English architecture. Only Thomas Jefferson had found the English model inadequate and discovered a new prototype for classical architecture in France. Jefferson's comments were the first to criticize American houses in terms of their overall style, as he was the first to pioneer in building his home in accordance with a unique model.

In his *Notes on the State of Virginia*, Jefferson lamented that "the genius of architecture seems to have shed its maledictions on the land." Costly and simple dwellings alike suffered from the limitations of their architectural style. It would have been, he said, "impossible to devise things more ugly, uncomfortable, and happily perishable." The last comment was Jefferson's cynical comfort in the lack of durability of wood, a popular building material he strongly disapproved of.

Taste and beauty, argued Jefferson, were not expensive, and a shortage of funds in no way excused ugliness in houses.

To give symmetry and taste would not increase the cost. It would only change the arrangement of the materials, the form and the combination of the members. This would cost less than the burden of barbarous ornaments with which the buildings are sometimes charged. But the first principles of the art are unknown, and there exists scarcely a model among us sufficiently chaste to give an idea of them.[8]

Jefferson's "Monticello" demonstrated his own taste in and knowledge of architecture. When the Marquis of Chastellux visited America, he delighted in Monticello, which he said "shows the owner's fondness for the language of Italy and even more for the fine arts." He recognized that Jefferson's home was unique, "The house in nowise resembles the others to be seen in this country; in fact it may be said that Mr. Jefferson is the first American to consult the fine arts in regard to his dwelling place."[9]

Despite Jefferson's example, English styles prevailed, and Georgian, Adamesque, and Palladian models succeeded one another in English pattern books and American houses until the Greek Revival swept over America, strewing pediments, porticoes, and columns over all of the settled parts of the country. The advent of the Greek Revival occurred during the period of strong anti-British feeling following the War of 1812. Despite the fact that Greek Revival architecture had appeared in England nearly a generation earlier, Americans seemed to feel that to build their houses after the model of Greek temples would free them from the domination of English styles. Furthermore, with a new architectural model available, the problem of taste was solved, if briefly; taste and style—a particular style—became one.

An 1815 essay in Philadelphia's *Analectic Magazine* addressed the problem of architectural style, condemning British models and praising "Grecian simplicity." American taste was at the threshold, the writer determined, ". . . taste has been widely diffused among the mass of the community," and although "this taste may not be very enlightened or critical . . . it is sufficient for the purpose of bringing forth and rewarding talent. . . ." But in architectural matters, national taste still languished, suffering from the emulation of British models. "In architecture, it must be confessed, we are still very far behind hand. Our domestic architecture is for the most part copied, and often very badly copied too, from the common English books, with but little variety, and no adaptation to our own climate or habits of life." Palladian architecture was particularly corrupt, reminding the writer of "the tawdry and tarnished finery of a strolling company of players." Palladian houses suffered most in comparison to those built in the Greek style, he added.

> . . . in its very best estate, this style [Palladian] of architecture can rise to nothing nobler than ponderous stateliness, and cumbrous magnificence; and the effect which it produces with infinite labour, is always poor and contemptible when compared with the grandeur and beauty of Grecian simplicity.[10]

The ideas in this essay were not fully developed, but the general conceptions the writer presented would become familiar in numerous essays on architecture in the years following. The necessity to avoid architectural imitation would be a common theme, as would the assertion that the newest style, no matter what its source, was non-imitative, was American. The most recent of the older styles would typically come in for the severest criticism, attacked for its gracelessness, its unsuitability, and its imitativeness.

The Greek Revival was the first architectural mode to be promoted in America as a style. Through its formal qualities contemporary taste was offered an acceptable form and cultural nationalism was appeased. In the eye of the beholder, the Greek temple became the perfect expression of America. For the first time, a style appeared that was celebrated as "American" and that made previous houses, no matter how elegant and opulent, look old-fashioned. Greek Revival houses were built in great number, for it was a time of prosperity in the older colonies and of the development of new towns in the west. For the wealthy, the Greek Revival style provided a new model for the mansion and for the villa; the more modest house, as well, could follow fashion, since the addition of a columned portico added the respectability of fashion to a simple house. ·

For a brief period Greek Revival achitecture offered the solution to the constantly perplexing question of where one would discover the ideal American house. But if American cultural nationalism could attach itself to the image of the Greek temple, it is obvious that it could learn to attach itself to other forms as well. The succession of styles that followed the Greek Revival all claimed to represent the essential attributes of American life and civilization.

The most delightful accounts of the exigencies of fashionable house-building appear in James Fenimore Cooper's *The Pioneers* and *Home as Found*. The house of Marmaduke Temple represents, in its earlier form in *The Pioneers*, the work of the combined artistry of Richard Jones, a fanatic for "the composite order," and Hiram Doolittle, "a certain wandering eastern mechanic, who, by exhibiting a few soiled plates of English architecture, and talking learnedly of friezes, entablatures, and particularly of the composite order, had obtained a very undue influence over Richard's taste." Temple's house had started out as "a tall, gaunt edifice of wood, with its gable toward the highway." But the combined efforts of Jones and Doolittle have transformed it into the distant cousin of a Greek temple through the addition of such classical members as a portico and a theoretically invisible roof. The roof, in particular, causes stylistic and structural difficulties because "the ancients always endeavor to conceal" it. Efforts to accommodate the invisible roof to the weight of winter snows result in the production of a roof which "was by far the most conspicuous part of the whole edifice," despite some remedial shingling and a series of whimsical paintjobs, from sky-blue, as a kind of camouflage, to a color Mr. Jones "christened 'sun-shine.'" The roof is finally completed with the addition of "gaudily painted railings" as well as chimneys designed to "resemble ornaments on the balustrades." Such low chimneys, however, do not carry off the smoke, and the raised stacks that correct that problem become "four extremely conspicuous objects in the view." Cooper concluded his description of the mansion with the observation that it soon became a local model for imitation.

> . . . as wealth and comfort are at all times attractive, it was . . . made a model for imitation on a small scale. In less than two years from its erection, he had the pleasure of standing on the elevated platform, and of looking down on three humble imitators of its beauty. Thus it is ever with fashion, which even renders the faults of the great subjects of admiration.[11]

In *Home as Found*, Cooper returns to the Temple mansion, now renovated in accordance with the newest architectural fashion, the Gothic Revival. Mr. John Effingham, an enthusiast for Gothic, is responsible for the changes in the house, which he has "considerably regenerated and revivified, not to say trans-mogrified." While the group gazes at the house, Edward Effing-ham inquires of John whether he is "quite sure that yonder castellated roof . . . is quite suited to the deep snows of these mountains?" John chooses to change the subject, for indeed the roof had proven an error; he turns Edward's attention instead to his neighbor's houses which "are a good deal worse off. Of all abortions of this sort, to my taste, a Grecian abortion is the worst."

And to Cooper's taste as well. For once the mild jokes have been enjoyed, Cooper makes it clear that he is a man of con-temporary taste. The Greek or Composite style of the old house was indeed laughable, but the new Gothic exterior is to be com-mended. The abortive Greek roof has been castellated and the porticoed porch replaced by "a small entrance tower," alterations that make the house, in Cooper's view, representative of respect-able age and solidity.

In truth, the Wigwam [Temple's house] had none of the more familiar features of a modern American dwelling of its class. There was not a column about it, whether Grecian, Roman, or Egyptian; no Venetian blinds; no veranda or piazza; no outside paint, nor gay blending of colors. On the contrary, it was a plain old structure, built with great solidity and of excellent materials, and in that style of respectable dignity and propriety that was perhaps a little more peculiar to our fathers than it is to their successors, our worthy selves.[12]

A Gothic entrance tower may not conjure up for us the dignity and propriety of America's past, but for Cooper it could, for the temple was out of fashion, and now another style appropriated to itself all the nobilities.

Even while the Greek Revival provided a solution, albeit temporary, to the problem of the correction of taste, other house-related issues continued to plague Americans. A developing double-think appeared in a good deal of writing about houses, applying one set of values to small, primarily rural, houses and another to great mansions and villas. The lavish homes of the rich were an announcement of national success; no colonial backwater, the United States would challenge England herself with its new residences. On the other hand, the log cabin, the cottage, and even the frame farmhouse needed other justification. A rationale for the small home was provided in the framework of the Jeffersonian ideal, celebrating the yeoman farmer, extended to include the mechanic or tradesman, on his own land, or merely in his own home. The major themes here were the dignity of labor and the rewards of property, occasionally sentimentalized to an idealization of the simple life in a humble dwelling.

Only the general notion of progress mediated between the different ideals associated with the mansion and the cottage. The idea of progress could be brought to the support of economic individualism as well as to the defense of an egalitarian ideal. But architectural progress presented its own dilemmas, for where was it to cease? The rich man's house grew larger, but at what point would the exhibition of financial power become antagonistic to American values? The farmer and mechanic, meanwhile, labored for money, more goods, and better houses, and if the cabins and cottages of an upwardly mobile population were to serve merely as temporary shelters on the road to the mansion or the villa, how could the fiction be maintained that such humble houses were themselves a blessed reward for honest labor? These contradictions were not resolved; as a result the several types of houses that became representative in this period—the mansion and the villa, the cabin and the cottage—received attention from men whose values were at bottom confused and ambiguous.

Many of the current American values about houses were revealed by Timothy Dwight in his *Travels in New England and New York*. Like his eighteenth century predecessors, Dwight believed in the house as the symbol of civilization's progress. Our houses distinguished us, for one thing, from the Indians, who had chosen to continue for generations along the "narrow track in which their progenitors had gone before them. They built their houses and formed their utensils in the same manner, without dreaming that either could be made in ways more convenient and useful. Their houses, through a succession of several thousand years, were still wigwams. . . ."[13] But the Indian was not sufficient cultural competition; Americans had to be com-

pared to one another and held up to the model of their own intense energy. American towns revealed progress in their decent
and comely houses, and when a town failed to come up to the
mark, Dwight could accuse the population of a failure of par-
ticipation in the general upward movement of our society.
Weathersfield, Connecticut, was a disappointing sight.

> The houses, taken together are neither so well built, nor so well
> repaired, as those of their neighbors. Forty years since, they ap-
> peared better than those of any town in the state. For some reason
> or other, imperfectly known to me, Weathersfield has not kept
> pace with the general improvement of the country.

A more heartening view was afforded by Worcester, Massachusetts.

> [Worcester] is situated in a valley and contains, as I judge, about
> one hundred and twenty houses, generally well built; surrounded
> by neat fences, out-houses, and gardens; frequently handsome, and
> very rarely small, old, or unrepaired. Few towns in New England
> exhibit so uniform an appearance of neatness and taste, or contain
> so great a proportion of good buildings and so small a proportion
> of those which are indifferent as Worcester. There is probably more
> wealth in it also than in any other which does not exceed it in
> dimensions and number of inhabitants.[14]

Dwight was paying no mere aesthetic complement to Worcester.
With faith in the perfect independence of the man who "lives on
his own ground," he believed this independence was forfeited
only by indolence or dissipation, for if a man were neither sick
nor decrepit, "he is absolutely his own master, and the master
of all his possessions." In such independence was forged the
chain of society's strength: "In consequence of this mode of
occupancy, every man has something to defend, and that something, in his own estimation, of incalculable value."[15] Defense
of one's own property, Dwight asserted, led naturally to the defense of one's neighbor's possessions as well; hence, the vigor
of a society, assured by the right to property, was accurately
reflected in the houses that society displayed.

While Dwight admired the indications of wealth in the houses
of many towns, he was aware at the same time of the potential

evil of excess. Berwick, he noted, was a town which displayed its "proofs of prosperity" in its houses, but it also pleased by revealing no "exhibitions of taste," that is, no ostentatious houses. In Salem, after recording his pleasure in the evidences of "industry, economy, sobriety, and perseverance," he warned that "In a republic where no chasms are formed by distinctions of rank between the classes of citizens, the propensity to follow expensiveness of living is much more powerful and much more to be dreaded than in countries where such distributions exist."[16] Having sounded his cautionary note, Dwight congratulated Salem's citizenry in having avoided the pitfalls of ostentation. In fact, for all of Dwight's caution about excess and luxury, he never actually found a town which overstepped the limits of architectural decorum.

Even in Newburyport, where the splendid domestic architecture apparently gave Dwight some second thoughts, he concluded that the dangers of wealth had been averted. "The houses taken collectively make a better appearance than those of any other town in New England. Many of them are particularly handsome. Their appendages also are neat. Indeed an air of wealth, taste, and elegance is spread over this beautiful spot with a cheerfulness and a brilliancy to which I know no rival." But despite the fact that "The wealth of this town is everywhere visible in the buildings and their appurtenances," Dwight came to the happy conclusion that "Their morals and religion . . . are on a higher scale than those of most other towns in New England of the same size."[17]

Caveats about the dangers of wealth aside, when Dwight arrived in Boston, it was not the opulent mansions but the older and plainer houses that distressed him. Given Boston's considerable prominence among American towns, Dwight wished it had fewer "indifferent buildings, indifferent, I mean, for a place of such distinction. . . ." He recognized, of course, that the very age and history of the city were responsible for a number of these "indifferent" houses, for many were "erected at periods when the inhabitants were in humble circumstances and their knowledge in architecture was very defective;" some, he confessed, were "mere relics of the seventeenth century." Furthermore, Boston was noteworthy for its high percentage of home-owners; Bostonians did not live in hired houses to the same extent as New Yorkers and Philadelphians. But even this virtue had its drawbacks, for "Each man, therefore, builds according to his ability, and you need not be informed that the greater number of people in any city must in this case fall much below the boundary of elegance." Dwight attempted to excuse much of the disappointing domestic architecture in Boston, but his rationalizations appear not to have satisfied him fully. Beacon Hill, on the other hand, proved a delight, for "A great part of this field is already covered with elegant houses, some of them superb, and in splendor of building and nobleness of situation is not on this side of the Atlantic within many degrees of a rival."[18]

The old and the simple houses of Boston could be comprehended in the light of historical and sociological information; dilapidated and ill-cared for houses could be neither understood nor forgiven. While Dwight saw in Cambridge "every gradation of building found in this country except the log hut," the houses that he concentrated his attention on were those that he labeled "ordinary and ill repaired." These houses called forth an outburst on the kind of house-owner Dwight apparently recognized from his years at Yale—the academic sloth.

> To my eye this last [type of house] appeared as if inhabited by men accustomed to rely on the university for their subsistence, men whose wives are the chief support of their families by boarding, washing, mending, and other offices of the like nature. The husband in the meantime is a kind of gentleman at large, exercising an authoratative control over everything within the purlieus of the house, reading newspapers, and political pamphlets, deciding on the characters and measures of an administration, and dictating the policy of his country . . . a being creeping along the limits of animated and unanimated existence, and serving, like an oyster, as a middle link between plants and animals. If such men are not found here, Harvard College may boast of exclusive privileges.[19]

Once out of the major towns and back on his journey through the smaller communities of New England, Dwight had an entirely different reaction to humble homes. The meager, if well-tended, houses of Lynn carried images of the simple pleasures of a humble life. "The houses with scarcely an exception, appear to be the abodes of industry, competence, and thrift. Few of them were large or expensive, but almost all were tidy and well repaired. At the sight of them a traveler could scarcely avoid concluding that a peaceful and comfortable fireside must be found within the walls."[20]

The houses in Lynn, Massachusetts, as Dwight described them, have nearly all the important elements associated in America with the cottage. They shelter families capable of "industry, competence, and thrift," they are "tidy and well repaired," and they each have "a peaceful and comfortable fireside." Only the vines are missing from the cottage stereotype. But Dwight did not use the term "cottage," which had not yet altogether shed its pejorative connotations. By 1815, some American writers began to use the word "cottage" in a positive sense, modified by the adjectives that were to become inextricably bound up with it, "humble" and "snug." The writer of the essay in the *Analectic*, who condemned Palladian architecture and houses imitative of English models, turned at one point from his remarks on style to chastise Americans for admiring the pretentious villa while "we despise or overlook the humble beauties and snug comforts of the cottage. . . ."[21]

By 1832, an essay for the *New England Magazine* pushed the cottage stereotype even further. The writer condemned the excess inherent in "the slavery to fashion and custom," which drove men to building larger houses than were suitable "for comfort, convenience, or beauty." Furthermore he warned, such houses brought "a load of debt" to the children, forced as a result to "yield their paternal acres to some stranger. . . ." In the place of the grandiose, he admired the "little cottage," which combined "neatness, and comfort, and taste."

> Its white walls peep out from among the trees. . . . You may enter the humble door of that cottage, over which a woodbine has been trained . . . you will find everything convenient. . . . And yet that is the dwelling house of a mechanic of humble means, who has made his own estate by industry, and knows how to enjoy it to the utmost.

Finally, he looked ahead to a time when "neat snug cottages and farm houses . . . where nature, and art, and economy shall all combine—shall be scattered through the land and mark the abodes of comfort, and true Republican independence."[22] In connection with the description of the cottage, the words "humble" and "snug" reappear and the image of the woodbine is introduced, an image to become essential to the vision of the cottage, now vine-covered. With the additional comment that the cottage represents the reward of a humble man's industrious life, the passage reflects the fully developed moral symbolism of the cottage.

Nowhere is the early ideal associated with the small house of the independent man so insistently expressed as in the work of Crevecoeur, especially in his *Letters from an American Farmer* (1782). Crevecoeur's "farmer" is a comfortably prosperous man; he owns a small acreage and lives in a good house, both left to him by his father and both of which he endeavors to improve. "My father left me three hundred and seventy-one acres of land, forty-seven of which are good timothy meadow, an excellent orchard, a good house, a substantial barn." An occasional remark suggests architectural improvements made possible by his prosperity; he has added a new parlor and he has the comforts of a piazza.[23]

More important than the land and the house in themselves, however, were their symbolic value as signs of a man's freedom and status as a citizen. The land that Crevecoeur's "farmer's" father had "converted . . . into a pleasant farm . . ." served as the basis of "all our right; on it is founded our rank, our freedom, our power as citizens, our importance as inhabitants of such a district. . . ." Essentially, it was the property rather than the house which stood for the freedom and self-respect Crevecoeur celebrated, "the bright idea of property, of exclusive right. . . ." But in his depiction of his life and of the world about him, he employed the image of the house in ways that at once reinforced his ideas and elevated the house to a symbolic value of its own. In a passage which described the American scene as it might appear to an Englishman, Crevecoeur painted a landscape and then filled it in with decent houses.

> We are all animated with the spirit of an industry which is unfettered and unrestrained, because each person works for himself. If he travels through our rural districts he views not the hostile castle, and the haughty mansion, contrasted with the clay-built hut and miserable cabin, where cattle and men help to keep each other warm, and dwell in meanness, smoke, and indigence. A pleasing uniformity of decent competence appears throughout our

habitations. The meanest of our log-houses is a dry and comfortable habitation.[24]

To Crevecoeur "The spirit of industry" was most apparent on the frontier, where the succession of houses, from log cabin to decent frame dwelling and at last to houses of brick or stone, signalled the advance of civilization. If the first group of settlers were a rough bunch, many of whom "exhibit the most hideous parts of our society," they would in a decade be followed by the next wave of settlers, "more industrious people, who will finish their improvements, convert the log-house into a convenient habitation . . . [and] change in a few years that hitherto barbarous country into a fine fertile, well regulated district. Such is our progress. . . ."[25]

The stages of architectural progress on the frontier were sufficiently interesting to occasion remarks by numerous writers. In *Notions of the Americans,* Cooper off-handedly alluded to the use of stone, where it is available, "in what may be called the second and third stages of the settlements."[26] And foreign visitors frequently outlined the stages of settlement in their books about America. The Count of Rochambeau described the process in his travel memoirs.

> They commence by firing the forests, which operation they call *clearing.* . . . They then build their habitations with the round branches of the trees, piled one upon another, and propped up by stakes. . . . At the expiration of twenty or thirty years, when they have succeeded in fully clearing the ground, they proceed to build more tidy and comfortable houses with planks cleverly joined and wrought with great art. . . . At length, twenty or thirty years later, the family's circumstances become more easy, and they then remove to a brick house, the complement of their architecture.[27]

The log cabin entered American lore as the rude and temporary shelter that announced the initial stage in the victory of civilization. Although the victory was not considered complete until the cabin had given way to the frame or brick house, the log cabin itself assumed symbolic value: it was the first round of artillery fire in a prolonged battle. Tocqueville's description of his visit to an early settlement near Lake Oneida carries such implications.

At last we heard the echoes of an axe-stroke, the first distant announcement of the presence of a European. Some trees cut down, trunks burnt and charred, and a few plants useful to the life of man sown in the midst of the confusion of a hundred shapes of debris, led us to the pioneer's dwelling. In the centre of the rather restricted clearing made by axe and fire around it, rose the rough dwelling of the precursor of European civilization. It was like an oasis in the desert.

Although the log cabin was not in these years viewed romantically, and was considered a suitable dwelling only under the rigorous conditions of frontier life, still no stigma attached itself to the man who built and inhabited a log cabin in the first period of settlement. Indeed Tocqueville remarked that "The Americans in their log houses have the air of rich folk who have temporarily gone to spend a season in a hunting lodge."[28]

Still, the log cabin, unlike the frame or brick house that succeeded it, did not carry with it the two significant values of American houses: individual respectability and societal success. David Thomas, who traveled through the west in 1816, saw many log cabins, but he tolerated them only in the rudest wilderness, asserting that "*log* buildings are commonly restricted with much propriety of taste, to the first openings of the wilderness." He especially approved of one town which, though it "claims no older date than ten years, when its site was a forest," has "about 100 houses, built chiefly of brick." The quick disappearance of log cabins was, for Thomas, particular proof of the energy of Yankees. The original population of Vincennes, Indiana, was French, and although the town was a century old, "it appears the cabin bounded their view in architecture." With the new wave of Anglo-Saxon settlers, however, came hope for Vincennes, for "this primitive indolence" was already somewhat "lessened in appearance by the influx of a northern population."[29]

Conversely, Washington Irving, in the person of Diedrich Knickerbocker, so disliked both the Yankee and his progress, that he insisted on the superiority of the log cabin to the pretentious frame house that followed it. Scorning Yankee "improvement," as he called it, Irving considered it nothing but a passion which goaded the frontiersman into replacing his serviceable log cabin with "A huge palace of pine boards . . . large enough for a parish church. . . ." The large house, having depleted either the financial or the emotional resources of the settler, typically remained unfinished, according to Irving, and slowly decayed: "The outside remaining unpainted, grows venerably black with time; the family wardrobe is laid under contribution for old hats, petticoats, and breeches, to stuff into the broken windows. . . ." Even the log cabin, now serving as cow-house or pig-sty, had represented a better shelter, for it at least "nestled this *improving* family snugly. . . ." Instead, the family became like "an aspiring snail" who determined "to crawl into the empty shell of a lobster—where he would no doubt have resided with great style and splendour, the envy and hate of all the painstaking snails in his neighbourhood, had he not accidentally perished with cold, in one corner of his stupendous mansion."[30]

Irving was not quite alone in attacking the efforts of the small farmer or tradesman to improve his housing. Criticism of this kind was, of course, infrequent, for it went against the grain of American idealism, particularly ideas of classlessness and free opportunity. But in the 1832 essay on "Domestic Architecture" in the *New England Magazine*, the author devoted a few paragraphs to tracing the typical course of events that led a "farmer or mechanic" to attempt a house beyond his means, "bringing ruin on himself and his family." He deplored the folly but excused the foolish on the ground that "our men of moderate fortunes" are brought to such ruinous extravagance by "honorable and praise-worthy considerations."

> There is a feeling of independence, and of republican equality among our citizens . . . which, if misapplied, makes them the veriest slaves. And this feeling may be traced in the style of our farm houses. . . . No man is willing to be out done, if he can avoid it, by his neighbor . . . he cannot bear with patience to be surpassed in the externals of style or independence.

The only remedy the author could suggest for this situation did not lie with the farmer or mechanic himself; rather it depended on the rich man whose responsibility it was to deny himself an overly luxurious house, particularly in rural areas, where it caused "lasting injury to a country village," by becoming "a sort of standard for others."[31]

These lasting injuries to country villages were the new and elaborate villas, the country houses of the urban rich. Perhaps even more than city mansions, these villas were designed with every consciousness of fashion and taste, for they were restricted neither by the confinements of a city lot nor by the pressures of urban architectural sobriety. Furthermore, architects found country houses more interesting to plan, for the rural landscape was more hospitable to their designs than were the ever smaller city lots. While the richest men had both a city and a country residence, many more men had incomes that limited them to one home; for them the American architect would create the compromise of the suburban villa. But before the suburbs, the villa emerged as the fashionable country house.

Crevecoeur, in his *Eighteenth Century Travels in Pennsylvania and New York*, took a boat up the Hudson River where he much admired "the homes of city merchants, almost all white and elegant," which adorned the shores between New York and New Jersey. The captain of the river boat supplemented the view with a vision of the villas of the future, foreseeing a time when

> agriculture, commerce, and industry have accumulated wealth and love of beauty will come here to build fine country seats, direct and guide these lovely waters, take possession of all the most charming sites, and convert these deserts, today so wild, into wholesome, cheerful, delightful dwelling places.

Nevertheless, the captain, a good environmentalist, did express concern over preserving the natural beauty of the landscape: "Can future generations preserve these beautiful cedars, these gigantic pines, these venerable hemlocks, these oaks, more than a century old. . . . Human ingenuity could never replace them."[32]

Although the villa was the newest country home, the rural landscape was still marked by the manor houses of the older families. Patterns were already established which separated the rich men of the eighteenth century, in their relatively decorous and quietly elegant houses, from the millionaires of the nineteenth, for some of whom no architectural flamboyance was excessive. While urban residences and neighborhoods in older cities reflected the differences between the two groups of affluent families, the architecture of country houses made these distinctions even more apparent. In 1838, to take one remarkable example, Alexander Davis designed a country house in Tarrytown for William Paulding, a New York merchant. "Lyndhurst" was a Gothic castle complete with turret and battlements, a structure in whose shadow the most sumptuous eighteenth century plantation house became a modest dwelling. The Barrell house near Boston, four decades earlier, had caused considerable comment, but the Barrell mansion was in fact simply an extension in size and in elegance of the typical fine house of the period. It looked like other houses. "Lyndhurst" was a fanciful interpretation of baronial architecture; it did not look like a house at all, but like the castles it emulated.

The older aristocracy whose family pride kept them immured in ruinous ancestral seats came in for occasional satire. Washington Irving created a comic prototype in the Cockloft family and its ancient manor house.

> The family mansion bears equal marks of antiquity with its inhabitants. As the Cocklofts are remarkable for their attachment to everything that has remained long in the family, they are bigoted toward their old edifice, and I dare say would sooner have it crumble about their ears than abandon it. The consequence is, it has been so patched up and repaired, that it has become as full of whims and oddities as its tenants; requires to be nursed and humored like a gouty old codger of an alderman. . . . Whenever the wind blows the old mansion makes a most perilous groaning; and every storm is sure to make a day's work for the carpenter, who attends upon it as regularly as the family physician.[33]

But whatever the eccentricities of the older aristocracy, it was the urban new rich, struggling to establish a foothold in a world dominated by fashion, who were the favorite target of satire. Cooper thought it "a fact that the parvenus are commonly the most lavish in their expenditures, either because money is a novelty, or, what is more probably the case, because they find it necessary to purchase consideration by its liberal use."[34] One kind of fashion that was available for purchase was a house in the right neighborhood, and Irving did not bother to weigh causes in his satire on the vanity of such fashion-conscious social climbers.

> —Broadway—great difference in the gentility of streets—a man who resides in Pearl street, or Chatham Row, derives no kind of

dignity from his domicile; but place him in a certain part of Broadway, anywhere between the Battery and Wall street, and he straightway becomes entitled to figure in the beau monde, and strut as a person of prodigious consequence!—Query, whether there is a degree of purity in the air of that quarter which changes the gross particles of vulgarity into gems of refinement and polish? A question to be asked, but not to be answered—[35]

As Tocqueville had noted, "The American is devoured by the longing to make his fortune; it is the unique passion of his life."[36] The stylish houses of the rich, in their fashionable neighborhoods or on country estates, advertised with a new blatancy the power of money in America.

As the American house assumed increasingly symbolic properties, writers began to associate particular character types with particular house types. Timothy Dwight saw a kind of house in Cambridge that spoke to him of the academic sloth who resided there. Rambling and unpainted farmhouses told Irving of Yankee "improvers." Log cabins signalled American progress for Crevecoeur and Tocqueville, conjuring up images of strong men and noble women forging civilization out of the wilderness. In fiction, writers began to go beyond the representational values of particular house-types and to employ houses as symbolic referents for their characters. Natty Bumppo, as Leatherstocking in Cooper's *The Pioneers*, dwells in a structure called a "hut," but which he, the antithesis of enthusiasm for progress, refers to as his "wigwam." Its simplicity reinforces Leatherstocking's own innocence; furthermore, it carries sentimental values, particularly those associated with "home." When the hut is burned down and Leatherstocking hears an offer to have it rebuilt he demurs:

> . . . can ye go into the place where you've laid your fathers, and mothers, and children, and gather together their ashes, and make the same men and women of them as afore? You do not know what 'tis to lay your head for more than forty years under the cover of the same logs, and to look on the same things for the better part of a man's life.[37]

The association of a man's house and his character could occasionally be developed along the lines of an economic sentimentality that connected great mansions with cruel or evil characters and simple dwellings with pious and honest persons. As early as 1799, Charles Brockden Brown played on this theme in describing the house of Wellbeck through the eyes of Arthur Mervyn.

> . . . a house of the loftiest and most stately order. It seemed like a recent erection, had all the gloss of novelty, and exhibited to my unpractised eyes, the magnificence of palaces. My father's dwelling did not equal the height of one story, and might be easily comprised in one-fourth of these buildings which here were designed to accomodate the menials. My heart dictated the comparison between my own condition and that of the proprietors of this domain. How wide and how impassable was the gulf by which we were separated! This fair inheritance had fallen to one who, perhaps, would only abuse it to the purpose of luxury, while I, with intentions worthy of the friend of mankind, was doomed to wield the flail and the mattock.[38]

By the 1840's, the American house clearly represented general cultural values, particularly as an index of progress, both personal and national. Also, particular house-types, the mansion and villa of the rich and the cabin and cottage of the poorer, had become associated with particular values, and in the case of the cottage, a stereotype had fully emerged. Furthermore, whether a house was a Gothic castle or a snug and humble cottage, it had begun to take effective power to represent the man, or the fictional character who inhabited it, becoming in effect his public face. However, as the American house assumed symbolic dimensions, it absorbed many of the contradictions inherent in American culture.

The richness and the power as well as the contradictions inherent in the symbol of the American house were all fully realized in the decade before the Civil War, a decade in which four major books were published that used the American house as subject, symbol, or cultural metaphor. In 1850, Andrew Jackson Downing's *The Architecture of Country Houses* appeared, a book that considered the question of house-form and style within a broad cultural and philosophical framework. In 1851 came Hawthorne's *House of the Seven Gables*, elevating the house to central symbolic importance within the structure of fiction. In

1854 Thoreau printed *Walden*, using the house as a primary metaphor through which to express the materialism of his society. In the same year, Rufus Griswold's *Republican Court* made the houses of prominent men an integral part of his history of "American Society in the Days of Washington." There are a number of reasons why the full symbolization of the American house should have been achieved by 1850. Most significant is the atmosphere of cultural nationalism brewing in this period, a desire for the intellectual and artistic independence of the United States that had been articulated over a decade earlier in Emerson's famous Phi Beta Kappa address of 1837. Like poetry and fiction, painting and sculpture, architecture needed to find an American expression. But with domestic architecture the situation was more complicated than it was with fiction or the fine arts, for houses were a necessity, and with or without a self-conscious interest in the aesthetic and nationalist characteristics of architecture, men would continue to construct homes.

Interest in American houses was stimulated as well by the wealth that America had earned by 1850. Rich business men of the United States already had a reputation for pouring all of their energies into business and none into the leisurely development of the arts. These men were building houses of some size and pretension, but not necessarily with any architectural refinement. The furious wave of Greek Revival enthusiasm had passed, and several architectural styles had been introduced, each asserting its special suitability for the wealthy American. A number of designers and writers undertook with special urgency the task of raising the national level of taste. But America's wealth lay not only in the riches of the few, but in the competency of the many, and in a land where property was available to all and where the house had become the primary symbol of property, significant interest developed as well in the style of small houses intended to bespeak the decency, dignity, and charm appropriate to American life.

Beyond cultural nationalism, developing national wealth, the discovery of new architectural styles, and the importance of establishing the image of a prosperous or at least self-sufficient class of farmers and mechanics, the symbolization of the house was probably enhanced as well by the development of a sense of national history. By 1850 Americans had grown conscious of their past, and with this consciousness came the nostalgia with which Americans have consistently looked at previous generations. Thus, old houses became important and the changing neighborhoods of rapidly developing cities began to stand as metaphors for the lost innocence of a happier time.

Such nostalgia marks Rufus Griswold's *Republican Court*, a codification and romanticization of our history. Tied in with both emphases in Griswold was his fascination with houses, a fascination partly attributed to his conservatism and snobbery. For example, Griswold provided a complete list of the addresses in New York of the President, Vice-President, and all the members of Congress in 1789, not only to preserve the facts themselves, but as Griswold said, to suggest "the limits of that part of the city which was occupied by the better classes of society."[39] Old New York had changed by 1854, as had Philadelphia, and Griswold defended against the present by setting each historic personality he dealt with, not only the famous but the wealthy and the socially prominent as well, in the house where he once lived.

Typical of Griswold's technique is his discussion of the Willing mansion in Philadelphia, a house that represented the vanished elegance of a simpler world. Independent of the Willing family, prominent and respectable Philadelphians, the mansion had a history of its own, boasting a string of distinguished tenants.

> The west end of this lot, fronting on Fourth street, Mr. Thomas Willing, son of the person here mentioned [Charles Willing], surrendered to his son-in-law and nephew, Mr. Thomas Willing Francis, who built upon it the beautiful mansion now occupied by Mr. Joseph Ingersoll. On the southern part, Mr. Charles Willing himself built a residence which has since given place to other buildings, for his son-in-law, Coloniel William Byrd, of Westover, in Virginia. General Washington for some time had his head-quarters at Philadelphia in this house. It was afterward the residence of Chief Justice Chew.[40]

Griswold uses the Willing house, and others like it, as emblems for his history. Nostalgia is complicated by snobbery. Looking back to an age of titans from a world he sees as corrupted by commerce and money, Griswold regards old houses that have for him the luster of age and association and he finds them more elegant than modern homes, reflecting a life nobler and simpler than that of his own time. As Griswold says, life in Philadelphia had once the "elegance of dignity, moral worth, and the consciousness of gentility." Although material wealth did contribute to this elegance, that wealth "less suddenly acquired and less generally diffused, had that honorable source, that repose of character, and that stability of endurance, which renders wealth more valuable for the respectability it imparts than as a means of material luxury."[41] Ironically, the Willing house itself fell victim to the newer prosperity. In the second edition of *Republican Court* (1867), Griswold observed that the Willing mansion had been torn down in 1856 to be replaced by the new offices of the Pennsylvania Railroad Company.

Henry David Thoreau would have concurred with Griswold only in his aversion to the growing contemporary drive for wealth and property. "Things are in the saddle," warned Emerson, but it was Thoreau whose rejection of materialism went beyond rhetoric to action. He discovered the most symbolic of "things" to sacrifice—the house. In the gesture of *Walden*, of the handmade cabin in the woods, Thoreau acted out a metaphor for America and established a parable for property.

In organizing his attack against property, Thoreau confronted the attitudes toward the house which were most ponderously self-congratulatory. His contemporaries asserted not only that shelter was one of life's basic necessities, but that the progress from primitive shelter, from the wigwam of the savage to the modern house, was the very measure of civilization. Thoreau granted the necessity of shelter, but insisted on redefining what was necessary.

> By the words, *necessary of life,* I mean whatever, of all that man obtains by his own exertions, has been from the first, or from long use has become, so important to human life that few, if any, whether from savageness, or poverty, or philosophy, ever attempt to do without it.[42]

He concluded that much less is necessary than we have come to believe so, either in the way of food and clothing or of shelter. As for civilization, Thoreau did not accept the nineteenth century enthusiasm for progress. He traced man's movement from the open world to the cave and to the roofed shelter, only to chafe at the effectiveness with which the hearth had removed us from nature.

For most Americans, furthermore, the construction of solid houses and the development of towns had been not only a desperate need for the early Colonies, but later a sign of the progress and security of the Republic. Thoreau was not convinced. He quoted both an unnamed secretary for the Province of New Netherlands and Edward Johnson's *Wonder-Working Providence* to describe the burrows in the earth or in the sides of hills in which shelter was first obtained in New England before time could be spared for the construction of houses. "Pressing wants" had forestalled the building of houses at the time of initial settlement, and Thoreau asked whether our "pressing wants [were] satisfied now?" By asserting moral rather than physical necessities, Thoreau concluded that the time had not arrived for building a luxurious dwelling: "I am deterred, for, so to speak, the country is not yet adapted to *human* culture, and we are still forced to cut our spiritual bread far thinner than our forefathers did their wheaten."[43]

Thoreau again took the offensive with moral artillery to combat contemporary praise of the beauty and convenience of the modern house. "While civilization has been improving our houses, it has not equally improved the men who are to inhabit them. It has created palaces, but it was not so easy to create noblemen and kings." In any case, Thoreau attacked the concept that beauty could be consciously created, and insisted on organic beauty, an outward expression of inward qualities. "What reasonable man ever supposed that ornaments were something outward and in the skin merely,—that the tortoise got his spotted shell, or the shellfish its mother-o'-pearl tints, by such a contract as the inhabitants of Broadway their Trinity Church."[44] The argument asserting that architectural beauty must somehow develop out of the character and spirituality of the inhabitant of the building is remarkable as paralleling the beliefs made current at the time by A. J. Downing and other pattern book writers, who used it to prove that men ought indeed to own, and preferably to have built for them, their own houses. But Thoreau employed the argument of the organic relationship between a man and his house to deny the necessity or even the propriety of building costly homes, for he saw beauty as a mystical accretion whose singular source lay in the spiritual goodness of man.

> What of architectural beauty I now see, I know has gradually grown from within outward, out of the necessities and character of the indweller, who is the only builder, —out of some unconscious truthfulness, and nobleness, without ever a thought for the appearance; and whatever additional beauty of this kind is destined to be produced will be preceded by a like unconscious beauty of life.[45]

Romantic organicism, with its metaphor rooted in the shellfish and tortoise imagery above, took a further turn in Thoreau's thinking to produce the idea of man creating his own house in the simple and natural way birds create their own nests.

> There is some of the same fitness in man's building his own house that there is in a bird's building its own nest. Who knows but if men constructed their dwelings with their own hands . . . the poetic faculty would be universally developed, as birds universally sing when they are so engaged? But alas! we do like cowbirds and cuckoos, which lay their eggs in nests which other birds have built, and cheer no traveller with their chattering and unmusical notes.[46]

This is, in fact the basic gesture of *Walden*. The significance of building one's house lay specifically in process and act and not in the accomplished architectural fact.

For those who could or would not build with their own hands, Thoreau suggested at least "a little Yankee shrewdness." For example, he has seen by the railroad a shelter made from a tool box six feet by three, which could probably be had for a dollar. Here, Thoreau's wit subverts basic American values, which promised the opportunity to earn a decent home by virtue of hard work and thrift. But Thoreau was no enthusiast for hard work, a life of drudgery that enabled one to buy what others had labelled necessities. Figuring the price of an average house near Concord at $800.00, and the average wage at a dollar a day, Thoreau calculated the consuming of ten to fifteen years of a laborer's life for the getting of a house—a very bad bargain.[47]

Thoreau attacked nearly all the attitudes that had grown up about the American house by 1850. He would not accept necessity, progress, or beauty as rationalizations for property. Only the organic metaphor had power with Thoreau, the intimate and expressive connection between a man and his shelter. But in his hands, even the organic argument was altered; the premise from which Downing and his colleagues sought to encourage the building of distinctive houses Thoreau used to condemn materialistic house-building. *Walden* is not, of course, a book about houses; nevertheless, Thoreau's principal metaphor, his $28.12½ cabin, was not picked at random. In developing the anti-materialist argument of *Walden*, Thoreau had unerringly discerned America's most potent symbol for property.

In *The House of the Seven Gables*, Nathaniel Hawthorne, like Thoreau, made the house a symbol for property, but Hawthorne both extended and complicated the meaning of the house in his novel. *The House of the Seven Gables* is the ancient home of the Pyncheon family, lived in now by old Hepzibah Pyncheon and her brother Clifford. The gloomy old dwelling is the physical counterpart of the family history. *The House of the Seven Gables*, whose "very timbers were oozy, as with the moisture of a heart," was "itself like a great human heart, with a life of its own, and full of rich and sombre reminiscence."[48]

It is in part through Clifford Pyncheon that Hawthorne articulated the novel's attack on the house as property, especially as inherited property. The "terms of roof and hearth-stone," Clifford declares, "are soon to pass out of men's daily use and be forgotten." As a result, much "human evil will crumble away."

> What we call real estate—the solid ground to build a house on—is the broad foundation on which nearly all the guilt of this world rests. A man will commit almost any wrong—he will heap up an immense pile of wickedness, as hard as granite, and which will weigh as heavily upon his soul, to eternal ages—only to build a great, gloomy, dark-chambered mansion for himself to die in, and for his posterity to be miserable in.

In fact, Clifford echoes doctrine very like that of Thoreau. Old houses, he says, emprison men whose "soul needs air; a wide sweep and frequent change of it." Once men had "dwelt in temporary huts, or bowers of branches, as easily constructed as a bird's nest," and when they built so, with their hands, they were in harmony with nature.[49]

Clifford, however, is not a dependable source; he is intellectually childlike, an idealistic dreamer, irresponsible. His views on houses are as idealistic and impractical as he. But Hawthorne has a second radical mouthpiece in the young daguerrotypist, Holgrave. Holgrave, like the Pyncheons, is a victim of the past, and he struggles against what he calls the power of Dead Men, whose wills, laws, books, jokes, diseases, forms, and creeds inhibit and even destroy the living. Furthermore, "we live in Dead Men's houses," he tells Phoebe Pyncheon, Hepzibah's young niece. But Phoebe is the voice of conservative moderation: "And why not . . . so long as we can be comfortable in them?" In his response, Holgrave does not, like Clifford, dismiss houses out of hand, but he does demand that each generation build its own.

> . . . we shall live to see the day, I trust . . . when no man shall build his house for posterity. . . . If each generation were allowed and expected to build its own houses, that single change, comparatively unimportant in itself, would imply almost every reform which society is suffering for. I doubt whether even our public edifices . . . ought to be built of such permanent materials as stone or brick. It were better that they should crumble to ruin, once in twenty years, or thereabouts, as a hint to people to examine into and reform the institutions which they symbolize.[50]

While the primary animus felt by both Clifford and Holgrave is directed specifically against the old Pyncheon house, their hostility becomes generalized, an attack on all houses as symbols of property and of the past.

The opposite point of view is expressed throughout by Phoebe whose judgment and emotional serenity are never threatened by the old house. When she arrives to stay with Hepzibah, innate female qualities enable her to bring some charm to the dismal old place. Hawthorne sees Phoebe as the very type of domestic female: "A wild hut of underbrush, tossed together by wayfarers through the primitive forest, would acquire the home-aspect by one night's lodging of such a woman." Under her genius, the old house loses its "grime and sordidness," its "dry-rot was stayed," even the dust ceases to fall. "Phoebe's presence made a home about her."

So effective is the home-instinct in Phoebe that love for her chastens the radical Holgrave, who begins to speak of building a home someday, a home that will shelter future generations. "I have a presentiment that, hereafter, it will be my lot to set out trees, to make fences—perhaps, in due time, to build a house for another generation—in a word, to conform myself to laws, and the peaceful practice of society." When, at the conclusion of the novel, the principal characters leave the old house to move to the "elegant country seat of the late Judge Pyncheon," Holgrave laments to see so fine a house constructed of wood rather than of a permanent material like stone.

> Then every generation of the family might have altered the interior, to suit its own taste and convenience; while the exterior, through the lapse of years, might have been adding venerableness to its original beauty, and thus giving that impression of permanence, which I consider essential to the happiness of any one moment.[51]

An amazed Phoebe finds Holgrave's ideas wonderfully changed. Holgrave can only confess that he is "conservative already."[52]

Hawthorne's notebooks reveal his fascination with the great houses of decayed families. Unlike Griswold, he did not see them as emblems of a gentler world, but rather as symbols of the vanity of pride and riches. But despite his refusal to fall victim to architectural nostalgia, Hawthorne could not adopt a radical Thoreauvian position toward houses. In *The House of the Seven Gables*, such views are relegated to the childlike Clifford and to the young, embittered Holgrave. Once Holgrave and Phoebe declare their love, the young daguerrotypist becomes socialized, surrendering his animosity toward family houses and planning someday to build his own.

Hawthorne's interpretation of the house was, finally, more profound and complex than Thoreau's, for Hawthorne was willing to face the dilemma of the effect on youthful radicalism of sexual love. For Thoreau, who like Clifford remained innocent and unattached, the house could be forsworn. But for Holgrave whose radical selflessness gave way to sexual love no such solution is possible. With marriage comes family, and with a family the requisite house, the conformity to society, even the desire to penetrate the future with a home built for one's posterity. Under the impact of domestic love, the house becomes home, and the notion of property is sunk under the weight of the

image of the hearth. Furthermore, Hawthorne made it clear that
women like Phoebe never experience the youthful radicalism of
Holgrave; they are, at their best, home-makers always, and their
mission is to search out the man who will build them the house
out of which they will create the family home. At bottom, the
dilemma of the house in Hawthorne, the double thrust of property and hearth, becomes a sexual conflict, one that the woman
necessarily wins.

The 1850's, with Downing, Griswold, Thoreau, and Hawthorne, saw the American house fully developed as a cultural
symbol, but as a symbol of complex and contradictory values. In
the years after the Civil War the significance of the house continued to grow, as did the complexities and contradictions it
carried with it. The house idea was exploited for aesthetic, domestic, social, economic, national, and moral arguments. Progress
boasted new houses; nostalgia cherished the old. Conservatism
looked to the house for stability; radicalism distrusted it as encouraging a blind adherence to the status quo. But the deepest
contradiction in the symbol of the house depended on the conflict between the premise of an egalitarian society and the
promise of a market place economy. The egalitarian dream en-
visioned a nation of farmers, and later mechanics, whose industry and sobriety were to be dignified by the possession of a
house. As a society without rigid class demarcations, America
would have no palaces and no hovels, but decent convenient
homes. But the market place, with its own body of myths,
promised more than decency and convenience; with the great
millionaires of the later nineteenth century came audacious
mansions, emblems of huge fortunes threatening the egalitarian
myth. Along with the mansions came the slums, the houses of
the poor, making a mockery of the house as property and denying
even the possibility of the house as home. The tenements of the
city clums replaced that older menace in American society, the
poorhouse. Thoreau had perceived the dichotomy of property
in 1854: "The luxury of one class is counterbalanced by the
indigence of another. On the one side is the palace, on the other
are the almshouse and the 'silent poor.' "[53]

But between the palace and the poorhouse, the middle class
home has survived and prospered. Downing's mechanic in his
cottage became the working-man in his small suburban house,

and later the World War II veteran in Levittown. For all the debate over mansions and tenements and despite the nostalgia that sentimentalized both log cabins and plantation houses, it is the ordinary houses, owned or dreamed of by the great majority of Americans, that came to express the most weighted symbolism. These houses are at once home and property, the center of family values and a membership card to responsible citizenship, a defense against personal immorality and a fortress against social and political radicalism.

The Authority of Architects

Chapter Three

From A. J. Downing
The Promise of Egalitarianism

> ... a home built and loved upon new world,
> and not the old world ideas and principles, a
> home in which humanity and republicanism
> are stronger than family pride and aristocratic
> feeling; a home of the virtuous citizen, rather
> than of the mighty owner of houses and lands.
>
> A. J. Downing,
> The Architecture of Country Houses

Over the last century and a quarter two major American architects have addressed serious social and cultural questions about the American house, Andrew Jackson Downing and Frank Lloyd Wright. Both men believed in the power of domestic architecture to effect personal and social betterment, and both saw domestic architecture as a reflection of and an index to the political and cultural institutions of a people. For Wright, architecture, like America, was on the defensive in an urban, technocratic, mobocracy. For Downing, in the decade before the Civil War, America provided more evidence for hope than for despair, and architecture would realize that promise.

Downing's America still perceived itself as a rural nation, despite the energetic growth of the cities, and as a nation in which the individual man, armed with industry and piety, was free to make what he would of himself and his life. Prosperity appeared widespread and increasing; the urban poor, not yet swelled by the freed slaves of the South or the great waves of immigration that lay ahead, was not an apparently menacing problem. Americans were beginning, as well, to flex their cultural muscles, and in their cry for national expression in the arts they included a plea for the American house, the house appropriate to so young, vigorous, and prosperous a people. In this

setting, Downing wrote *The Architecture of Country Houses*
(1850), bringing to the subject of the American house a mixture
of romantic organicism, American idealism, practical technology,
contemporary architectural fashions, and an egalitarian dream.

Between A. J. Downing and Frank Lloyd Wright other architects wrote about the American house, but none so extensively
nor so convincingly. In the 1850's, other books like Downing's
The Architecture of Country Houses appeared, but none revealed his breadth or his absorption in the American culture.
After the Civil War and through the end of the nineteenth century, published materials on houses became increasingly popular.
But the authors of these books and articles floundered in the
architectural and cultural contradictions of their time. The
growing gap between the rich and the poor, the increasing
problem of the urban poor, the great demand for middle-class
houses in the suburbs were not urgent problems for architects
engaged in designing fantastic mansions for the Vanderbilts and
their circle in New York City and Newport. Not until Louis
Sullivan, did an architect attempt to speak to the relationship
between the buildings of a society and the real texture of that
society. Finally, Wright turned Sullivan's lens from the public
buildings to the private home of America.

Social and political questions had played no part in American
architectural books before the 1850's. Like European and British
books, they concentrated on matters of style, construction, and
ornamentation. Furthermore, before the influence of Ruskin
reached America, architectural publications, limited to professional concerns, had addressed themselves to a small and special
audience of professionals, collectors, and educated amateurs.
Before the American Revolution, this audience had been supplied
with architectural publications from Europe, and especially
from England; after the Revolution, American builders began to
publish their own books, modeling them on the English ones
they had used previously, and borrowing freely from contemporary British architectural styles.

Asher Benjamin, a New England "housewright," published the
first American architectural book in 1797, *The Country Builder's
Assistant*, which ran to forty-four editions. Of the seven books
Benjamin wrote, the best known was *The American Builder's
Companion* (1806), a thoroughly instructive work intended for

the use of other builders. There are a limited number of plans and elevations, primarily for churches, but including as well three town houses and two country homes. The rest of the volume is taken up with drawings of architectural details and ornaments, such as plaster moldings, urns, and staircases. Indicative of the audience to which the book was addressed is a lengthy section on basic geometry, intended to assist rural carpenters.

Benjamin's book did not include material on the philosophy, the aesthetics, or the ethics of house-building; his volumes provided the practical information his readers wanted. The only general discourse Benjamin permitted himself was a two-page introduction, "The Origin of Building," a brief narration of man's progress from the houseless stage, when he "lived without care and without labor," to his discovery of nature's builders, "Swallows, rooks, bees, and storks." Employing his own "reasoning faculties," man "soon outdid his masters in the builder's art."[1]

The Modern Builder's Guide (1833), by Minard Lafever, turned immediately to practical ends with a chapter on "Geometry Adapted to Practical Carpentry." Subsequent material dealt with such matters as groin arches, stair railings, hand railings, and Grecian architecture, a section describing antique buildings taken from Stewart's *Antiquities of Athens*. The practical thrust of these early builders' books is best illustrated by a brief quote from Lafever.

> To give the strings of a circular stair their proper curvature and spiral twist, make for each string, a cylindrical block, that is, make two frames with battens or narrow strips of board nailed on longitudinally and rounded off at the outer edges, so that each frame shall, following the outline of the battens, be cylindrical, and have the respective curvatures of the circular wall and well-hole. Around these cylindrical frames bend your stair strings, gluing in the wedges as you proceed, and, if you please, gluing a piece of coarse canvas over the wedges.[2]

Seventeen years after Lafever explained the method of curving circular stairs, the publication of Downing's *Architecture of Country Houses* dramatically altered the purpose, tone, and anticipated audience of architectural books in America. In striking contrast to the practical information provided by Benjamin or

Lafever is much of the subject-matter and the rhetoric of Downing.

> . . . everything in architecture that can suggest or be made a symbol of social or domestic virtues, adds to its beauty, and exhalts its character. Every material object that becomes the type of the spiritual, moral, or intellectual nature of man, becomes at once beautiful, because it is suggestive of the beautiful in human nature.[3]

Andrew Jackson Downing (1815-1852) was a horticulturist whose first book concentrated on landscape gardening in America. In 1842 he published *Cottage Residences,* a work that introduced the aesthetic and moral interests fully developed in his major work, *The Architecture of Country Houses* (1850). With a profound respect for and knowledge of the work of Ruskin, Downing applied the Romantic idealism and organicism of Ruskin not to civic and ecclesiastic architecture, but to the architecture of the American house. Downing adopted, and carefully explained to his readers, Ruskin's theories of the beautiful and the useful in architecture, and his conception of the roles of harmony, symmetry, proportion, variety and unity.

Downing did not, however, limit himself to a recapitulation of Ruskin, nor did he assume that Ruskin's idealism was in itself sufficient for the realization of an American domestic architecture. Basic to Downing's work is the conception of a specifically American frame of reference in which he placed more generally current thories of romantic platonism and romantic organicism. The unique quality of the American experience, as Downing saw it, was the great significance of the home and the universal possibility for home-ownership in America. In the Preface to his book, Downing listed "three excellent reasons why my countrymen should have good houses." His first reason depended on the now-familiar theory of progress: ". . . a good house . . . is a powerful means of civilization. A nation, whose rural population is content to live in mean huts and miserable hovels, is certain to be behind its neighbors in education, the arts, and all that makes up the external signs of progress." Secondly, Downing believed in the formation of character in the family home. Through the formation of strong individual characters, the nation was served; thus, "the *individual home* has a great social value for a people." Finally, "there is a moral influence in a country home. . . . where the family hearth is made a central point of the Beautiful and the Good."

For Downing the importance of the individual home was to be fully realized in America "where every man may have a home."[4] If individual homes were to be virtually universal in the United States, it was imperative to educate "the national taste." "A young and progressive people," must develop "ideas of beauty, harmony, and moral significance in their daily lives." Therefore, the purpose of Downing's book was to alleviate the general ignorance of his public about architectural matters, an ignorance he ascribed to architects who have chosen to write in a "dry and barren manner" about their art. With enlightenment will come an improvement in taste, an awareness of ideas of beauty, appropriate for every citizen "in a country where the ease of obtaining a house and land, and the ability of almost every industrious citizen to build his own house, constitute a distinctive feature of national prosperity."[5] *The Architecture of Country Houses* is rooted in the premise that the health and strength of a culture are insured by the quantity and quality of its private houses.

The Architecture of Country Houses belongs to a type of publication known as the pattern book. Basic to these works are the elevations and the floor plans they provide, along with some textual material about each house. Frequently, pattern books would include other matter, essays ranging from the most philosophical material to the most mundane information. Downing's book, for example, includes passages on Absolute Beauty; The True in Architecture; Principles for designing farm-houses, as regards utility and beauty; Ignorance of the principles of building Chimneys; Cheap Varnish; The true meaning of the republican home; Extravagance of modern fashion in interior decoration; and the Use of air in purifying the blood. Also typical of nineteenth century pattern books is a much greater interest in country (or suburban) houses than in urban residences; hence, there is a major concentration on cottages and villas, and occasionally on farm-houses. Since the farmhouse, the cottage, and the villa represented housing for all types of Americans, the rural and the urban, the rich and the poor, pattern book writers assumed a very wide audience. The titles of pattern books published in the fifties frequently implied a universal audience: *Poor Man's House and Rich Man's Palace* (1854) and *The Modern House Builder from the Log Cabin to the Mansion* (1857).

Downing, like most other pattern book writers, confined his interests to rural residences. The general lack of interest in town houses reflected in these books, in architectural essays, and even later in the twentieth century writings of Frank Lloyd Wright stems from several causes. At its root, the preference for conceiving ideal homes in the country or the suburbs matched a developing American distrust of the city. Certainly, as the eighteenth century town turned into the nineteenth century city, real dangers and discomforts could be pointed to in urban life, and while more and more wage earners came to the cities for work, an increasingly insistent warning urged them to set their families in some conveniently located suburb where fresh air and a garden provided the suitable place for the raising of children and the preservation of the family hearth.

The advantages of the country house were both real and symbolic. For one thing, it stood on sufficient land to include a garden, perhaps a small orchard; therefore, it more closely approximated the American concept of property and of independence. Furthermore, such a house more closely conformed to ideas of home, to the homelike and wholesome atmosphere in which to raise children. Moreover, the designers of country houses, from cottage to villa, had a great deal more freedom than did urban builders. Not only were the rural architects not confined to specified lot sizes (twenty-five front feet in New York City), but they did not have to create houses whose facades and roof-lines fitted the block in which they were built. For pattern books, the more fanciful, "picturesque" houses sketched in a rural setting, provided much more appealing illustrations than did four or five story town houses.

In his consideration of country houses, Downing continually asserted that it was not only the right but even the duty of every "industrious citizen" to build his own house. In building his own house, that citizen could express his individual character, and Downing insisted that the expressive possibilities of domestic architecture are virtually unlimited. Domestic architecture "ought to be significant of the whole private life of man— his intelligence, his feelings, and his enjoyment."

. . . if [a house] plainly shows by its various apartments, that it is intended not only for the physical wants of man, but for his moral, social, and intellectual existence; if hospitality smiles in ample parlors; if home virtues dwell in cosy, fireside family-rooms; if the love of the beautiful is seen in pictures or statue galleries; intellectuality, in well-stocked libraries; and even a dignified love of leisure and repose, in cool and spacious verandas; we feel, at a glance, that here we have reached the highest beauty of which Domestic Architecture is capable—that of individual expression.[6]

Furthermore, Downing argued, "the character of every man may be read in his house." Nor could character be disguised; let a vicious man buy the house designed for and once lived in by a virtuous man, and we will discover that his viciousness "deadens or destroys its beauty by overlaying its fair features with a corrupt or vicious expression." The moral quality of a house, be it admirable or contemptible, was visible, and the moral quality of a house was no more or less than the reflection of the moral character of the inhabitant. Downing warned that "The basis for enduring beauty is truthfulness, no less in houses than in morals. . . ." The ideal house, therefore, would be one built by a virtuous man, or built for him by an architect who knew him "so completely as to make his work express the individual truly." Clearly, such an ideal contradicted the very purpose behind presenting a book of house patterns, as Downing admitted in a footnote. But he added as a justification that "All that we can do, is to offer to the feelings and judgments of our readers a number of designs. If their own character is more or less typified in any one of them, that design will be at once preferred by them."[7]

As prepared designs were antipathetic to absolute individuality of expression, so borrowed architectural fashions were hostile to the development of an indigenous American style. Downing's approach to this dilemma was, typically, to consider not the styles in themselves, but the motivations that controlled the choice of a particular style.

So far as an admiration of foreign style in architecture arises from the mere love of novelty, it is poor and contemptible; so far as it arises from an admiration of truthful beauty of form or expression, it is noble and praiseworthy.[8]

But while Downing did not condemn the imitation of foreign styles, unless they were done *"for the mere sake of the imitation,"* he did celebrate the hope of a developing American architecture, and like Emerson "would suppose that a cultivated American would exult and thank God for the great Future which dawns on him here, rather than sigh and fondle over the great Past which remains in Europe." Finally, like many American architects before and after him, Downing believed in an indigenous architecture emerging from the interaction of European influences and American conditions.

> Our own soil is the platform upon which a genuine national architecture must grow, though it will be aided in its growth by all foreign thoughts that mingle harmoniously with its simple and free spirit.[9]

Nowhere was the "simple and free spirit" of America so celebrated as in the idealized character of the independent farmer or working man. In designing farmhouses and cottages for such men, Downing paid his tribute to the republican ideal. Indeed, unlike many pattern book writers, Downing gave considerable attention to the cottage. He divided his book into three major sections, devoting one to cottages, one to farm-houses, and the last to villas. Each section opens with its own philosophical chapter and presents its own set of elevations and floor plans. A more common pattern of organization in pattern books was a serial presentation of plans after a general opening essay. While each pattern may have been accompanied with a page or two of text, there was no need to consider the cottage at length nor to come to grips with major socio-economic questions. Furthermore, since most pattern books moved from the cheapest to the most expensive plans, the simpler cottages were more or less sunk under the weight of the forty-room villas that followed them.

Downing's discussion of cottages assumed as a thesis the unique character of the American working-man—his independence, his dignity, his intelligence. In the United States such men could own their own homes, homes that were seen as at once the cause and the result of this independence, dignity and intelligence. No one, Downing insisted, should be ashamed to live in a cottage, nor should he wish to live in a cottage that decked itself out as if it were a villa. Indeed, the cottage was the symbol of the special qualities of the life of the working class in America; therefore, "intelligent working men . . . ought, more than the same class anywhere else, to feel the value and the dignity of labor, and the superior beauty of a cottage home which is truthful, and aims to be no more than it honestly is. . . ."[10]

The American cottage, like the American working-man it housed, was distinctive. While what passed in England as a cottage might well be a country house of "fifty apartments, with all the luxury of a first-rate villa," the same was not true in America. Here a cottage, as Downing defined it, "is a dwelling of small size," characterized by a family which managed "the houshold cares itself, or, at the most, with the assistance of one or two servants." The special distinction of the American cottage, however, lay neither in its size nor in the self-sufficiency of the family; rather its uniqueness depended upon the independence of the working-man for whom the cottage was private property.

> The majority of . . . cottages in this country are occupied not by tenants, dependents, or serfs, as in many parts of Europe, but by industrious and intelligent mechanics and working-men, the bone and sinew of the land, who own the ground upon which they stand, build them for their own use, and arrange them to satisfy their own peculiar wants and gratify their own tastes.[11]

Downing admitted that it was a good deal more difficult to design a cottage than a villa, for "the architect is bound down by rigid notions of economy." Nevertheless, good cottages could be designed to fill a demand that came, as Downing believed, not only from the basic need for shelter, but from the desire of "tens of thousands of working-men . . . who now wish to give something of beauty and interest to the simple forms of cottage life. . . ." No less than the rich, "these families were desirous to have their home of three rooms tasteful and expressive."[12] In the texts that accompany specific cottage plans, Downing continued to elevate and ennoble the simple American family. For example, Downing presented one cottage-plan that included a parlor although, he observed, "in most cheap cottages, the living-room is virtually the parlor. . . ." Nevertheless, "The American cottager is no peasant, but thinks, and thinks correctly, that as soon as he can afford it, he deserves a parlor, where he can receive his guests with propriety, as well as his wealthiest neighbor. We respect this feeling entirely."[13]

The farm-house, like the cottage, assumed importance from the class of men who inhabited it, and the farmer in America was a free landholder. Foreign architects, argued Downing, found the farm-house "little worthy of their attention," and not surprisingly, for in countries like Russia or England the serf or the tenant "has no property in the soil he cultivates." In America the situation was far different, "a large portion of the farmers are intelligent men. . . ." American institutions did not prevent the farmer from being included "among the wisest, the best, and the most honored of our citizens." Therefore, American farmers had attempted to build themselves something better than a mere "comfortable shelter for their heads;" unfortunately, there had been no suitable models and the farmer had too often aimed at a taste and elegance inappropriate to his life.[14]

But the farmhouse, like other houses, needed architectural truthfulness, and Downing set himself the task of providing suitable models, expressive of their owners and reflecting the life of the genuine farmer. Farmhouses should "show an absence of all pretension," for farmers were "more sincere, more earnest than men of any other class," as well as being "less sophisticated either in manners or heart. . . ."

> His dwelling ought to suggest simplicity, honesty of purpose, frankness, a hearty, genuine spirit of goodwill, and a homely and modest, though manly and independent, bearing in his outward deportment.[15]

Downing elaborated on the expressive function of farmhouses by listing a few of the specific architectural characteristics which were appropriate: "Extended space on the ground . . . a certain rustic plainness . . . a substantial and solid construction." Each of these characteristics was in itself expressive; for example, the rustic plainness he advocated "denotes a class more occupied with the practical and useful than the elegant arts of life."[16]

The sections on cottages and farmhouses in *The Architecture of Country Houses* are earnest and convincing; still it is in the chapters on the architecture of villas that Downing revealed his deepest excitement and enthusiasm. Attractive and expressive cottages and farmhouses would illustrate the general progress and prosperity of America, but beautiful villas would demonstrate that in the United States a special few can achieve unique success and live with taste and elegance. In a country where "there are neither the castles of feudal barons nor the palaces of princes," the villa was the residence of greatest dignity, "the most refined home of America—the home of its most leisurely and educated class of citizens." Acknowledging republican virtues in his essay on cottages and farmhouses, and refusing the temptations of European aristocratic values, Downing did find in the houses of the economically privileged class a particularly seductive ideal. Architecturally, large villas provided opportunities for the realization of beauty; moreover, "it is in such houses that we should look for the happiest social and moral development of our people."[17] The relationship between beauty and morality is always close in Downing's work, although the nature of the relationship is never carefully examined. Therefore, while Downing asserted that utility and beauty must go hand in hand in architecture and that truthfulness in architecture is the expression of the purpose of the structure, he seems finally to have preferred that kind of beauty which was relatively uninhibited by restraints on size or utility. "The cottage is too limited in size, the farm-house too simply useful in its character, to admit of that indulgence of beauty of form and decoration which belongs properly to the villa."[18]

Because the villa was freed from the constraints of size and from the demands of utility, Downing argued, it could more easily achieve not only beauty but also expressiveness. Most significantly, the freedom of the villa permitted the expression of individual rather than class characteristics. Unlike the cottage or farmhouse which reflected the type of life appropriate to a mechanic or a farmer, the villa could make a much more specific statement about the personality and taste of its particular inhabitant. "The man of common-sense views" may have himself "a symmetrical, regular house;" while "the man of sentiment or feeling" will build a house that "must nestle in, or grow out of, the soil." For "the men of imagination" there is the "picturesque" villa.

The villa, then, had great advantages in its freedom from

constraints of size and expense, but in this freedom lay potential dangers. A rich man must not be misled into assuming that the architectural qualities of his villa could conceal any deficiencies in his character. Downing continued to insist on the moral relationship between a man and his house; the owner and his dwelling must be at one, and the finest house could not conceal a shabby character.

> To find a really original man living in an original and characteristic house, is as satisfactory as to find an eagle's nest built on the top of a mountain crag—while to find a pretentious, shallow, man in such a habitation, is no better than to find the jackdaw in the eagle's nest.[19]

Furthermore, opulence in architecture held communal as well as personal perils. A republic, as Downing believed, could not afford the unlimited opulence that turned the house into the baronial hall. Downing was not, of course, unique in his warning against overly-ambitious houses. The earliest documents relating to Jamestown and the Massachusetts Colony had expressed a distrust of great houses. But in Downing we find the first considered attempt to set political and moral limits on the size and cost of the American house.

The question, as Downing posed it, asks "what a villa should be, in order that in its cost and duration, it may be true to its own time and country?" Having observed signs that "our wealthy builders of country-seats are about to go far astray," in committing themselves to "expenditures in domestic architecture quite unmeaning and unwise in a republic," Downing asserted that large and costly country seats "are always and inevitably failures in America," because they are "contrary to the spirit of republican institutions." To establish a great country seat was to depend on feelings that "can never take root, except in a government of hereditary rights . . . they are wholly in contradiction to the spirit of our time and people."[20]

Not only the American spirit, but American law as well militated against the establishment of great houses. The absence of a law of primogeniture, Downing warned, meant that a man's wealth must be divided among his children, leaving no one of them rich enough to maintain his splendid residence. The laws of inheritance, as Downing cited them, seem designed to frustrate and punish the overly-ambitious for their defiance of the republican spirit. A house built in excess of the appropriate republican limits frequently passed from its owners into the hands of strangers, a meet fate for a "fine establishment which has been built in defiance of the spirit of the time and nation." Some, Downing continued, may regret these conditions, for they inhibit the development of ancestral houses in America. Admitting that "There is something beautiful and touching in the associations that grow up in a home held sacred in the same family for generations," Downing concluded that this pleasure was rightly denied to Americans; for "it is only an idyl, or only a delusion to us. It belongs to the past, so far as we are concerned. . . . It could only be reanimated at the sacrifice of the happiness of millions of free citizens." Americans, however, could forego the pleasure of the ancestral house, for "The just pride of a true American is not in a great hereditary home, but in greater heredity institutions."[21]

The same institutions that frustrated the would-be aristocrat made possible the open economic system characteristic of America. True Americans, according to Downing, know that "It is better . . . that it should be possible for the humblest laborer to look forward to the possession of a future country house and home like his own, than to feel that a wide and impassable gulf of misery separates him, the lord of the soil, from a large class of his fellow-beings born beneath him."[22] Similarly, the true American house represented by its self-restraint and absence of ostentation that it was the "republican home, built by no robbery of the property of another class, maintained by no infringement of a brothers' rights. . . ."[23]

The country houses built by wealthy Americans had, then, a double responsibility. These houses represented in their beauty and tastefulness the perfection the republican house could achieve, and since each such house reflected the character of its builder, a significant quantity of these houses indicated the refined and honest character of a whole segment of the population. At the same time, the restraint displayed by the fine villas of republican America lent credence to the egalitarian promise of the society. What had formerly been acknowledged as the essential drawbacks of domestic architecture in America, as Cooper had blamed the absence of first-class homes on the democratic conditions of the society, were transformed in Downing's work to the advantages under which both architect and house-owner conceived and constructed houses at once aesthetically and socially ideal.

Indeed, the designs that Downing provided were relatively modest. The number and the size of rooms and the overall cost-estimates from two of the largest villas in *The Architecture of Country Houses* indicates a control of ostentation and excess. "Southern villa—Romanesque Style" is made up of two wings, the smaller one housing the working areas, kitchen, laundry. The family rooms in the major wing include, on the first floor, a drawing room (19 x 28), a boudoir (12 x 12), a library (16 x 22), an ante-room (12 x 16), a vestibule (13 x 13), a dining hall (20 x 26), and an interior corridor and exterior arcade and pavilion. The main wing of the second floor contains seven chambers, ranging in size from 10 x 12 to 19 x 20, with two dressing rooms, a "W.C.," and bath.[24] This house, without question, overwhelms the first cottage presented in the book, with a first floor consisting only of a 12 x 18 living room and a single bedroom, 12 x 12, with two similar rooms in the attic story.[25] Nevertheless, the villa is not usually large or pretentious, and its estimated cost of $14,000 was not a fortune even by the standards of 1850.

One other design, "Large Country House," boasts a similar set of family rooms on the principal floor: drawing room, library, boudoir, dining room, and hall. The sizes of the rooms range from the boudoir, 12 x 18, to the drawing room, 18 x 32. There are five bedrooms, not including those for the servants, and again two dressing rooms, on the "Chamber Floor." The estimated cost is $13,000, according to Gervase Wheeler from whom Downing had taken this plan.[26] It is worth note that a number of the plans for the villas were taken from the work of other architects, but the cottage designs were all original.

Comparison with a contemporary architect's more ambitious and expensive plan is useful for indicating how carefully Downing followed his thesis in choosing the designs to include in his book. One example, "Villa on a Large Scale," was designed by Calvert Vaux and published in *Harper's* in 1855. Vaux was an Englishman, working in London as a draughtsman in 1850 when Downing met and hired him. He worked with Downing in Newburgh, New York, until Downing's death and subsequently moved to New York City where he worked as an architect and as a landscape architect, cooperating with Frederick Law Olmstead in the designs for Central Park in 1857. In 1864 he published *Villas and Cottages*, a pattern book generally similar to *The Architecture of Country Houses* but with a number of marked and significant differences. One such difference is apparent in the plan for "Villa on a Large Scale" which Vaux reprinted in his book. The cost-estimate for this design is $60,000. Although both Downing and Vaux worked on the plan (for a commission that never materialized), it is unthinkable that Downing would have included in his book any so grandiloquent a residence. Vaux did note that the house "is more extensive than is usually called for in the United States. . . ," but he included it nonetheless. The family quarters on the first floor are surrounded by arcades, a pavilion, terraces, and a veranda. A large entry hall (27 x 20) with a fountain has access to two lateral corridors and to an octagonal parlor (20 x 20). The parlor is flanked by the dining room and the drawing room (both 30 x 20). There are, as well, a boudoir (17 x 20), and a library (20 x 34). An equal amount of space on the first floor is given over to a family bedroom (24 x 30) with dressing room and bath, as well as to the servant's quarters and kitchens.[27]

Villas and Cottages is a much less philosophical book than *The Architecture of Country Houses*. Vaux was not only less interested in presenting theoretical material than was Downing, but he reflected an unusual blend of prejudice and insight in his writing. In his approach to the problems of domestic architecture in America, several subtle but pervasive attitudes reveal his English origins, and indicate his confusion over some American values and his partial misconception about others.

One instance of Vaux's miscomprehension of American values can be discovered in his design for a log cabin. The design itself is intelligent and practical, setting aside two small sleeping areas, a storeroom and a sink room, so as to leave one large room (16 x 20) free for the common life of the family. Vaux carefully labeled his design a log house, rather than a log cabin, because the term *cabin* indicated a "single room, in which a family of men, women, and children, eat, drink, sleep, wash, dress, and undress all together." The house that Vaux designed was meant to elevate the quality of frontier life, making it suitable for the "well-educated, active, energetic men, who are the pioneers of civilization. . . ." Such houses, furthermore, would raise the tone of these new districts. The practicality of this design, Vaux believed, came from the fact that these primitive houses "are frequently occupied, for years . . ." by the pioneer and his family.[28] All of what Vaux said is, of course, true, but he had, nevertheless, run directly in the face of a deeply held American belief: that log cabins, or log houses, were only temporary shelter. To make a real dwelling out of such temporary shelter would be to belie the faith in the immediate future, when the substantial and permanent family house would be erected. Americans might have needed, but did not want, plans for more convenient log cabins.

It is, however, in the introductory material to the book, that Vaux revealed the most marked discrepancies between his thinking and that of Downing. Like Downing, he was impressed with the amount of money available in America, and with the large number of country houses being built with this money. Vaux delighted in the fact that "Nothing like it has ever yet occurred in the world's history. . . ." Again, like Downing, Vaux was distressed by the quality of these houses and he determined to remedy the taste for "meagre, monotonous, unartistic" houses by showing Americans that they were not getting their money's worth.[29] Vaux isolated two characteristics of American life that combined to hold back the advance of taste: the Puritan ethic and the business ethic. In these excursions into American cultural history, Vaux's thinking was distinctly unlike Downing's. For Downing, American history and tradition resided in the republican, egalitarian ethos. He did not examine this ethos, trace its development, nor analyze its contradictions. Actually, Downing was like many of his contemporaries in assuming that our history lay in the future, and that the American character remained to be made.

Vaux, on the other hand, saw America with a foreigner's eye, remarked on our unique qualities, and attempted to explain them historically. From this point of view, he arrived at the conclusion that the Puritan ethic was responsible for a general distrust of beauty in America. According to Vaux, Downing had recognized and combatted this tendency, using "every effort to break down the foolish barrier that ignorance had set between the artist and the moralist." Downing made "manifest in all his works the glorious truth that the really 'beautiful' and the really 'good' are one."[30] But Vaux's ideas here were essentially shallow; he was no Hawthorne in dealing with the tension between beauty and goodness in America. For in another context, Vaux changed his terminology and blamed the failure of national taste on the republican ethos. "The awakening spirit of republicanism refused to acknowledge the value of art," because art had been the preserve of the rich and the aristocratic. Vaux conceded that such a mood was temporarily necessary, so that art could move out of the hot-house and flourish in the open air of democracy. But, he argued, for a century now "The great bulk of money that is laid out on building in the United States belongs to the active workers. . . . The industrious classes, therefore, decide the national standard of architectural taste."[31] Having laid the ghosts of Puritanism and mistaken republicanism, Vaux could proceed with the education of those industrious classes, by which he meant, apparently, men of manufacture and trade, not mechanics and laborers.

The business ethic, however, now stood in his way. Vaux attacked the values that adhered to money-making in America, and he attempted to create a new set of criteria applicable to "money-spending." The dichotomy Vaux established was, obviously, a false one for nineteenth century America, where money-spending was the proof of one's success in money-making. Nevertheless, he continued with this argument, asserting the necessity of a new leisured class in America. "The born rich," said Vaux, were in a predicament in America where "The science of spending is imperfectly understood." Since Americans abhorred idleness, they sent their rich sons into the professions; "Then follows a failure, in the majority of cases," for these men lacked any real incentive to work.

It is neither fair to the individuals, nor to the society of which they are responsible units, that the sons of rich men should be tied down to one or two money-making pursuits; they ought to be in every department of literature, science, and art, not as diletanti connoisseurs, but as earnest laborers, striving boldly for a higher national excellence than has yet ben achieved. This is *their* proper post.[32]

From such a class, whose fathers would be understood as having had reason to labor for the money to support such sons, would come the development and the promulgation of a national taste.

Vaux was much more closely attuned to American values when he wrote about the laboring class in America than when he spoke of the wealthy. He saw in the "Square boxes, small and large," in which these families lived the tale of "the migratory, independent spirit." These houses "offer interesting evidence of the genuine prosperity of the country," showing "that the landlord and tenant system is disliked," and that "almost every storekeeper and mechanic can contrive, even when quite young, to buy his own lot and live in his own house." But these same houses told as well that the men who lived in them underwent "a system of education in which the study of the beautiful in its most simple elements is neglected and apparently despised." Turning to the same premise that informed the work of Downing, Vaux spoke of the proper house of a nation which enjoyed "a full exercise of freedom of speech and action. . . ." Thus, "a refined propriety and simple, inexpensive grace ought habitually to be the distinctive marks of every habitation in which a free American dwells."[33]

While Vaux appreciated fully the American idealism that recreated the mechanic and the farmer as types of the "thoughtful, noble, and refined worker,"[34] he could not fully grasp the implications of a theoretically fluid society. As a result, he was capable of misjudging his audience, both in designing log houses to serve as the relatively permanent home of the pioneer family and in promoting the idea of a leisure class from which would come the new ideas of American art and culture. He was also capable of errors in tact. Having grasped the significance of money-making in America, he attempted to tell Americans that they were not getting their money's worth in the houses they built, at least insofar as taste was concerned. And although there has seldom been a man engaged in building his house who has not worried about getting his money's worth, Vaux was wrong to assume that this base anxiety was a proper subject for the idealistic pattern book of the fifties. In other words, he failed to realize the extent to which the sentimental values of the home excluded from house books any crass discussion of dollar value.

Villas and Cottages has interest, however, insofar as it sets in relief a number of Downing's theories and attitudes by filtering them through the mind of an intelligent and perceptive Englishman. Two other pattern books of the fifties are worth note as well for their interpretation of the house-ethos of the period. While neither of these writers came at the American house so philosophically or so universally as Downing, each revealed in his book a number of the same basic attitudes that informed *The Architecture of Country Houses.*

Lewis F. Allen (1800-1890) was a stock breeder and agricultural writer who addressed his *Rural Architecture* (1852) specifically to farmers.

> . . . the farm house is the chief nursery on which our broad country must rely for that healthy infusion of stamina and spirit into those men who, under our institutions, guide its destiny and direct its councils. They, in the great majority of their numbers, are natives of the retired homestead. It is, therefore, of high consequence, that good taste, intelligence, and correct judgment, should enter into all that surrounds the birth-place, and early scene of those who are to be the future actors in the prominent walks of life. . . .[35]

Believing in the farmhouse as the nursery of America's future leaders, Allen argued that the character of that house would provide a formative influence, both personally and nationally: "As the man himself—no matter what his occupation—be lodged and fed, so influenced, in a degree, will be his practice in the daily duties of his life." Although the farmer himself benefitted from a suitable house, the most obvious benefit fell to his children. These benefits came partly from the farmhouse itself, partly from rural living, and partly from the successful struggle the family waged against poverty. It was morally incumbent on a man and his family to resist a domestic environment that signalled the defeat of architectural, and hence personal, ambition. Any rude dwellings were pernicious, but particularly dangerous conditions existed when a family lived without a struggle in some noisome house or tenement. "A squalid, miserable tenement, with which they who inhabit it are content, can lead to no elevation of character, no improvement in condition, either social or moral, in its occupants."[36]

In order to encourage the building of farmhouses capable of

carrying such a significant social and moral weight, Allen presented some designs and a number of suggestions and criticisms.
The designs ranged in cost estimates from $100 (for the farm
cottage to house a laborer) to $8000 for a fairly extensive es-
tablishment. By the standards of the 1850's, Allen presented relatively simple designs. He believed that the farmer, a "plain
man," should have a plain structure for his house.[37] Where any
ornamentation was included in his designs, Allen noted that it
could be eliminated, sacrificing fashion to economy. Not only
ornamentation, but some new-fangled amenities displeased Allen,
who saw them as deeply implicated in the spread of urban
values. He strongly disapproved, for example, of interior water-
closets:

> [There are] some things which in a country establishment, par-
> ticularly, ought never to be there, such as privies, or *water-closets*,
> as they are more *genteelly* called. These last, in our estimation,
> have no business in a *farmer's* house. They are an *effeminacy*, only,
> and introduced by *city*-life.[38]

Allen grew exercised, as well, over the spread of country
villas built by the new rich in a style more gorgeous than was
suitable for the simplicities of the countryside. The consolation,
however, was the ephemeral nature of these dwellings, for American law, "with no privilege of entail to our posterity," assured
that luxurious houses lasted but one generation in the family that
built them.[39]

> It is a happy feature of our republican institutions, both social and
> political, that we can afford to let the flashy men of the *day*—not of
> *time*—flaunter [sic] in all their purchased fancy in house-building.
> . . . The man of money, simply, may build his 'villa' and squander
> his tens of thousands upon it . . . he may even hang his coat of
> arms upon it . . . but it is equally sure that no child of his will
> occupy it after him. . . .[40]

Allen's strong aversion to country villas for city men and his
overall belief in architectural simplicity did not always prevail
over the charm of some particular designs. While his designs
are in no way extravagant, he did present a number of large

and gracious houses in the fashionable styles of the period. Further, he suggested in relation to one of his "more ambitious and pretending" houses that it would be suitable not only for "a large and wealthy farmer, who indulged in the elegances of country life," but also for the retired business man, that enemy from the city.[41] Thus, like many other writers about American houses, Allen was not able to draw a firm line between acceptable and unacceptable elegance.

O. S. Fowler (1809-1887) whose interests included phrenology and the correction of perverted sexuality, was another major enthusiast for reform in domestic architecture, specifically for the development of the octagonal house and the gravel wall. In *A Home for All, or The Gravel Wall and Octagon Mode of Building* . . . (1854), Fowler presented his arguments and his methods for revolutionizing house-building in America. Fowler argued both scientifically and philosophically for the advantages of the gravel wall (i.e. cement) as a building material and for the octagonal shape as a building form. Fowler's premise was that "Every living thing must have its HABITATION,"[42] or as he put it more choicely: "Beautiful birds build tasty nests." In fact, man was the "most perfect exemplification" of the "great home law" and was "Endowed with the primitive faculty called 'inhabitiveness,' created for the express purpose of COMPELLING him to provide an abiding-place. . . ."[43]

Fowler, however, was not satisfied with the humble home; he made it a moral issue to insist that no one should "be content with a poor home only till they can better it, but provide the *best they can*."[44] Although Fowler explained that he would not have a man court bankruptcy or spend beyond his means, it is clear that he would encourage every sacrifice that served to add money to the building fund. In the section of "The Poor Man's Cottage," Fowler was quite specific about costs and sacrifices. He described a one-room cottage designed to be expanded, eventually, to four rooms on the first floor with sleeping space above. The initial construction "can be rendered comfortable for from $30 to $50 to $100," and Fowler explained how such amounts of money could be saved. Using Thoreau's argument that "*Nature's* wants are few—artificial wants consume by far the largest part of human time and earnings,"[45] Fowler altogether altered the ends for which Thoreau had argued. One can live cheaply, Thoreau contended, and therefore could afford to work less. Fowler, on the other hand, demanded more work and cheaper living in order to accumulate greater savings. And while for Thoreau anything but the most primitive house was an "artificial" want, for Fowler the primitive house was merely the first step on the way to a larger and finer house.

Fowler contended that the only real expense one had to face in this period of saving was that of food. He then devised a diet for "the poorest laboring man [who] can earn at least twelve and a half dollars per month, or $150 a year, and save $4 per month for a prospective home." This diet consisted of "One pound of wheat and a few sweet apples per day. . . ." "Buy a bushel of wheat with your first labor," he counseled, "Boil a pound per day —not overboil, but leave something for the teeth to do; and, if married, it will last yourself and wife a month—less, if you have children." Furthermore, all luxuries had to be foresworn, including tea, coffee, and tobacco. With earnings of $150 a year, a man could save $50 toward the construction of a house if he persisted in this regimen.[46]

Although Fowler fulfilled his duty to the poor man and the one-room house, his interests really lay in the large and beautiful octagonal house. Fowler asserted the superiority of the octagon over more conventional house forms on several grounds. The octagon house contained, he claimed, twenty per cent more floor space than a rectangular house with the same amount of wall. He preferred the arrangement of rooms necessitated by the octagonal shape, and argued for its superior beauty. But square or octagonal, the houses Fowler preferred and promoted were sizeable and stylish. "The domiciles of all animals bear a close resemblance to their respective characters;" therefore, men's houses would reflect their characters as well. The man who was "little refined, will build some outlandish tenement. . . ," while the "slack, low-minded, and 'shiftless,' aspire only to some hut or hovel, dug out of a bank. . . ." On the other hand, "the spirited, ambitious, and enterprising, whose aspirations are lofty, and minds high-toned, select eminences, and build high houses." Fowler admitted that perfect expressiveness in a house was sometimes confounded, as when an inferior man hired a superior architect; nevertheless, the general rule provided for a mirror representation of the man in his house.

. . . a fancy man will build a fancy cottage; a practical man, a convenient home; a substantial man, a solid edifice; a weak man, an illy arranged house; an aspiring man, a high house; and a superior man, a superb villa.

"Indeed," Fowler asserted, "other things being equal, the better a man's mentality, the better mansion will he construct, and the characteristics of the house will be as those of its builder and occupant."[47]

Basic to Fowler's house-philosophy was the necessity for every man to have his own house built for him. Nature had ensured this arrangement "by rendering the very building [of houses] itself most pleasurable." Again like Thoreau, Fowler made an analogy between the happiness of "yon birds, ingathering materials, and building up day by day, a sweet little home for themselves and their prospective offspring," and the man who found joy in building, a joy Fowler labeled as "almost intoxicating." Nature endowed mankind with two faculties, "Inhabitiveness" and "Constructiveness," and the building of houses continued "and should continue till all are supplied with comfortable homes."[48] Concluding this section on the joys of building, Fowler turned briefly to the benefits of the hereditary family mansion, and dismissed them. Unlike Downing, however, Fowler did not argue against the ancestral house on grounds of egalitarian brotherhood, but by insisting on the necessity of each man's building his own house.

One may well be content to live in the old family mansion, consecrated by the joys and sorrows of his parents and ancestors, and by the sacred reminiscences of his childhood; but give me a relatively poor house of my own erection, in preference to one built by some stranger.[49]

Fowler shared with Downing a number of premises about houses, primarily the insistence on the intimate, expressive relationship between a man and the house he built. But Fowler did not have Downing's social vision; nowhere did he suggest that with each self-denial in domestic splendor, a man returned some credit to the egalitarian dream. Furthermore, Fowler never spoke of the "American" or "republican" house, and while he contended in his preface that the purpose of his book was

"To cheapen and improve human homes, and especially to bring comfortable dwellings within the reach of the poorer classes . . . ,"[50] his emphasis on the superior value of larger homes undercut his reformist sincerity. The limitations perceptible in the social vision of men like Vaux, Allen, and Fowler throw into relief the breadth and complexity of Downing's architectural and social philosophy. After the Civil War, Downing's influence continued to make itself felt in American architectural writing, but in the altered America of the later nineteenth century, that influence was called into the service of viewpoints remarkably different from those of Downing himself.

Chapter Four

To Frank Lloyd Wright
The Preservation of Democracy

In America each man has a peculiar, inalienable
right to live in his own house in his own way.
He is a pioneer in every right sense of the
word. His home environment may face for-
ward, may portray his character, tastes, and
ideas, if he has any, and every man has some
somewhere about him.
    Frank Lloyd Wright,
    Ausgeführte Bauten und Entwürfe, (1910)

The pattern book as it was developed by Downing and those
who followed him addressed itself to a wide, but generally
middle-class audience. Because the plans in pattern books embraced a wide range of houses, from the small cottage to the
extravagant villa, it was possible to conceive of this audience as
representative of the whole spectrum of American economic
classes, despite the omission of such marginal groups as the poor
farmer, the Southern tenant, the urban poor, and even the new
millionaire. The pattern books, of course, sought not only an
audience, but also potential customers. To an extent, even Downing's *The Architecture of Country Houses,* for all its philosophical, ethical and aesthetic base, addressed in its audience a new
consumer class. Even before the Civil War, the pattern book
had become an advertising medium attempting to create and to
capture a new market. The pattern book writer wished not only
to sell his own designs but participated as well in the general
campaign to develop and increase the employment of architects
by prospective home-owners.

After the Civil War pattern books began to address a somewhat more limited audience. While books continued to be
printed that courted the wealthier middle class, many more

books addressed themselves specifically to those potential house-builders who were less moneyed and less sophisticated. For this audience, paradoxically, the ready-made designs in the pattern books of the later nineteenth century eliminated the need for professional architects, for contractors could follow the ready-made plans. Pattern books served a practical function, but they probably had an entertainment value as well, if only to permit the readers to indulge in dream-house fantasies. For both reasons, the popularity of pattern books increased, and for a time this vogue was exploited by major monthly periodicals like *Harper's* and *Scribner's*. *Harper's*, as has been mentioned, had published material by Vaux as early as 1854. Even earlier, *Godey's Ladies' Book* had begun, at first sporadically, the publication of a monthly pattern for cottage or villa. But is was not until after the Civil War that the house pattern became a dependable subject for occasional articles in popular magazines.

Godey's Ladies' Book is a barometer for the popularity of house patterns. The first plans appeared in 1846, and from 1846 to 1853 *Godey's* published designs taken from English sources. Not until four years after the publication of *The Architecture of Country Houses* did *Godey's* begin to use American materials. In 1859, the magazine started to commission its own designs, and eventually one designer, Isaac Hobbs, took over most of this work. The influence of *Godey's* was very significant; in 1868, the editors announced that more than four thousand cottages and villas had been built from plans published in the magazine.[1]

The elevations, floor plans, and descriptive texts in *Godey's* are not markedly different from those in contemporary pattern books, except in an exaggeration of current fashions and an occasionally bizarre design. In 1847, for instance, they printed the plan for "A Castellated Cottage" with corner piers imitating crennelated towers pierced with cross-shaped windows suitable for defending a seige with bow and arrow. In 1850 an "Anglo-Grecian Villa" showed five rooms in a cruciform pattern with the four corner angles filled in with a porch, a green house, and two verandas. Like pre-war pattern books, *Godey's* appealed to a wide audience, featuring houses that varied greatly in cost. The cruciform villa was estimated at $8500, while a small cottage displayed in 1847 could be built for $421.76.[2]

When Isaac Hobbs took over the patterns for *Godey's*, he

tended to publicize fairly expensive houses. Generally, the advertising motive was strong in Hobbs' work. Whenever he was able, he used plans he had already built, and he often dropped the names of his successful middle-class clients through whom he intended, apparently, to influence other potential customers. In 1873, Hobbs presented the homes of Mrs. Eshleman in Lancaster, Pennsylvania, Albert Dilsworth, near Pittsburgh, and William M. Lloyd, a banker from Altoona, whose house cost between $35,000 and $40,000. In 1874, he featured the house of John W. Stoddard of Dayton, built for $25,000, about which Hobbs announced "We are willing to contrast it for beauty or elegance of effect or costly appearance with any other building in the vicinity for $50,000." Now and then his monthly piece concluded with the notice that "We have ready our book of designs which we will send to any point in the United States and Canada per mail upon receipt of $3. It contains nearly a hundred different buildings."[3]

The occasional work done for monthlies like *Harper's* and *Scribner's* was of an altogether different cast from that in *Godey's*, Whereas *Godey's* treated house plans rather like their monthly fashion plates with a set of illustrations supported by brief texts, the more sophisticated magazines set their patterns in a considerable amount of text. Typically, these articles stated certain premises about the meaning and importance of the house, the necessity to elevate the national taste, and usually, the superiority of one style over another. Following this material were sample plans by the architect-writer.

In 1875 and 1876 Henry Hudson Holly did four articles for *Harper's* on "Modern Dwellings," going beyond the house proper to questions of decoration and furniture. Holly, a devoté of Queen Anne style, opened his articles with statements about the quest for an indigenous house-style and a plea for truth in architecture. Holly's comments are like an echo of Downing's philosophy reduced to formula, to ritual phrases prefacing the real business of the article, the designs themselves. We hear that "In America it is the privilege of nearly all classes to build for themselves homes in the country. . . ." Personal expression was touched on as well, but primarily as a method of promoting the profession of architecture, for Holly attempted to prove that one's own character was enhanced by, rather than submerged in, the technique of a professional architect. "A gentleman, by frequent communication with his architect, necessarily to a very great extent imprints his own character upon his house . . . and [this] proves how possible it is to express in a manner even the most delicate idiosyncrasies of human character."[4]

One element in Holly's writing cannot, however, be traced back to Downing, and that is his nostalgia over a lost heroic American past. Holly's nostalgia for a vanished America was not unique to him, and it marks a significant new aspect in the conceptualization of the American house after the Civil War. Throughout the seventies *Harper's* printed articles on old towns in America. The older houses of Marblehead, Cambridge, Baltimore, and Philadelphia were seen as the homes of a more stable and elegant civilization. Holly specifically turned to the houses of Colonial America, romanticizing them, and occasionally designing a house to recall, even to recreate, that American past. Overall, he paid homage to older American house-types, to specimens of "real Puritan architecture of 'the good old colony times' in New England, of the old stone Revolutionary Dutch farm-houses on the Hudson, or of the plantation houses of Maryland and Virginia. . . ." The rapidity of American prosperity had brought with it "pretentious display, without the refinement of education. . . ."[5]

Holly's designs, published in book form in 1878 as *Modern Dwellings in Town and Country,* varied in size and price, but generally appealed to a relatively affluent audience. He did provide plans for an inexpensive cottage costing $2200, but pointed out its suitability as an attractive "lodge" for a mansion.[6] The great majority of his plans were for much more substantial dwellings, and Holly did not feel any necessity to balance these with designs for modest homes. In a passage that appeared in both the article and the subsequent book, Holly asserted that the mansion "as compared with the cottage, is like the full-grown man to the child, not only in aspect of size, but of general comprehensiveness and refinement. . . ." Holly's most grandiose plan far exceeds anything in Downing or Vaux. This enormous country house included, on the first floor alone, an entrance lobby, a hall (22 x 40) with a fireplace (itself 7 x 9), and a reception room (17 x 21), a parlor (17 x 34), tea rooom (13 x 16), conservatory (12 x 48), billiard room (16 x 22), library (16 x 22), office (13 x 16), and dining room (17 x 28), as well as an entire servants' wing with a hall and a housekeeper's room, and a number of closets and pantries, even a gun-room. There is no price estimate.[7]

In 1890, *Scribner's* ran four articles by the architects John Wellborn Root, Russell Sturgis, Bruce Price, and Donald G. Mitchell; these were also published in book form, as *Homes in City and Country* (1893). Price's essay appeared first, a discussion of "The Suburban House" revealing the same set of assumptions observable in Holly's articles. Price celebrated life in an older America, "a society, intelligent, refined, and almost chivalric in its intercourse," and he attacked modern vulgarity, the "*noveaux riches*, who gauge the beauty of their house by its cost. . . ." Despite the nostalgia and pessimism inherent in these views, Price believed optimistically in the emergence of an American architecture which would come from "its source in a thousand well-springs deep down in the national character." The national character, furthermore, continued to demand the house as a means of expression.

> It is a vivid expression of that American trait which inspires every man, no matter how subordinate his position in the business world, to assert his individuality and independence by owning a home which is the outgrowth of his special tastes and needs. Amid the pretences and shams of which American life is often accused, this at least has the instinct of truth, and an honest purpose.[8]

But for Price, self-expression was no longer the natural result of an organic relationship between a man and his shelter; now it was a necessary form of self-assertion and an escape from contemporary hypocrisy.

Root, writing of "The City House in the West," defended the houses of Chicago against eastern attacks, by asserting that self-expression was much greater in western than in eastern dwellings. This was true because the westerner "is much less governed by artificial conditions than his brother in the East, and very much more freely expresses himself." Root's article is much more "architectural" than the others in the series; he paid a great deal more attention to details of form and ornamentation, and less to philosophical generalizations. Nevertheless, he took time to insist on the emergence of a national style:

"With wholesome quality of mind and life in the layman, and with imagination and discrimination in the architect, what may not our domestic architecture become?"[9]

At the end of the nineteenth century and the beginning of the twentieth, more outlets developed for the publication of architectural writing. New architectural journals were established, *Architects' and Builders' Magazine* in 1882 and *The Architectural Record* in 1891; in 1899 *House and Garden* began publication. Generally, although not exclusively, the architectural magazines, as well as *House and Garden*, focused their attention on the homes of the upper middle class and of the very wealthy. The cautiously upper-middle class thrust of the articles in *Harper's* and *Scribner's* gave way to a more open interest in architect-built houses for those who could afford commodious and luxurious residences.

Although Downing-like premises continued to be articulated and the search for an American style and an expressive house went on, the architectural journals more or less assumed that self-expression, and a national style, could be realized only in the houses of the rich. This premise reveals a callous dismissal of the problems of mass housing, to be sure; on the other hand, self-expression could not be looked for in slums, in rented houses, or in the contractor-built suburbs of the working class. The advocates of self-expression in American houses had always assumed that a man would have his own house built, and if rising costs and more complex domestic machinery made individual houses an impossibility for poorer Americans, that was not, in 1900, the problem of the professional architectural journals. But as a result of the concentration on the houses of the affluent in these magazines, the concept of the American house also underwent subtle but profound changes in their pages. As style became the paramount factor in any consideration of individual or national self-expression, vaguer and more idealistic concepts of a romantic interconnection between a man and his house and of a republican ethos in domestic architecture were muted or disappeared altogether.

The professional necessity to give space to excessively opulent houses built for showy clients by fashionable architects frequently led the professional journals to debase the currency of American idealism about houses. The presentation of such houses within a context of sentimental rationalization touching on self-expression, the intimacy of the home, or the republican ethos, resulted in a grotesque distortion of romantic American values. For example, in 1910 *The Architectural Record* featured a new town house in Boston, a highly conventionalized Louis XVI limestone mansion. The writer ingratiatingly observed that this stylized exercise in self-aggrandizement represented "The urban residence of today, designed to be the 'home' of its occupant, rather than a place which expressed only the owner's abundance of wealth. . . ."[10]

Four years later, a long article described "The Practical Farmhouse of a Country Gentleman," an enormous house with eleven bedrooms (ten with fireplaces) and eight baths in the main house, and a collection of outhouses including a studio house, a superintendent's cottage (with eight rooms), a laborer's cottage, a stable and a garage. The owner, not named, was a financier who had built his house in memory of "a dear old home" in Virginia. We are informed that "Houses, like persons, have individuality," and that here the distinctive note is hospitality "since the owner cherishes all those delightful traditions of men born in the Southland. . . ." The architectural expression of hospitality, the writer added with what one hopes is irony, is "able to overcome the appearance of a hostelry, which a Colonial house of between sixty and seventy rooms must inevitably present."[11]

For these architect-writers, an important goal was the encouragement of a clientele for the architect-designed house. Since expressiveness had become inextricably linked to the values of the house, it was necessary to promote the intimate relationship between man and house even in those cases where the pretentiousness of the house could legitimately indicate nothing but the pretentiousness of its owner. Therefore, homey or homelike qualities were discovered in even the most formidable residences. On the other hand, houses designed and built by contractors were said to lack not only home atmosphere but taste and individual expression as well. The professional necessity to criticize contractor-built houses bought by lower-income families sometimes moved a writer from an attack on the houses themselves to an attack on the people who bought them. An *Architectural Record* article from 1893-1894 castigated not only the "average man" but the general "democratic standard" as well.

> When [most people] build or buy houses they aim only at equaling or excelling the standard set by their neighbors; at doing the customary thing, approved by the divine majority, which we all worship. The 'average man'—that democratic standard of perfection, toward which his superiors must bow, as his inferiors may aspire— the average man is quite satisfied if his house is provided with the fashionable crudities of the moment. . . .[12]

The same article went on to justify fashionable ostentation, arguing from, and distorting, the romantic premise of an expressive relationship between a culture and the houses it boasted. Ostentation, it asserted was the sign of the times; it was, in fact, "a necessity of business, that is of life." Therefore, the role of the private house was to advertise commercial success: "So must our houses testify that our business is reasonably prosperous; indicate if possible that we could, if we wanted to, do things even more lavishly." These circumstances were not to be criticized by the architect, but merely comprehended; when "Pretense is so necessary to existence," the architect's purpose is to enhance the quality of ostentation. American culture might indeed be materialistic and vulgar, but such a problem demanded not social change, but more tasteful design: "a polished villain is a pleasanter companion than the most virtuous bore. . . ."[13]

Gradually, the romantic idealism associated with both the individual and social values of the American house gave way in the architectural journals to a consideration of style, and style became the primary—if not the only—criterion by which American houses were evaluated. At the turn of the century, however, there were two attitudes toward an American style, one attached to the revival of Colonial architecture, the other insisting on the benefits of eclecticism. The eclectics believed that an American style could emerge only out of a fusion of the architectural styles of the past. Architectural support for this point of view came largely from enthusiasts for the work of firms like McKim, Mead, and White, designers of many of the chateaux and palaces of Fifth Avenue and Newport, whose clients delighted in the recreation of European symbols of aristocracy and nobility. A tendentious philosophical argument for eclecticism rested on an analogy between the fusion of architectural styles and the fusion of national types in the United States.

> We are a nation of composite extraction and it is therefore not unreasonable that the architecture of our houses should betray some evidences of a composite origin. A few of us it is true, can point with satisfaction to American ancestry on both sides of our family trees for two hundred years or more, but because the majority of our compatriots are less fortunate, they are none the less Americans and it would be extremely unjust as well as snobbish to deny them the title. It is precisely the same with architecture.[14]

In a purer world, the writer seems to sigh, perhaps a purer architecture. In any case, the concept of "American" has been reduced here altogether to a question of style.

The Colonial enthusiasts, conversely, asserted that there was no need to create an American style since one already existed, and in those houses which, from the late nineteenth century on, had been designed in imitation of the spirit of Federal or Georgian architecture, could be found at last the realization of the American House. Joy Wheeler Dow wrote a series of articles subsequently published as *American Renaissance* (1904). Dow's ideal was the 100% American house, one embued with "Anglo-Saxon Home Feeling." Dow illustrated one article with a pair of contrasting houses, followed by percentage analyses of their characteristics. One illustration shows a contemporary imitation of an eighteenth century mansion; the other a moderately "modern", two-story house with an arch over the doorway and a marked absence of pillars. Under each is an "Analysis" which reckons the percentage of eight "architectural" features devised by Dow: "Moresque Spain," "Moresque Algiers," "Moresque California Mission," "East Indian," "Newly reclaimed land," "Chinese ornament," "Modern invention," and "Anglo-Saxon home atmosphere." The "American Renaissance" house has 0% of all qualities but the last, in which it scores 100%. The house representative of "Newly Invented Architecture" has 5 or 10% of each characteristic, except for 50% of "Modern Invention, pure" and 0% of "Anglo-Saxon home atmosphere."[15]

Dow's presuppositions, where they are not purely stylistic,

are a mixture of arch-conservative elitism and sentimental
nostalgia, both depending on a concept of an American past in
which elegance, taste, and aristocratic manners prevailed. In
those better days a house-builder would no more have "thought
of departing from what I shall call 'the straight and narrow
path' of precedent in architecture than he would have been
guilty of a religious defection. . . ." That happy world perished
under the presidency of Andrew Jackson.

> Previous to this advent of rabid democracy there lingered a vestige
> of a certain code of social restrictions which once regulated archi-
> tecture almost as absolutely as it did the private affairs of every
> family in the land.[16]

From Andrew Jackson to Henry Hobson Richardson was, for
Dow, but a short step. Dow analyzed the trouble with the
houses of Richardson and his like as a contempt of American
tradition. "They did not reckon with their grandparents for an
instant. . . . They apparently took the keenest delight in walking
roughshod over every sacred home memory."[17]
Unfortunately, not all of Dow's readers had an eighteenth
century mansion in the family. Therefore, the problem was to
build a new house that incorporated the characteristics of the
old and that, furthermore, created the illusion of one's having
had a family history. Of such qualities was "home" composed.

> [The home] must presuppose, by subtle architectonic expression
> . . . that its owner possessed, once upon a time, two good parents,
> four grandparents, eight great-grandparents, and so on . . . that
> *bienséance* and family order have flourished in his line from time
> immemorial . . . and that he has inherited heirlooms, plate, portraits,
> miniatures, pictures, rare voulmes, diaries, letters and state archives
> to link him up properly in historical succession and progression.[18]

It would appear from these passages that Dow himself could
not be swerved from the straight and narrow path of old money,
family tradition and colonial architecture, but this was not the
case. New money, in large enough amounts, overrode any other
considerations. The late nineteenth century palaces of the
fabulously rich, despite their provenance in French chateaux or

Italian pallazzi, seemed American to Dow. The W. K. Vanderbilt house at Fifth Avenue and Fifty-Second Street, built by Hunt in imitation of a French chateau, may have looked French in 1883, said Dow, but it "had gradually grown to look to us what it really is, i.e. good American Renaissance adapted from the Valois propaganda of architectural composition." Even "Biltmore," the vast country estate of the Vanderbilts in South Carolina, which "We call French Renaissance now . . . ," Dow securely believed would be "American Renaissance later on."[19]

The houses designed for less affluent Americans were promoted not through the major magazines in architect-written essays, but through the descendants of the pattern book. Immediately after the Civil War, pattern books had resumed publication in much the mold established by Downing. *Woodward's Country Houses* (1865) declared the countryside to be the most advantageous setting for the house and insisted on the need for the cultivation of the popular taste. He spoke as well for the expression of personal and national character and criticized the house that attempted to "attract attention as blazoning the wealth and money importance of the owner." Woodward acknowledged his debt to Downing and expressed gratitude for the effect of Downing's work in elevating national taste.[20]

In the 1870's pattern books continued to seek a general audience, as their titles reveal: *House Plans for Everybody* and *Villas and Cottages, or Homes for All* (both 1876). In 1881 Appleton's started a series of inexpensive books on houses. The first in the series, A. F. Oakey's *Building a Home*, combined general information on site, drainage, construction costs, and the decoration of interiors, with a number of plans and a limited amount of high-flown rhetoric—debased Downing—on the general meaning of the house.

These later pattern books were more and more obviously forms of advertisements directed to a market unreachable by professional architects. Cost-control and the influence of mass production become apparent, significantly in the development of interchangable exterior designs and interior floor plans. If a buyer liked one elevation, he might be able to choose among three or four floor plans; conversely, suitable floor-plans could be dressed up in several different exterior styles. In an address in 1900 to the Chicago Architectural League, Frank Lloyd

Wright attacked the use of "stock patterns" as a money-making system borrowed from the world of business: ". . . it is in the ready-made article that the money lies, altered to fit by any popular 'sartorial artist;' the less alteration the greater the profit; and the 'architect.' "[21]

The profit in stock patterns was great enough, by the beginning of the century, so that a western designer, Henry L. Wilson, author of *The Bungalow Book* (1908), could call himself a "Designer of Artistic Homes," and announce that he did no building and no supervising since it took all his time to prepare the plans for his books. *The Bungalow Book* cost one dollar and advertised full specifications costing from $7.50 to $15.00. Most of Wilson's plans permitted interchangable elevations and floor plans. The houses ranged in cost between $800 and $5500, and no plans were aimed at attracting an affluent or sophisticated clientele. Wilson's pitch was the bungalow itself, a newly popular descendant of the cottage, originally associated with a one-story house indigenous to the American southwest, particularly Southern California. But Wilson's elevations show every popular contemporary house-style, indicating that the bungalow, like the cottage, was a state of mind.

While Wilson's book has no extended essay section, the prose commentaries accompanying each design suggest the values these bungalows represented. Plan #37 promised an appearance of solid middle-class wealth at half the apparent cost; while estimated at about $4400, "it always looks as if it must have cost nearly double that amount." Like mid-twentieth century car commercials, Wilson's houses promised romance as well as respectability. He offered one $800 house, four rooms, overall dimensions 28 x 40, as a "type of the famous 'Bungalow built for two,' " and added that it "makes an ideal home for the young couple just starting on their wedded career." Another four-room house, 33 x 33, is "a charming little home as snug as the traditional bug." Furthermore, "The prospect of a home like this ought to hasten matrimonial arrangements for the slowest swain or the shyest maid." The book closes with a page of letters from happy customers: "A PLEASED CUSTOMER IS THE BEST ADVERTISEMENT."[22]

Despite the commercial impetus apparent in publications like *The Bungalow Book*, idealism and reformism remained motives in a small number of pattern books. Gustav Stickley's *Craftsman Homes* (1901) combined the familiar idealism of Downing with the craft enthusiasm of William Morris and the philosophy of Edward Carpenter in England, and showed as well the influence of Japanese architectural simplicity. Stickley had begun the *Craftsman Magazine* to encourage handicrafts; subsequently, the interests of the magazine extended to include architecture, the arts, and social and political issues, as well as agricultural matters. In 1909 he opened Craftsman Farms in New Jersey to encourage men and women, and especially to educate children, to a life of simplicity, agriculture, and handicrafts.

Craftsman Homes has an unusually large proportion of text to illustration; like Downing, Stickley had a great deal to say about the meaning of the American house. Also, like Downing, Stickley concentrated on smaller and simpler houses, and he insisted on the intimacy between a man and his house and on the relationship between the house and the American experience. Much like Frank Lloyd Wright, Stickley connected architectural with social reform, and he stressed the contrast apparent between American independence in most matters and the sheep-like conformity of Americans where their houses were concerned. However, Stickley was not advocating architectural reform alone, and it was not for him simply a question of having more individualistic homes. Through such homes American ideals would be preserved or restored.

> And to what extent can we hope for finer ideals in a country that is afraid to be sincere in that most significant feature of national achievement—the home. We are a country of self-supporting men and women, and we cannot expect to develop an honest significant architecture until we build homes that are simple, yet beautiful, that proclaim fine democratic standards and that are essentially appropriate to busy intelligent people.[23]

At its most developed Stickley's philosophy posited architectural reform as the spearhead for social reform.

Reform is the major theme in the closing essay of *Craftsman Homes*, "The Craftsman Idea of the Kind of Home Environment that would Result from More Natural Standards of Life and Work." With a belief in progress, and in "the reality of the world-wide movement in the direction of better things," Stickley asserted that reform begins with the individual and "that the life of the individual is shaped mainly by home surroundings and influences. . . ." A proper home, set in the country, simple but individually expressive, would provide a setting in which the false values of urban civilization could be replaced by "individual life" and "the vigorous constructive spirit" of the pioneers.[24]

More significant figures than Stickley, however, had begun to insist on architectural reform as an initiator of social reform. Louis Sullivan and Frank Lloyd Wright both operated from the premise that architecture and society were intimately tied to one another, and that a truly democratic society would find expression in truly democratic architecture. However, in the writing of both Sullivan and Wright, there is frequent confusion of cause and effect. They believed that the corruption of democratic ideals had led to an architecture equally corrupt, an analysis emphasizing the effect of culture on architecture. Nevertheless, both men could assert their belief in the meliorative effect of architecture on culture. Architecture was to initiate the reform of American society.

In *Kindergarten Chats* (1901), Sullivan addresses a young architect whom he is slowly weaning away from the values and beliefs inculcated by a conventional education in falsehood and hypocrisy. Sullivan takes the young man to the corrupt city where public and private buildings are testimony to the viciousness of society. There, he demonstrates to the young man that American architecture is a mirror of American life. "Our architecture reflects us, as truly as a mirror . . ." he says, and "architecture today in our benighted land—[is] an art without pretense of honesty, feeling or regard for consequence." Still, democracy retains the promise of a new era of independence, enlightenment, and spiritual fulfillment. Like a latter-day Walt Whitman, Sullivan leads the young architect to the countryside, to the healing and inspiring power of Nature, and he instills in the youth the Idea of Democracy.

> Democracy, as you may now infer, is an IDEA: It is a function of such infinite spiritual fertility, it is so unitary, so concentrate, so diffusive, it is so charged with power that it may well seem the latest and most potent of nature's spiritual forces to arise within

the domain of MAN'S DESIRE: even though in truth it be of the primordial and the eternal.[25]

The young architect, through these experiences, is cleansed of his false education and infused with a new spirit with which to perform his life's tasks.

While Sullivan saw in all kinds of architecture the evidences of a bankrupt society, he concentrated his remarks on public buildings. Never greatly interested in domestic architecture, Sullivan wrote only occasionally of houses, and the houses he spoke of, either particular examples or general types, served essentially as emblems of the chasm between economic classes in America. Not the middle class suburban home, but the tenement and the mansion appear in Sullivan's books. In *Democracy: a Man-Search* (1908), Sullivan roams through Great City, passing the mansions on the boulevard, continuing on to the streets of the poor. He depicts a scene of drunkenness and violence behind the closed door of one miserable home, a home we have been told we cannot enter "because there is no trail and all are safe in solitude." But Sullivan denies the solitude and blazes the trail from "the forlorn home direct to the working-man's saloon," and from there in two lines "one to the brewer, the other to the rectifier—both poisoners, both cowards. . . ." And from these wretched poor and the brewer and the rectifier "run lines straight as the crow flies to you and me (we also brutalized the man, struck the woman, terrified and degraded the children). . . ." These lines, concluded Sullivan, "connect us in endless combinations."[26] Democracy, as Sullivan wrote in "Consent to Listen," "implies the brotherhood of man, and universal love because of universal accountability."[27]

In Sullivan's vision of a democratic society, hovels and mansions could not exist side by side. Downing had spoken of the true republican who would not profit at the expense of his brother and, therefore, restrained the size and luxury of his house. But Sullivan, who hoped himself for "universal accountability," looked at the evidence that belied Downing's optimism, he looked at the Fifth Avenue chateau of W. K. Vanderbilt.

Must I show you this *French Chateau*, this little Chateau de Blois on this street corner, here, in New York, and still you do not laugh!

Must you wait until you see a 'gentleman' in a silk hat, come out
of it before you laugh? Have you no sense of humor, no sense of
pathos? Must I tell you that while the man may live in the house
physically, (for a man may live in any kind of a house physically),
that he cannot possibly live in it morally, mentally or spiritually,
that he and his house are a paradox, a contradiction, an absurdity,
a characteristically New York absurdity; that he is no part of his
house, and his house is no part of him?

Joy Wheeler Dow was capable of finding the Vanderbilt chateau "American;" Sullivan isolated it as one symbol of New
York City, where "Gold is God" and dismissed as absurdities
the house, the architect, and the man who lived in it, "a vulgarly
rich absurdity because he lives in a costly house which is an
ostentatious solecism."[28]

Unlike Sullivan, Frank Lloyd Wright spent a great deal of his
talent and energy on domestic architecture, and his writings
reflect a continuing concern with the houses of the middle
class. The houses of Americans, as Wright spoke of them, were
both reflections of the society and inhibitors of human development. The late nineteenth century suburb, "the fiasco alfresco,"
as he called it in 1903, elicited Wright's concern and his contempt. He questioned the "theatrical desire on the part of fairly
respectable people to live in chateaux, manor houses, Venetian
palaces, feudal castles, and Queen Anne cottages."[29] In 1943
he recalled Chicago's Oak Park as it had appeared half a century earlier.

The buildings standing around there on the Chicago prairies were
all tall and all tight. Chimneys were lean and taller still—sooty
fingers threatening the sky. And beside them, sticking up almost
as high, were the dormers. Dormers were elaborate devices—
cunning little buildings complete in themselves—stuck on to the
main roof—slopes to let the help poke their heads out of the attic
for air. . . . These overdressed wood house walls had cut in them,
or cut out of them to be precise, big holes for the big cat and little
holes for the little cat to get in or get out or for ulterior purposes
of light and air. These house walls were becorniced or fancy-
bracketed up at the top into the tall, purposely, profusely complicated roof. . . . The whole exterior was bedeviled, that is to say,
mixed to puzzle-pieces with corner-boards, panel-boards, window-

frames, corner-blocks, plinth-blocks, rosettes, fantails, and jigger-work in general. . . . Unless the householder of the period were poor indeed, usually the ingenious corner tower as seen in mono-garia, eventuated into a candle-snuffer dome, a spire, an inverted rutabaga, radish or onion.[30]

Since these houses, consisting of "boxes beside boxes or inside boxes,"[31] served as a visible sign for the condition of the society that had built them, Wright could ask himself about the homes in Oak Park, "Were these meaningless monstrosities like the people whose houses they were—like the men and women who lived in them? Was all this waste what they deserved?"[32]

An idealist asserting, as had Downing a century earlier, both the intimacy between the man and his house, and the connection between a democratic society and the houses it displayed, Wright brought to his statements about the house an emphasis on expressiveness, on romantic organicism, and on the meaning inherent in the "democratic" house. But Wright's career was a long one and the vicissitudes of his life brought about marked changes in his attitude toward the society as a whole, toward the family, and toward the individual in both familial and social contexts. Wright's statements about democracy, for example, swing from Sullivan-like enthusiasm to bitter cynicism. He could speak, as Norris Smith comments, of "the 'pseudo-civilization' of our Usonian 'mobocracy' as barbarous, degenerate, servile, and wholly lacking in anything that might conceivably be called a genuine culture."[33] Yet he could insist as well that democracy held as its potential "the highest possible expression of the individual as a unit not incompatible with a harmonious whole."[34]

Wright did not lose faith in democracy as an ideal, but he did grow increasingly dismayed by evidences he saw of the failure of that ideal. In 1939 he attributed the corruption of democracy to the hang-over of feudal elitism, now expressed in terms of economic power. America had begun, said Wright, "with the truly great idea of making life an even break for every man." And like Downing, he went on to argue that "every real man must want the prosperity for others he wants for himself."[35] However, aggressive economic individualism had negated this implicit brotherhood, and the complement of the feudal baron of industry was the common man who, beaten down by a spurious democracy, believed only in "the Gospel of Mediocrity."[36] Such men lived in houses that reflected both this mediocrity and the nervous competitiveness of the American middle class, in houses that evoked in Wright's head a "monologue reciting in monotone . . . *Nobody home! Nobody home! 'They stay here but they don't live here. We never knew life. But we are just as good as anybody's houses, just as good: just as good as 'they' are—better, maybe."* [37]

In the place of these characterless houses with their empty self-assertion, Wright envisaged the democratic house, a structure freed of sham in which the owner and his family would be themselves freed to realize their individualism. In 1953 Wright recalled his prairie houses, built half a century before, and he emphasized the effective role of democracy in the conception of these houses.

> To say the house planted by myself on the good earth of the Chicago prairie as early as 1900, or earlier, was the first truly democratic expression of our democracy in architecture would start a controversy with professional addicts who believe architecture has no political (therefore no social) significance. So, let's say that the spirit of democracy—freedom of the individual as an individual —took hold of the house as it then was, took off the attic, and the porch, pulled out the basement, and made a single spacious, harmonious unit out of living room, dining room and kitchen, with appropriate entry conveniences.[38]

The "democratic expression of our democracy in architecture," however, had a broader implication in Wright's thought than the physical reordering of space. In such a house, men underwent a transformation; the democratic, the "organic" house would have, Wright promised, "a salutary effect morally." In a house built with "integrity," people could "derive countenance and sustenance from the atmosphere of the things they live in or with. . . ."[39] Children, especially, would benefit by growing up "in an atmosphere that contributes to serenity and well-being and to the consciousness of those things which are excellent. . . ."[40] To live in a democratic house, therefore, was to become liberated for a self-discovery and self-expression, and by extension, to participate in the birth of a new social order.

This architecture we call organic is an architecture upon which true American society will eventually be based if we survive at all. An architecture upon and within which the common man is given freedom to realize his potentialities as an individual—himself unique, creative, free.[41]

Once again, an architectural revolution was seen as the fore-runner and spearhead of a social revolution.

The democratic house and the insistence on individual expression, as Wright developed these ideas, recall Downing, but Wright extended and altered the simpler romanticism of *The Architecture of Country Houses* to suit a more complex and threatening environment. Other concerns of Downing's can be found as well in Wright's material, and similar changes noted. Downing had outlined the benefits of country living; Wright, after his period of suburban architecture, also argued for a country site. But his arguments are often nervous and shrill, revealing an increased hostility toward the modern city. Is the modern city, Wright asked, "a natural triumph of the herd instinct over humanity," or "only a persistent form of social disease?"[42] In either case, build your house far from the urban environment.

When selecting a site for your house, there is always the question of how close to the city you should be, and that depends on what kind of slave you are. The best thing to do is go as far out as you can get. Avoid the suburbs—dormitory towns—by all means. Go way out into the country—what you regard as 'too far'—and when others follow, as they will (if procreation keeps up), move on.

. . . go far from the city, much farther than you think you can afford. You will soon find you never can go quite far enough.[43]

In a rural setting, the house could be realized as part of nature. Wright conceived Taliesen in these terms, as the house in the hill and of the hill, rather than upon the hill, a house made out of local materials, "a house that hill might marry and live happily ever after."[44] Frequently, Wright employed the metaphor of a tree or a plant to capture the natural quality of the organic house. The prairie house was designed so that "an entire building might grow up out of conditions as a plant grows up out of soil and yet be free to be itself. . . ."[45] Architecture, "is no less a weaving and a fabric than the trees are," he said, again about Taliesen.[46] And of the organic house, ". . . it is in the nature of any organic building to grow from its site, come out of the ground into the light. . . ." From this kind of architecture comes "A building dignified as a tree in the midst of nature."[47]

But it was not only the necessity to avoid the city that persuaded Wright to encourage exurban house-building. In a rural setting it was possible for a man to own some land, and there is a strong dose of the Jeffersonian ideal in Wright's statement that "A free country and democratic in the sense that our forefathers intended us to be free, means *individual* freedom for each man on his own ground."[48] Throughout the nineteenth century, architects had encouraged country building, promising the benefits of fresh air, exercise, and a garden of one's own. But Wright based the plea on different grounds: the ownership of land itself. In a significant way, Wright attempted to reverse a long-term American conceptualization by which the house had preempted the land as property; he insisted on the urgency of establishing the "Citizen in his own Life in his own Home with his feet on his own Ground: truly a Free man."[49]

Wright's architectural and social theories led him to an ever-increasing concern about the houses of the less affluent middle class and about the housing of the poor. "The house of moderate cost," he said, "is not only America's major architectural problem but the problem most difficult for her major architects."[50] Downing, too, had developed numerous designs for simple cheap houses, but in 1850 the cheap house was a much more realizable possibility than in Wright's time. A house without plumbing, heating, and wiring could be easily constructed, perhaps by the owner himself. Wright wanted to find ways of constructing houses with twentieth century amenities and at twentieth century labor costs to suit very modest budgets.

In the 1930's Wright experimented with small, moderate-priced houses. In California he worked with concrete block construction for Mrs. Alice Millard's "La Miniatura." In 1937 he did the first Jacobs house in Madison, Wisconsin; the cost, including Wright's fee was $5500. Expenses were cut by means of the elimination of non-essentials such as a visible roof, a garage, and a basement, as well as by the consolidation and simplification of "the three appurtenance systems—heating, lighting, and sanitation."[51] Wright employed the term "Usonian," borrowed from Samuel Bulter's "Usonia" for USA, to describe the small, inexpensive, but thoroughly organic and individualistic house. For Wright, it was not sufficient that a house like the Jacobs' be merely economical; it had to be, as well, a piece of professional architecture: "It is not a builder's nor an amateur's effort." Unlike Downing, whose designs were published for general imitation, Wright insisted that there was "considerable risk in exposing the scheme to imitation or emulation," and added that the architect was necessary to oversee construction, and even to advise on furnishing and planting.[52]

With the "Usonian Automatic" developed after the Second World War, Wright had to forego the architect's privilege. The Usonian Automatic was a house made of pre-cast concrete blocks which could be assembled by the owner. Wright intended this house for the G. I. who "cannot pay a plasterer, mason, bricklayer, carpenter, etc., twenty-nine dollars a day. . . ." Despite the standardization of the materials, Wright contended that the Usonian Automatic provided for individuality since it was "capable of infinite modification of form, pattern, and application, and to any extent." Such housing was "becoming to a free society because, though standardized fully, it yet establishes the democratic ideal of variety—the sovereignty of the individual." The Usonian was "a natural house" for "the free man of our democracy. . . ."[53]

The Usonian Automatic may appear to compromise individual expression despite Wright's argument to the contrary. However, the alternative, as Wright saw it, was the pernicious influence to come from government interference, from the federal mortgaging system that brought Levittown to America. Wright despised government intervention in housing. The buildings themselves were inimical to a free spirit.

> Cubicles in rows or shelves on shelves in hard military array wholly remote from the reflex of democratic nature and architecture, inspiring as any coffin. Decent? Maybe. But just for that, as things are—deadening strait jackets in which human life is to be the 'beneficiary'? But not blessed. Ingenious officering all this by Government order, of the army of the Poor: the Poor who are to be poor and *stay* decently poor.[54]

Furthermore, the payment of rent absolutely stifled freedom, making men themselves "grim Rent to fortuitous Fortune in the form of Rent."[55] But even the guaranteed mortagages provided by the FHA, mortgages which permitted home-ownership to a very large population in the late 1940's and the 1950's, was dangerous in Wright's eyes. According to Wright's criticism, the FHA would mortgage only resalable houses, houses that were, therefore, commonplace and mediocre—suiting anyone because they expressed no one's particular individuality. As early as 1938, Wright had challenged the Association of Federal Architects in Washington:

> I stand here and challenge our America to reflect that any honest, willing, *busy* workman of today with his family can own no home of his own at all unless by grace and beneficence of Government. That should make it time to sit up and raise hell with what made it that way.[56]

There is a curious mixture of the idealist and the reactionary in Wright, and this mix is particularly apparent in his conceptualization of the democratic house. He may not, himself, have been unaware of the nineteenth century values inherent in his vision of the independent man. He took care to differentiate between individualism and individuality: individualism was the characteristic of the "rugged individualistists of capital," and between that quality and "true individuality" lay the same vast difference as lay between "selfishness and selfhood," "sentiment and sentimentality," and "liberty and licence."[57] True individuality was spiritual and creative, and it was the special role of democracy to encourage "the highest possible expression of the individual as a unit not incompatible with a harmonious whole."[58] Individualism, on the other hand, was a reflex of feudalism, presently expressed in economic power. In a democracy, Wright insisted, "every real man must want the prosperity for others he wants for himself,"[59] recalling Downing's statement about "the republican home, built by no robbery of the property of another class, maintained by no infringement of a brother's rights."

The creation of a domestic environment in which free and individual spirits could flourish was for Wright not merely the answer to the dilemma of modern life, it was as well the salvation of the democratic system and even the source for the alleviation of the woes of the world. In such houses dwelt the World Citizen who, "because of well-founded confidence in his own strength . . . is eager to share the work of the World. The World will be invigorated by the happiness and vitality of his own actual practice of the Democracy he preaches. The results of his Democracy would become Ideal for all the world."[60] Most remarkable in these comments is the echo of an earlier American sense of power and of mission—of universal reform emanating from the New Jerusalem.

Behind this idealism lie old and dangerous currents of American chauvinism and missionary zeal, more dangerous because so easily misunderstood and vulgarized. In 1955, *House Beautiful* devoted an entire issue to Frank Lloyd Wright and his work: what *House Beautiful* called his "CONTRIBUTION: A Beauty of Life equal to the Great Concept of America." In the pages of this magazine, nearly all of Wright's concepts are found, vulgarized to accord with the muscle-flexing nationalism of the 1950's. The thesis here is that America has produced "probably the greatest domestic architecture in the history of the homes of man," and the problem to which the editors address themselves is that of explaining "Why [it was] *America* that produced him," "him" being Wright. All the stops are opened: "We might start with the Declaration of Independence and say that 125 years later America finally achieved an architecture for man's right to 'life, liberty and the pursuit of happiness.'" In fact, the Declaration of Independence is cited five times in one article alone; in one context: "every man . . . has a right to a life of beauty, privacy and noble spaciousness. That is the meaning of the American Declaration." (An interpretation which would probably have astonished Jefferson.) America, the magazine continues, has "been acknowledged the leading country of the world in terms of the life of its people," and "Architecture (we'll risk stating it bluntly) is the great art of America." Proof, they tell us, lies in the 10,000,000 homes built in the last ten years—how many of them constructed by Levitt and financed by the FHA, they do not tell us. As for the architecture itself, the houses Wright designed, *House Beautiful* blandly analogizes the opening up of interior space with the opening up of economic and social opportunity. If we can break through the old social pattern of Europe, they ask, "Why not break through the walls of our homes?"[61]

In the hands of popular journalism, the vulgarization of Wright's political and architectural philosophy exaggerates both the ideal and the reactionary elements. But both were part of Wright's thought as he conceived the ideal house for an America that might well have ceased to exist, if it ever did, long before the first prairie houses astonished the conventional householders of Oak Park, Illinois.

Plutocrats and Paupers

Chapter Five

The Houses of the Rich

Our leading object has been to furnish encour-
agement to the young, from the contemplation
of success resulting from a suitable combination
of those sterling qualities, Perseverence, Energy,
Carefulness, Economy, Integrity, Honesty.
> A. Forbes and F. W. Greene,
> *The Rich Men of Massachusetts (1851)*

The imaginations of most men are fired by the
spectacle of the few achieving great fortunes;
each believes that a like fortune lies somewhere
within his own reach, and with blind fatuity he
tolerates conditions which he instinctively feels
to be inequitable, simply because he expects
himself to master them.
> J. W. Ghent,
> *Our Benevolent Feudalism (1902)*

American attitudes toward the mansions of the rich reflect American values about the more general problem of the acquisition of huge fortunes and the development of an aristocracy of wealth. As the house in America became the most visible and the most potent symbol of property, the complex and confused attitudes about great wealth in America focused in the second half of the nineteenth century on the mansions and the country houses of the new millionaires. Value judgments about the houses of the rich, however, were complicated not only with social and economic preoccupations, but also with older concepts of the house as these had developed in the eighteenth century and in the early years of the nineteenth. In accord with these inherited attitudes, houses continued to be seen as symbols for the individual success of their owners and as representations of general national prosperity. Furthermore, great houses stood as proof of the progress of the arts and of taste in America. Such congratulatory views of mansions might, conversely, be tempered or altogether discarded as a result of egalitarian idealism or simply as a consequence of an instinctive American distrust of excessive display. Thus, nineteenth century views of the houses of the rich revealed the dilemma of basic, but antithetical, American values: the oportunity for unlimited personal economic success versus the egalitarian vision of a relatively homogeneous society.

Post-Civil War attitudes toward the mansion depended on a manipulation of these values within the context of any writer's particular social, economic, historical, moral, or aesthetic framework. Economic theories, for example, affected the views of both admirers of millionaires, willing to extol their houses, and radical thinkers, who attacked mansions as symbols of an economic system they deplored. Historic sentiment developed a dichotomy between the old mansions and the new. The old were preferable, in many eyes, to the new; they had the luster of history and association, and no taint of new money. Furthermore, in cities like New York and Boston, where an older aristocracy was being pushed aside by the new rich, older mansions symbolized a more decent past as against a vulgar new wave. Sentimental morality differentiated on yet other grounds, focusing on the manner of the acquisition or the construction of the house. Overall, these were values demanding that an owner "earn" both financially and spiritually, the house he lived in. For example, the inheritance of an old mansion was sentimentally preferable to acquisition by purchase or marriage. New mansions were better built than bought, for if built by the owner, they at least stood for his taste and reflected his character. Even less attractive than buying a ready-built mansion, was renting one; for renting denied both ownership and personal commitment. Finally, questions of architectural style were loaded with sentimental considerations, particularly in respect to the discovery or the creation of an American style.

Points of view toward the mansion also revealed a fairly sharp distinction between the concepts expressed in general expository prose, whether conservative or radical, and the attitudes expressed in fiction. Novelists used the mansion almost exclusively as an emblem of character; an individual might, of course, typify a class of people, but his personal history and even his psychological make-up were represented in the mansion. Non-fiction, on the other hand, tended to deal with the mansion as the representation of a general social condition. Non-fiction pointed out dangers or celebrated achievements. Fiction repeated familiar plot-lines in which the mansion was frequently employed as a moralistic symbol.

Over all, Americans were uncomfortable with the great houses of the rich. Long before the houses of the rich had become distinguishable from the houses of the successful middle class, Americans had shown a certain amount of suspicion at their relative ostentation. Bulfinch, as has been noted, thought the William Bingham house in Philadelphia overly large and costly, and Josiah Quincy had been uneasy about the life-style emblemized by Miles Brewton's house in Charleston. Furthermore, Downing and his followers had warned that a republic could not support aristocratic pretension in American houses.[1] But the houses that Bulfinch and Quincy and Downing distrusted were nothing like what emerged in the late nineteenth century in millionaire architecture. Previously, rich men built bigger houses than other men, but for the most part, their houses were similar in conception and style to more modest American homes. This similarity disappeared in the last decades of the nineteenth century, so that by the end of the century, millionaires had created imitations of European chateaux and palazzi, and had, in these versions of the residences of European nobility, assumed an aristocratic pretension altogether inimical to egalitarian republicanism.

A comparison between two publications, one from 1844 and the other from 1881, devoted to the celebration of large and ostentatious houses, reveals these differences in scope and style between pre- and post-Civil War mansions. Between 1841 and 1843 George W. Carpenter of Philadelphia built himself a mansion in Germantown; in 1844 he had a pamphlet printed describing his house, "Phil-Ellena." The pamphlet was intended for free distribution and was dedicated to the workers who had constructed the house; the last pages of the little book list all the artists and mechanics who worked there, as well as those who furnished the materials and all the "operatives" whose names Carpenter could recall. Despite this attention paid to the workers, it is clear enough that Carpenter's purpose was self-congratulatory. Not only had he accumulated sufficient money for the project, but he had used no architect, "the plan being that of the proprietor."

The house itself was enormous, but for all its expanse and expense it was built in Carpenter's version of the popular Greek Revival style. A central pavillion was flanked by wings, each made up of a higher and a lower portion. Since the central mass was higher than the wings and thrust forward, both the floor plan and the elevation showed a sort of step-pattern. A three-layer round tower topped the central pediment. All the wings boasted full-size columns, and the most exterior wings also held niches for imitation Greek statuary. The grounds, thirty-six acres, contained a Greek temple for a museum, a hothouse, a summer house, a cottage, barn, coach house and wagon house, and several artificial lakes. Inside were frescoes and friezes, ornamented ceilings and paintings, all but the paintings imitations of European treasures. Although the house itself was vast, 165 feet across the front, the rooms themselves were typical of those in smaller houses; the first floor had a drawing room, a dining room, two parlors, a hall, a library, a breakfast room, a conservatory, and a kitchen. "Phil-Ellena" was simply more, certainly a great deal more, of what every middle-class house-builder was constructing.[2]

In contrast with the thirty-five page, soft-covered pamphlet that Carpenter had printed is the ten-volume publication, *Mr. Vanderbilt's House and Collection.* The over-sized volumes are printed on fine paper with watered silk inside covers and include both black and white and color illustrations. Printed in a limited edition of one thousand copies, they were not "for free distribution." In these ten volumes, Earl Shinn, (pseud. Edward Strahan) conducted the reader on a guided tour of the William H. Vanderbilt house on Fifth Avenue.

The Vanderbilt house was, by 1884, a set of twin houses separated by an atrium; two of Vanderbilt's sons-in-law lived in the second house. From the façade and on through each of the rooms, it is apparent that the Vanderbilt house was not simply more of what the middle-class American lived in or might hope to live in. The exterior style was Italianate, one might say Imperial, with a great deal of ornamental carving. Within were a number of unusual kinds of rooms; added to the parlor, library, dining room, and drawing room, were such innovations as the atrium, antichamber, saloon, Japanese parlor, upper library, and the picture and sculpture gallery. Like Carpenter, Vanderbilt was proud of his *objets-d'art*, and again like Carpenter, he owned a number that were copies of originals. But while Carpenter had merely imitated European frescoes and friezes, Vanderbilt went so far as to have casts made of Ghiberti's Gates of Paradise, have them covered with gold, and set in his vestibule.

Of course, a great number of Vanderbilt's treasures were the real thing, and the reader, on his guided tour, has opportunity to take note of many of them. Nevertheless, as the illustrations of entire rooms show, and this includes the ill-named Japanese parlor, the general display is one of nineteenth century clutter, no more attractive done in antique sculpture than in rubberplants and antimacassars. The prose, in contrast to the straight-forward language of Carpenter's pamphlet, is on a par with the interior décor.

> Mother-of-pearl, very freely used in both the architecture and the furniture of this saloon, strikes the highest key in the octave of colors in the decoration, of which the lowest is the crimson of the walls and carpet, while a middle value is attained by a very lavish use of gold.

Most striking in the Vanderbilt volumes is the attempt on Shinn's part to establish a series of justifications for the mansion; nothing parallel appears in the Carpenter pamphlet. Two rationalizations are expressed, and these are the principal justifications in American culture for any large house. The Vanderbilt house is at once architectural proof of the success of civilization in America and a sample of the typical personal "home." Shinn announced that through these volumes we are afforded "a revelation of a private home" which indicates, "like a more perfect Pompeii," "the vision and the image of a typical American residence." Since men are curious about the houses of a Sallust or a Flemish banker, Venetian merchant prince or Tudor gentleman, so they will be curious about the houses of Americans, particularly "at the moment when the nation began to have a taste of its own, an architecture, a connaisseurship [sic]." He went on to connect the house with the particular character of its owner. There are "three senses" according to Shinn, in which the house is understood. One may erect a residence according to the five architectural orders or he may choose to construct a building to display fashionable collections, like tapestries or hangings. The Vanderbilt house was built according to "the third sense [which] regards the House as a Home. In the mind of such an owner, the residence is only the last shell or envelope of the man, the rooms express the habits . . . the house appears to have grown over this mass of individual needs." Therefore, Shinn argued, this was not an unusually ostentatious house; rather, it was representative. Further, it was expressive and even organic, appearing "to have grown" out of Vanderbilt's unique requirements.[3]

The Vanderbilt volumes indicate both in their sumptuousness and in their rationalizations a response to American attitudes about the mansion. If the justifications were intended to allay suspicions about grandiose residences, the braggadoccio catered to a wide-spread popular fascination with the life of the very rich. Popular journalism also appealed to this fascination by featuring illustrated articles on new mansions, and the guide-books to major cities directed tourists to the most remarkable examples of architectural conspicuous consumption. For example, in 1867 *Appleton's Illustrated Guide* pointed the visitor to the A. T. Stewart mansion at Fifth Avenue and Thirty-fourth Street. Stewart, a new millionaire who had amassed a fortune in the dry goods business, built his mansion between 1864 and 1869. Constructed of marble, inside and out, it was four stories high and more than one hundred feet square, the cost has been variously estimated at between two and three million dollars, including such amenities as imitation classical statuary and a gold-encrusted bathtub.[4]

The history of Stewart and his house is marked with ironies that grow familiar in reading about great American mansions. Downing had warned that such houses would pass from the original family in one generation, but Downing's estimate was generous in this case. Stewart lived only eight years in his mansion, and during none of them was he accepted by the society to which he aspired. His widow continued to live in the house until her death in 1886, after which the executor of the estate moved in himself for five years before renting it, for another nine, at $37,000 a year. In 1901, it was torn down, much of its marble sold to stone-carvers for tombs. But long before 1900, the Stewart house had lost its significance and grandeur; society moved further uptown, and the newer millionaires constructed houses that far overshadowed the Stewart palace. By the time of the death of Stewart's widow the words of *Appleton's Guide* were a curious anachronism, for no longer was Stewart's mansion "the most famous building on Fifth Avenue," one for which "words are absolutely inadequate to describe its beauty and unique grandeur."[5]

The *Times*, more abstractly and more prophetically, had celebrated Stewart's architectural achievement by declaring that "Nothing denotes more greatly a nation's advancement in civilization than the erection of palatial private residences."[6] If so, Fifth Avenue was the major signpost of American advancement, and the Vanderbilts participated generously in the progress of our civilization. Allen Churchill, in *The Upper Crust*, lists thirteen Fifth Avenue addresses where "at one time or another, Vanderbilts built or resided in mansions." The sums of money spent by the Vanderbilts make Stewart's three million dollars seem only a modest fortune. Land-prices alone were enormous. Cornelius Vanderbilt II paid $600,000 for property at Fifth Avenue and Fifty-Seventh Street, five blocks up from W. K. Vanderbilt's "little Chateau de Blois." But the Vanderbilts did not restrict their building to the city, and their summer residences as well cost vast fortunes. W. K. spent two million dollars for the construction of "Marble House" (1892) at Newport, and another nine million for the furnishings. For the rebuilding of "Idle Hours" (1899), with one hundred and ten rooms and forty-five bathrooms, Vanderbilt spent another six million.[7]

New York produced the greatest quantity of the most spectacular mansions and Newport the most fantastic "cottages." Nevertheless, other American cities produced their own millionaires and they in turn, their own architectural monuments. In Chicago, the McCormick and Potter Palmer mansions, in St. Paul the James Hill residence; even in Eureka, California, the Carson House. In Boston, Henry James's friend, Isabella Stewart Gardiner had an Italian palace dismantled, transported and reconstructed on the Fenway. Still, New York and Newport outdid their rivals and their mansions and cottages became representative of the houses of the gilded millionaires. A Fifth Avenue mansion was the seal of success, and not infrequently the most successful provincial millionaires moved from their provincial palaces to New York to build anew; in some cases, they finally moved on from New York to Europe in search of the aristocratic life. Andrew Carnegie passed from Pittsburgh, through Fifth Avenue, to his castle in Scotland. Hearst established his castle in Wales.

Such aristocratic, even royal, living had seemed a foreign innovation to pre-Civil War Americans. Attacks on mansion-living in the earlier nineteenth century suggested the anti-American character of "fashionable" life. In 1845, Anna Cora Mowatt's *Fashion* was produced in New York, and in its satire of the life of the new rich expressed all the popular antipathies to the mansion. The Tiffany family lives in grand style, Mr. Tiffany a slave to his business and his wife the fool of fashion and of her venal French maid, who pretends to assist her mistress in achieving a *"jenny-sans-quoi"* look. When their situation becomes intricately endangered by business and matrimonial difficulties, they are saved by Mr. Trueblood, an elderly American gentleman of perfect probity and no pretensions. He labels their home "a fashionable *museum*," in which no one would ever "feel *at home*." Mr. Trueblood promises to rescue the Tiffany family from their financial confusion, but "upon one condition." "You must sell your house and all these gew gaws, and bundle your wife and daughter off to the country. There let them learn economy, true independence, and home virtues, instead of foreign folies."[8] The mansion the Tiffanys must surrender stands for several qualities hostile to the American experience—the city, luxury, and the folly and viciousness of the idle woman. All these antipathies remained a part of the American repertory of condemnation for the mansion; however, Mr. Trueblood also sees the mansion and its life-style as imported, as "foreign follies." After the Civil War this concept passed away; the mansion was no longer an importation, but a representation, good or bad, of one aspect of the American experience.

While the ornate and ostentatious mansion lost its foreign taint, it did not disembarrass itself of its other antipathetic qualities. Critics continued to point to the great houses of the rich, lamenting the excessive money spent for them and decrying the lives of luxury that were passed within them. To many minds, the growing inequality in the distribution of wealth and the evidence of lives of extraordinary sumptuousness remained, as they had long been, inimical to the American ideal. Meanwhile, the defenders of the rich, of the economic system, and of the mansions that symbolized both, presented counter-attacks to justify the building of these houses.

Justifications for large and opulent homes had appeared in American writing since the eighteenth century. Fine homes provided evidence of individual hard work as well as of the general advancement of the American nation. By the 1850's, the arguments in favor of luxurious homes were fully developed responses to current attacks on opulence. Great private homes added luster to the American image, said a writer for *Putnam's* in 1854. "Private dwellings in a country like the United States, where every man labors for his own individual comfort, and not for the glory of the state, or the ambition of the monarch, offer the best evidences of the prosperity, the intelligence, and the general taste of the people." Further, he argued against the "Objections [that] have been made, on moral and economic grounds, to the display of wealth and luxury in architectural decoration." For one thing, such display was natural, and "luxury is a vice, only when it is extravagance in an individual." Such domestic luxury, he found, was not private only; rather, it led to "public benefits to trade and industry." Even private sumptuousness could be defensible on the grounds of the familiarity of the rich with great comforts as well as by the fact that "every external indication of prosperity tends to add attractions to a city." The writer of this piece was not, apparently, deaf to hostile voices and he did admit that it was true that all the wealth and "intelligent labor" might "better serve the cause of human happiness by being employed in other ways." He concluded with the old caution about the wheel of fortune in American business: "The wealthy merchant builds himself a palace today which will be inhabited by the son of his porter tomorrow."[9]

The *Putnam's* article justified mansions both individually and societally; a more sophisticated argument from the same decade proved that general social betterment resulted from individual self-aggrandizement. The mansion, as a visible symbol of financial success, served as an incentive to young men to strive for similar success. In the 1850's success was popularly attributed to a set of Christian virtues rather than to any particular shrewdness, and never to illegal or immoral methods. According to Forbes and Greene, who in 1851 put together a small book called *The Rich Men of Massachusetts*, success comprised "Perseverence, Energy, Carefulness, Economy, Integrity, Honesty." In listing the rich men, the estimated amount of their fortunes, and the methods by which these fortunes were accumulated, Forbes and Greene revealed two sets of value judgments which enhanced their definition of success. Philanthropy was praised wherever evidence for it could be found, and self-made men were preferred to those who had inherited or married their money.

Further indication of the attitudes embraced by Forbes and Greene appears in the brief biographies included in some of their listings. Occasionally, one comes upon the archetypal rags-to-riches plot of American mythology. For example, a Mrs. Sarah Hale, whose fortune was estimated at $450,000, inherited it from her grandfather, Moses Brown, a wheelwright who rose to great wealth.

> [Moses Brown] Went himself to Mr. Dalton's splendid mansion in State street after the chaise . . . much surprised at the elegance and richness of the place he had seen. Mark the changes of fortune: Mr. Dalton died, leaving the property to his son; the son was lazy, extravagant, intemperate, and soon brought the elegant mansion 'into market.' Mr. Brown's opposite qualities had brought *him* into a condition to purchase just such a mansion, he bought, lived and died in the very house from which he had 'hauled off' by hand the first job that was ever given to him.

In this short biography are the elements of much of the American dream and many of the symbolic qualities, both good and bad, connected with the mansion-dweller. The wealthy man is succeeded by a wastrel son; the prophetic warning is realized, and the house is lost. The virtuous man, however, wins the mansion, for he has proven his right to it.[10]

After the Civil War, justifications for the mansion underwent some changes. While defenders of the rich and their houses continued to employ the ideas of national progress and individual incentive, the increasing acerbity of the attacks against the mansion necessitated more sophisticated defenses. In *Dream*

and Thought in the Business Community, Edward Chase Kirkland reviews the attitudes of the late nineteenth century toward
the mansions of the rich, isolating a number of justifications for
the mansion. For one thing, expensive houses were seen as
spreading around the assets of the country; to the extent that the
working-class received wages for their part in construction,
they were personally enriched. Secondly, by building a fine
house a man beautified the community he lived in; thus, he was,
voluntarily or not, a benefactor. Another argument, an extension
of business laissez-faire, insisted that what a rich man did with
his own money was no one's business but his own. Some voices
argued that the rich had a responsibility to live grandly.[11]

Opponents of the luxurious architecture of the rich insisted
that great houses absorbed money that could better be used for
investment capital. Some writers worried about the increasingly
apparent chasm between rich and poor and warned that the
presence of such houses led directly to social unrest. In a period
when socialism and anarchism loomed as fearful threats, this
last critique was less an argument than a menacing warning.
Finally, luxury itself was seen as unwholesome, threatening the
rich themselves by sapping their moral fiber, and providing not
an incentive but a dangerous model for the young. Since at its
most extreme the celebration of the life-style of the rich equated
money with happiness, it confused and corrupted young men
and women. To make this point, Theodore Dreiser ironically
described Sister Carrie's response to Chicago's North Shore
Drive.

> [Carrie] imagined that across these richly carved entranceways,
> where the globed and crystalled lamps shone upon panelled doors
> set with stained and designed panes of glass, was neither care nor
> unsatisfied desire. She was perfectly certain that here was hap-
> piness.[12]

The economic debate over luxury climaxed in the 1890's. In
an essay in the *North American Review* of 1899, F. Spencer Baldwin, "Professor of Economics in the Boston University," discussed
"Some Aspects of Luxury." He argued in favor of luxurious
living and spending on the part of the rich, contending that
"If luxury itself tends to slacken the energy of individuals, the

desire for luxury tends to quicken their energies." Therefore, if some of the rich are weakened, the general working force is encouraged by the sight of luxurious living, which is "a very powerful motive to industrial activity." In the course of his article, Baldwin attacked every argument against luxury. Others had argued that investment capital was necessary for the increase of production, but he pointed out that we were in danger of over-production, and that as a result "luxurious expenditure really promotes the economic interests of society." As for the idea that luxury wrongs the poor, "This notion that there is necessarily any causal connection between opulence and poverty is too crude to require a serious refutation;" there is no fixed amount of capital in any society, he added. And while he grudgingly admitted, without specifying, that there were some unjustifiable luxuries, bad both for the individual and for society, on the whole luxury was an unmixed blessing.

> Luxury is a main factor in this onward movement of the race. It deepens and enriches the content of life. The desire for it furnishes a chief motive to social advancement. Without it, existence would become a stagnant monotony. It stands for much of the beauty, grace and variety which alone make life really worth the living.[13]

The opposite point of view was taken by E. L. Godkin in *Scribner's Magazine* in 1896. In "The Expenditure of Rich Men," Godkin attempted to convince the rich to give their money to urban beautification. Possibly in order to make his argument more palatable to the rich, Godkin kept his rhetoric mild; nevertheless, he struck cannily at all the arguments in favor of the building of great houses, while developing a strong attack against the mansion, including the old charge of "foreignness." The principal thesis of the essay is the necessity of rich, private individuals to spend their money for display. Such examples of "tangible, visible property" are determined, whether the rich man is aware of it or not, by the "ways in which the public in general expected him to spend it." Godkin had no quarrel with this fact; however, he wished to point out that America had no traditions about the ways in which money was to be displayed.

Until the present, Godkin continued, European history has been marked with the union of money and nobility. America

has no such history. Indeed, even our early estates on the James
and the Hudson were "simply moderate sized mansions which,
on most estates in England or France, would be considered
small." Unlike England or France, where great houses were
"intended to maintain and support the influence of the ruling
class by means which were sure to impress the popular mind,"
these eighteenth century mansions in America are "mainly interesting as showing the pains taken to put up comfortable
abodes in what were then out-of-the-way places." Given such
an absence of tradition, it is not surprising that Americans have
aped Europeans and used their money to create imitations of
English and French estate houses. But this is an error, said
Godkin. European houses have always meant large and aristocratic hospitality depending on "society," which has never appeared in America, or on "great territorial possessions." Since
there are no great land-holders in America, there is no reason
for great houses.

More important than these mistakes about the meaning of the
great houses of Europe, Godkin maintained, is the radical error
about the relationship of such houses to American society. The
most significant idea about "American polity . . . is equality of
conditions, that there should neither be an immoderate display
of wealth, nor of poverty." "Above all," he added, "wealth should
not become an object of apprehension." This is no minor matter,
as Godkin developed it, and houses are no random symbol of
the expenditures of rich men. The houses that men live in are
a uniquely clear index to the condition of a society.

> In short, it may be truly said that dwelling-places, from the
> Indian's tepee up to the palace of the great noble, indicate, far
> more clearly than books or constitutions, the political and social
> condition of the country.[14]

While this argument went on in the monthly magazines, the
rich themselves continued to build and to inhabit their gorgeous
mansions, limiting their statements on the subject to such publications as *Mr. Vanderbilt's House and Collection.* There was,
of course, a notable exception in Andrew Carnegie. In "Wealth,"
published in the *North American Review* in 1889, Carnegie discussed luxury and houses and the responsibilities of the man of

wealth. Carnegie picked up some of the themes associated for over a century with the American house. He opened his essay with a nod in the direction of progress. "The contrast between the palace of the millionaire and the cottage of the laborer with us to-day measures the change which has come with civilization." Such a change is highly beneficial; it is "essential for the progress of the race." Progress, as Carnegie saw it, comes through the advantages of the most fortunate. It is better that some men live in great houses than that none at all should. He cited as proof the fact that all classes at present live in better conditions than the rich had at one time lived. Therefore, progress should be left unimpeded; anarchists and socialists should understand that "upon the sacredness of property civilization itself depends." Nevertheless, Carnegie argued for moderation on the part of the millionaire, whose duties included the necessity to "set an example of modest, unostentatious living, shunning display or extravagance." In attempting to answer the old American question of the limits of ostentation, Carnegie responded that "Whatever makes one conspicuous offends the canon."[15]

Architectural critics were no more successful than Carnegie at discovering those limits, but for them, beauty and tastefulness frequently excused excess. Mariana Van Rensselaer wrote a series of architectural articles for *Century Magazine* between 1884 and 1886. She noted that from 1870 on showiness marked New York houses, but "Fortunately we too may already count dwellings not a few where evident costliness is amply justified by beauty." Beauty, however, did not justify the Stewart mansion, which she could call only "very showy." And of the Vanderbilt chateau, she could say she found it good enough to override the general desirability of simplicity. "While it is necessary that the virtues and possibilities of simplicity should be praised, it is well to be reminded occasionally that they are not the only virtues or the finest possibilities."[16]

Russel Sturgis, in his architectural essays, ignored the problem of limits and sought magnificence. He was dismayed at the lack of real grandeur displayed by the homes of the rich, labeling them almost all "small houses looked at through a magnifying glass." An American who had multiplied his fortune a hundredfold had built houses only "perhaps ten-fold larger than he would otherwise have done." Basically, Sturgis believed in the right, indeed the responsibility, of the rich to appear rich and to create a life-style commensurate with their wealth. Unfortunately, "the necessary conditions of a stately house, a sort of palazzo, have hardly been considered."[17]

Sturgis was not alone in demanding more magnificence from the rich. In an essay for *McClure's* in 1905, Ida M. Tarbell criticized Rockefeller for his relatively simple living. Although he had city houses in both New York and Cleveland and three country houses, none of them was particularly costly or architecturally interesting. Tarbell felt a man's character could be read in his houses, and that Rockefeller's homes "show his cult of the unpretentious," but "they are all unpretending even to the point of being conspicuous." In other words, Rockefeller had failed to build an "appropriate mansion."[18]

One particularly acerbic critic of the American millionaire employed a two-edged sword in his attacks on their houses. Gustavus Myers, in the *History of the Great American Fortunes* (1909, 1936), saw great mansions as indicative of the crass vulgarity of the rich and lesser houses as examples of their inhabitants' stinginess. Commodore Vanderbilt, for example, was a notorious skin-flint, according to Myers. "His closefistedness was such a passion that for many years he refused to substitute new carpets for the scandalous ones covering the floors of his house No. 10 Washington Place." As for his son, William H., he lived until 1864 in "a small, square, plain two-story house facing the sea, with a lean-to on one end for a kitchen. He was driven to this kind of living by his father's attitude toward "leisure and luxury;" therefore, "William H. Vanderbilt made a studious policy of standing in with his father, truckling to his every caprice and demand." But once the Commodore was dead, his son showed his true colors. "It was at this time that he, in accord with the chrysalid tendency manifested by most other millionaires, discarded his long-followed sombre method of life and invested himself with a gaudy magnificence," the Fifth Avenue mansion.[19]

With the beginning of the twentieth century, sufficient criticism had been leveled at the houses of the rich to make defenders of opulent residences avoid the word "mansion." In 1903, Harry W. Desmond and Herbert Croly, editors of the *Architectural Review*, published *Stately Homes in America*. The title itself is an exercise in tact, and the language throughout is cautious. The authors spoke of "expensive and magnificent private dwellings," "the greater contemporary residence," "the house the millionaire has built," and "'palatial' private building."[20]

Stately Homes in America is a history of fine houses, an assertion of the meaning of the American house, and a defensive argument for the continued building of splendid residences. The earliest American houses of size and style are placed in historical perspective. Rather than drift in a nostalgic sentiment for the return of the old days, Desmond and Croly asserted that Colonial homes were established for an aristocracy which had for standards "very modest dwellings," like those of second-rate country squires in England. While the inhabitants were respectable and endowed with "some notion of good form," their houses reflected the limits of the "range of expression" in their lives, and lacked "the richer tone, the deeper harmonies, the grander style of some French and Italian models." They had, after all, very little originality.[21]

It was not until after the Civil War that American houses began to be built which attempted something original and something grandiose. A few earlier men of means had tried to move away from Greek Revival or Brownstone uniformity, but there was no architectural taste as yet to support them. Desmond and Croly saw a favorable new turn of events in the domestic architecture that was undertaken in America from the late 1870's, architecture that signaled the distinctive quality of its builders. The authors singled out the most significant characteristic of these new houses: they were built as the homes of the very rich, "for men whose chief title to distinction is that they are rich." They were "the peculiar product . . . partly of the tastes, the ambitions, the methods, and the resources of contemporary American captains of industry."[22]

Not Louis Sullivan nor the most radical economic thinker of 1900 would have argued this point with Desmond and Croly; American mansions certainly were the reflection of American tastes, ambitions, and commercial methods. But for Desmond and Croly both the ambition and the architectural style were defensible, and so was the character of the American millionaire-builder. As for the borrowed styles of these mansions, their provenance in the aristocratic architecture of Europe, they conceded that "there is a manifest incongruity between the lives of these men and their dwellings." So said Sullivan. But Desmond and Croly concluded that "it is not the aspect of truth on which it is helpful at the present time to dwell." The point is that Americans had no fully developed social forms as yet, and as a result no fully developed native architectural forms for the rich. Despite any architectural incongruity in American mansions, Desmond and Croly discovered one overriding form of suitability in the houses of the rich; "there is some propriety between the generous habits of mind of the men who live in these houses, their love of splendor and distinction, and the peculiar character of their homes."[23]

Desmond and Croly were willing, however, to go further in celebrating the nature of the American millionaire and his house. These mansions are architectural monuments to business success.

> Unlike any previous type of residence erected in this country, these great modern dwellings are something more than personal and domestic products, something more than pleasant and appropiate houses in which to live and bring up a family; and this 'something more' stands for a different point of view. . . . They indicate on the parts of these gentlemen, not the pride of station and position of a European noble, but a very conscious delight in the opportunities to be publicly effective, which are offered to them by their wealth and by the freedom of American life. They exist, in part at least, in order to display that wealth, and to celebrate those opportunities in a worthy and conspicuous manner.

Thus, this defense of the millionaire's house rested precisely on its distance from the "home." The display of fortune, for so long discouraged in American domestic architecture, was not only condoned and even encouraged, but that very display became in this passage the "American" aspect of the house by advertising the financial opportunities the nation offered. The advertising, at last, excused even the vulgarity. If the architectural tastes of this class "are somewhat barbaric" and altogether lacking in the sense of economy which brings simplicity, "what else can be expected?" If the architects had acquiesced in the mere imitation of European styles, they had done so because they were happy to imitate what they loved. And if the millionaire was a bit crude, well, the effect of all this finery on his children would be "pervasive and profound." Civilization was on the march in America, and the mansions of the rich were a species of "monumental 'posters,' advertising to the world both American opulence and American artistic emancipation."[24]

Even the question of the distribution of wealth was not one from which Desmond and Croly altogether shrank. They were willing to raise the question, much in the air in these years, as to whether the concentration of great wealth was good or evil, but they raised it only to dismiss it. Capitalism was the basis of American society; to oppose the concentration of wealth was to give up on American civilization.

> If wealth, whether widely distributed or concentrated in a few hands, or both, is as bad a thing as some passages in the Prophets and the Gospels make it out to be, there is little hope for American civilization, for our civilization is assuredly conditioned on the belief that a high standard of comfort is not of necessity morally stupifying, or the possession of a large fortune inevitably a source of evil and corruption.

Determining that, "Unless we are to go back on the whole trend of our development, we must find some way of reconciling prosperity with heroism, and great wealth with moderation, refinement, and distinction," the authors brought to their argument the support of the novels of Mr. Henry James.[25]

The Wings of the Dove, particularly, struck Desmond and Croly as proof of "the finer promise of certain current tendencies" in regard to the connection between high moral character and large material fortune. Milly Theale, the heroine of The Wings of the Dove, is both rich and noble. In general, the authors admired James's recognition of the importance of houses, deriving "even his motives from the actual effect on the lives of people of noble, memorable, and beautiful houses."

> In "The Spoils of Poynton," the whole motive of the book is derived from the passionate devotion to a beautiful house, which is aroused in the woman who planned it, by the danger of it falling into the hands of people who will impair its perfection.[26]

But in "The Spoils of Poynton," it seems necessary to add, the passionate devotion to her house on the part of Mrs. Gereth not only leads inexorably to the misery and frustration of Fleda Vetch but, indeed, to the destruction of the house itself.

Probably no American writer has given us the architectural richness of James. Desmond and Croly were correct in noting that James "is always peculiarly solicitous about effecting some suggestive propriety between the man or the woman and the house." Certainly, James's novels are rich in houses, and the greater number of these are fine mansions and country houses. Of these rich houses, however, very few are untainted by intrigue and evil. One can find an occasional house like an apparent Eden, for example, "Gardencourt" in *The Portrait of a Lady*. But it is at Gardencourt that Isabel Archer's exposure to wealth initiates her downfall. Much more frequent than the Gardencourts in James's fiction are houses like "Roccanera," where Isabel is immured by her evil husband, the sinister rue de l'Université residence of the Bellegarde family in *The American*, the cursed country house in *The Turn of the Screw*, or the great Venetian palace in which a betrayed Milly Theale turns her face to the wall and dies.

Henry James's treatment of houses is somewhat atypical, in part because of the great majority of foreign settings in his work and in part because of his remarkable subtlety and ambiguousness. James does maintain the general American fictional connection between the mansion and immorality, even evil. However, the importance James placed on beauty and on the maintenance of social forms, notwithstanding the presence of evil, creates a particular lustre about the great houses in his novels. In effect, James manipulates his grander domestic settings in order to evoke both great beauty and an oppressive sense of evil. In "The Spoils of Poynton," to return to Desmond and Croly's example, James never diminished the aesthetic perfection of the house as a means of underscoring a moral warning. But such treatment of fine houses is anomalous in American fiction. Most American novelists have revealed a more single-minded moral purpose in their work and typically chosen for their immoral characters an environment of vulgar ostentation rather than tasteful beauty.

Therefore, typical attitudes toward the mansion in American fiction concentrate on the negative qualities of the lives of the rich, transmuting beauty into excess and vulgarity. In Mark

Twain's settings in *The Gilded Age,* in the naturalist novels of Norris, Frederick, and Fuller, and in the New York novels of Edith Wharton, opulent houses are treated with heavy and moralistic irony. For Twain, any attempts at architectural upward mobility—except his own—from the first expression of tasteless home improvement to the final realization of self-styled magnificence are comical. In *The Gilded Age* (1873), Squire Hawkins begins to make his fortune. Having appeared first in "a double log cabin, in a state of decay," he soon finds his way to a new, two-story house, with " 'store' furniture from St. Louis," and "oilcloth window-curtains [with] noble pictures on them of castles such as had never been seen anywhere in the world but on window-curtains." But Twain is equally acerbic about the White House, "a fine large white barn, with wide unhandsome grounds about it. . . . It is ugly enough outside, but that is nothing to what it is inside. Dreariness, flimsiness, bad taste reduced to mathematical completeness is what the inside offers the eye."[27]

It is not, however, a case of the simple dismissal of the architectural taste and the moral standards of the rich, although the mansion obviously symbolizes both of these. Much more significantly, the mansion stands at the heart of a plot-pattern insistently repeated in late nineteenth and early twentieth century American literature. This plot, a counterpoint to the story of rags-to-riches, depicts the fall from success and riches. At its center is the mansion, achieved and then lost; in effect, it is the story not of Moses Brown who earned the mansion of Mr. Dalton, his former employer, but of Mr. Dalton and his son, who lose their right to the great house.

The pattern of the fall from fortune has several variations in progression. The hero may start poor, reach success, and end poor; or, we may meet him at the height of his success and witness only his decline. The hero, furthermore, may betray himself, or he may be the victim of the ambition of his wife or of his children. An important distinction must also be made between the man who engineers his own downfall as a result of his greed or immoral behavior, and the man who is interpreted as the victim of the economic environment in which he lives. Generally, the American novel of the turn of the century tended toward pity rather than censure, and essential to this viewpoint was the vision of the hero as a victim of his culture.

The victimization of the successful business man and of his wife, is basic to the plot-line of Frank Norris's *The Pit* (1903), a moral tale of the corruption worked by money and ambition. Curtis Jadwin marries the beautiful Laura Dearborn and they move into a mansion facing Lincoln Park in Chicago. The mansion is so large that Jadwin claims not to know its precise extent; in response to a friend who asks how many rooms he has in the house, he replies, "Upon my word, I don't know. . . . I discovered a new one yesterday." In another passage Laura's aunt exclaims, "Why, it's a palace! . . . Why, it takes in the whole block, child, and there's a conservatory pretty near as big as [my] house." There are, as well, an art gallery with the requisite Bourguereau, and a music room with an organ.

Jadwin, a simple man at heart, grows intoxicated by the wheat exchange, forgetting even his wife in his wild enthusiasm for profit. Laura, too, is a sympathetic character, but she is unhappy in the mansion, lonely without her wheat-drunken husband, nearly seduced by an artist-friend in her misery. But the very night of her planned elopement, her husband returns from the exchange, a ruined man. Faced with economic privation, husband and wife rediscover one another as they leave the mansion to move to the West, where they will begin life again. In short, economic disaster saves the Jadwin's marriage by freeing them from the ostentation of wealth. As Jadwin says, reminiscing about his youth,

> Lord love me, I can see that kitchen in the old farmhouse as plain! The walls were just logs and plaster, and there were upright supports in each corner. . . . And the fireplace was there . . . and there was the wood box. . . . Honey, I was happy then. Of course, I've got you now, and that's all the difference in the world. . . . We've got a fine place and a mint of money I suppose—and I'm proud of it. But I don't know. . . . If they'd let me be and put us two—just you and me—back in the old house with the bare floors and the rawhide chairs and the shuck beds, I guess we'd manage.[28]

But manage they could not in the mansion, a domestic setting inimical to successful marriage.

In Henry B. Fuller's *With the Procession* (1895), the older generation is the victim of the younger, the children corrupted by the values of the world around them. David Marshall and his wife have continued to live contentedly in their older Chicago home despite the great fortune that he has accumulated. "Taken altogether, a sedate, stable, decorous old homestead, fit for the family within it." There are a number of children, but among them it is the beauty Rosamund (Rosie) who forces the family to build a new mansion: "Are we going on forever living in this same old place?" At last, the Marshalls accede to Rosie's pleadings and to the added insistence of their married daughter Alice The great house is built out on the prairie, where other "new houses [were] placed dispersedly about."

The symbolic menace of the new house is intensified by two incidents in the plot. Marshall, tricked by a deceitful partner, loses his business as the house is completed, and as the family moves into the house, the sick old man dies. Even Rosie, now married to an Englishman who had deceived the family about his wealth and connections, is stricken with conscience; "I am to blame for it all," she cries. There is nothing to salvage but their pride, and only old Mrs. Marshall can rise to the necessity. She announces to a haughty visitor that the house "is one of the handsomest on the street. . . . We feel completely at home here." "But in truth," adds Fuller, "the poor soul was homesick, heartsick, as lost and forlorn as a shipwrecked sailor on the chill coast of Kamchatka."[29] Fuller, like Norris, not only forcefully denies any connection between human happiness and great houses, but absolutely asserts the incompatibility of the mansion with peace of mind.

Particularly striking is the fact that Fuller did not equate misery with great wealth in general; the old Marshalls were rich and happy as long as they did not spend their money for an ostentatious house. In this particular novel, the existence of a great amount of money served as a temptation to the young to create a symbolic setting for their lives. That setting, the great house, leads to their ruin. Fuller is willing, however, to grant the possibility of the coexistence of a mansion and happiness under very special conditions. With the Procession also gives us Mrs. Bates, a woman with an extraordinarily grand house, who escapes its curse by maintaining her own inner simplicity of heart, symbolized by a real cottage hideaway deep within the mansion.

The Bates house is described in great detail; through some

twenty-five pages of text, we move from the granite façade, by the liveried footman, through the hall, music room, and library, Grand Salon, and the "Sala de los Embajadors," at last into Mrs. Bates bedroom, a "spacious room done in white and gold. . . . To one side stood a massive brass bedstead full panoplied in coverlet and pillow-case, and the mirror of the dressing case reflected a formal row of silver-backed brushes and combs." When an awed young visitor, Jane Marshall, asks if this is where Mrs. Bates sleeps, the older woman cries, "Sleep here! . . . I don't sleep here. I'd as soon think of sleeping out on the prairie." The great bed, she adds, is simply for ladies to leave their hats and cloaks on. At this point Mrs. Bates leads Jane to the room she does sleep in, to the cottage deep within the mansion.

> . . . a small, cramped, low-ceiled room which was filled with worn and antiquated furniture. There was a ponderous old mahogany bureau, with the veneering cracked and peeled, and a bed to correspond. There was a shabby little writing-desk. . . . On the floor there was an old Brussels carpet. . . . In one corner stood a small upright piano . . . and on one wall hung a set of thin black-walnut shelves strung together with cords and loaded with a variety of well-worn volumes. In the grate was a coal fire.

And Jane, we are told, understands: "How good you are to me!"[30] This room is more stuffed with symbols than with furniture. A bed for single slumber, a piano for playing, books that have been read, a real fireplace. From such a stronghold, Mrs. Bates can well defend against the moral incursions from the world of her mansion.

Mrs. Bates' two beds are, in themselves, especially rich symbols. While the novels of this period in American literature avoid any explicit investigation of sexuality, it is evident that the houses of the rich are hospitable to illicit sexuality. In James's *The Golden Bowl* (1904), "Matcham" is one setting for the adultery between the Prince and Charlotte, as well as for the vulgar affair between Lady Castledean and the piano-playing Mr. Blint. In *The House of Mirth* (1905), Edith Wharton creates an atmosphere of illicit sexuality in "Bellomont," the Newport home of the Gus Trenors. And in *Hudson River Bracketed* (1929), Wharton presents Mrs. Jet Pulsifer, who resides in a colossal mansion in New York City, where she tries to seduce the young hero. Both her seductive charm and her sexual immorality are implicit in her home, rich, costly, vast, and a bit vulgar.

Harold Frederick, in *The Damnation of Theron Ware* (1896), also connects adulterous sexuality with a mansion setting. The protagonist is a protestant minister who indulges in a long flirtation with Celia Madden, a young Catholic girl. The mansion where she lives is "huge and ornate." When her father built it, he put "to shame every other house in the place [and] gave an effect of ostentation to the Maddens." This is not, however, to Mr. Madden's discredit, rude "Connemara peasant" though he is. The house "had been built to please, or rather placate his wife." Furthermore, such a setting is suitable for the charming and seductive Celia, "the only one who really belonged there." Indeed, Celia lounges about in a room "furnished with only divans and huge, soft cushions, its walls covered with statues not too strictly clothed."[31] It is tempting to see the wild forest where Hester Prynne and Arthur Dimmesdale fell into sin now replaced by the city mansion or country house. Not nature but excessive civilization provides the temptation for lawless love.

Mansion settings in American fiction in general were established for characters who exceeded societal restraints, particularly economic and sexual restraints. But no class of mansion-dwellers provided so egregious an example of vulgarity in getting and spending, or in ensnaring and marrying, than the parvenus. Hostility toward the new rich was particularly bitter on the part of older families whose standards of taste decried new ostentation and lavishness. As a result, older mansions not only escaped any general denigration, but they became symbolic of an earlier society where restraint and decorum ruled. In New York, where the incursion of the new rich meant the building of new houses in a continuous uptown wave, nostalgia for a former way of life was concentrated on the old neighborhoods. In 1883 Richard Grant White, the father of architect Stanford White, wrote about "Old New York and its Houses," for *Century*. Old New York, he lamented, had "been swept out of existence by the great tidal wave of its own material prosperity." The old neighborhoods boasted houses "of a stately elegance which would now be sought in vain between Washington Square and the Central Park." New houses were built by a "mob in good clothes with money in pocket," in whom "pretension is united with vulgarity."[32]

Fiction reflected the same sentiment for the older houses of New York and the same animadversion for the newer. In fact, any mansion not indecently new could be treated with respect, particularly if the owner had removed himself from the competitive world. An example, in Edith Wharton's *The Age of Innocence* (1920), is Mrs. Manson Mingott who had showed her audacity and courage by building "a large house of pale cream-coloured stone (when brown sandstone seemed as much the only wear as a frock coat in the afternoon) in an inacessible wilderness near the Central Park." Here she lived among the "visible proof of her moral courage," and watched fashionable society move up to and beyond her in its northward migration. The house perfectly symbolizes old Mrs. Mingott, a character of "moral courage" and absolute convictions, and a character who, both financially and matrimonially, is *hors de combat.*[33]

American fiction after the First World War continued to use the mansion as a central symbol for the new rich. In *The Great Gatsby* (1925), F. Scott Fitzgerald created a parvenu hero who, like the protagonists of late nineteenth century fiction, is the victim of the values of his society. But Fitzgerald replaced the sentimental morality of earlier fiction, in which the victimized hero is let off with a warning, with a sterner ethical base. Gatsby's insatiable ambition, although first stirred not by greed or lust but by love, is punished by death. In the novel, Gatsby's rented mansion is symbolic of the corrupt values of money and society. Neither building nor buying his house, Gatsby fails of any kind of self-expression, merely donning a temporarily empty shell, "a factual imitation of some Hôtel de Ville in Normandy." It had been built by a brewer, whose "children sold his house with the black wreath still on the door."[34] Furthermore, Gatsby does not "live" in his house, he entertains in it, spreading the net with which he hopes to ensnare Daisy Buchanan. It is a temporary set for a sentimental adultery.

In William Faulkner's novels, the use of the mansion is altered slightly by the southern setting. After the Civil War, old southern mansions, even more than those in the North, were celebrated as the setting of a genteel, pastoral aristocracy. As in the North, these houses represented a bulwark against the intrusion of the new rich, but in the South the pattern of the progress of the new rich was not realized in a continuing wave of new houses, but rather in the takeover of an old mansion, once the seat of an aristocratic family, by a representative of the new rich. In Faulkner's Yoknapatawpha County, the Snopeses are the most egregious example of the new rich. In his trilogy of Snopesism (*The Hamlet, The Town,* and *The Mansion*), Faulkner moved the Snopeses up the ladder of domestic architecture. In *The Hamlet* (1940), Flem Snopes wrests possession of the Old Frenchman's Place from Will Varner, the closest thing to an aristocrat in Frenchman's Bend. *The Mansion* (1959) finds Snopes in the old De Spain mansion where the front porch has been torn off and the "colyums" extended "to reach all the way from the ground to the second storey roof." Flem needed this old house as "the physical symbol of all them generations of respectability and aristocracy."[35]

Where Faulkner does not mark the defeat of the old aristocracy by the usurpation of their houses, he accomplishes it by the destruction of their family homes. The Compson estate is whittled away by the continued sale of pieces of property; finally, the house is destroyed by a fire set by the idiot Benjy. As a last irony, Jason Compson uses the site of the house for the construction of jerry-built houses for returning war veterans.

In *Absalom, Absalom!* (1936), Faulkner's protagonist builds a mansion in the ante-bellum South, a mansion intended as his bid for membership in a still vital aristocracy. Thomas Sutpen struggles out of a life of utter poverty and ignorance, acquiring money by means that remain—like those employed by Jay Gatsby—shadowy. In the midst of one hundred square miles of land, Sutpen builds himself a Southern mansion, but his ambition is doomed to failure. The curse of black blood, and of incest, proves inescapable. Like Gatsby in his rented palace, Sutpen is murdered in his incongruous mansion. The house itself falls into decay before it is finally destroyed by the fire set by Sutpen's idiot, black grandson.

Both Fitzgerald and Faulkner avoided the squeamish sentiment of earlier American novelists in dealing with their mansion-dwellers. Like Norris and the other naturalists, Fitzgerald and Faulkner took cognizance of the social pressures which drove their heroes into their extravagant economic aggressiveness and self-aggrandizement, of which the mansion is the visible symbol. However, these later novelists insisted on the moral responsibility of their protagonists; the pressure of social forces can not mitigate their guilt nor minimize their punishment. As a result, the mansions in these novels symbolize not only the folly of Gatsby and Sutpen, but the corruption of the culture from which they spring.

The mansion has disappeared from the American city but neither economic-political debate nor fictionalized philosophy drove them away. The fate of the mansion was resolved not by rhetoric but by changing economic and domestic conditions. In 1925, Herbert Croly wrote an essay for the *Architectural Record* in which he discussed the disappearance of the city mansion. The Astor house was being demolished after only thirty years; on its 125 x 100 lot an apartment house was to be constructed. Income taxes and the servant problem, as Croly noted, made the mansion no longer feasible. Therefore, the rich were moving into the new apartments on Fifth Avenue, apartments that rented, in 1925, for thirty or forty thousand dollars a year and that could be run on a "minimal staff" of twelve or fifteen servants. "It is just as well that palatial dwellings should pass," determined Croly, "they are economically a waste and socially an anachronism."[36]

Even without the real mansion, however, the values that it represents continue to reappear in popular materials. Fictional representations of the houses of the rich are physically altered, reduced from luxurious grandeur to mere luxurious comfort. But settings of upper middle class suburban homes are still used to establish social and moral dilemmas; often, they are prizes for which the hero must sacrifice certain perogatives and independences. John P. Marquand's *Point of No Return* (1949) is studded with houses: the suburban house Charles Gray and his family live in, the Richardson house of his boss Tony Burton, and the homes in Clyde, Massachusetts, where Charles grew up in a common frame house and fell in love with the daughter of the Johnson mansion. In the final scene of the novel, Charles and his wife are at dinner at the Burton's where Charles is prepared to hear that he has not received a crucial promotion. He broods about the consequent necessity to sell his house: "He could sell the house at Sycamore Park. Suburban real estate was still high. They could move to a smaller place." Four pages later, Charles learns that he has received the promotion; inwardly he exults, "They would sell the house at Sycamore Park and get a larger place."[37] Such successes, however, continue to be psychologically costly in American fiction; Marquand lets the reader know that the victory is ashes in Charles's mouth.

A peculiar form of democratization has taken place at last in respect to the mansion. Its dangerous moral qualities have been transferred to smaller houses; upper middle-class suburbia has taken the place of Fifth Avenue. As for the actual mansions of the nineteenth century, those that have not disappeared have gone the way of older American houses of size and splendor, either into debased use or into the itinerary of tourism and nostalgia. Here and there, old mansions house boarding schools or similar institutions, in other instances they have become museums, empty structures suggesting in their hand-carved woodwork, frescoed panels, and gilded ceilings the life of the American millionaire.

Chapter Six

The Housing of the Poor

Put it this way: you cannot let men live like
pigs when you need their votes as freemen; it
is not safe.
Jacob Riis, *The Battle with the Slums (1902)*

There is a wide distinction between homes and
mere housing. These immortal ballads, Home,
Sweet Home, My Old Kentucky Home, *and*
The Little Gray House in the West, *were not*
written about tenements and apartments.
Herbert Hoover *(1931)*

An essential component in the self-image of early Republican America was the belief in the absence of a permanent class of urban poor. Indeed, this was a principal distinction of the United States, the land where thrift and industry inevitably led to an economic competence. In both city and country, to be sure, examples of individual poverty could not be denied, but isolated examples could be laid to individual shiftlessness rather than to any inequities in the social system of the new country. And in those instances where slum areas could be discerned in the busy cities of the Northeast, yet another cause was discovered: an alien population had brought its background and experience from Europe and had been unable to escape their pernicious effect. But the houses in which the urban poor were forced to live served as the most egregious evidence of their poverty, hard proof of the failure of the universality of American prosperity.

In 1828, James Fenimore Cooper described in considerable detail the houses of Americans, pointing to the widespread prosperity evident in the homes of "merchants, or professional men, in moderate circumstances," compensation of some sort for the absence of any really palatial residences like those in European countries. Unlike England, America had little poverty, he asserted, and few squalid dwellings, although he must confess to having seen, "always in the cities," rare examples of "filth, and squalid, abject poverty." His companion, Cadwallader, however, had made inquiries at more than one "dreary hovel" and found the tenants to be immigrants, proving "that his own country had not given birth to the vice and idleness which here could alone entail such want." In Cooper's short passage from *Notions of the Americans* are included all the defenses against the evidence of an oppressed economic class in America: examples of squalor are rare; they are individual examples of vicious idleness when discovered in native Americans; and on the whole such examples are restricted to new immigrants who are not Americans at all.[1]

In the nineteenth century, as the cities grew and the rate of immigration continued to increase, the urban poor became an ever more pressing problem. Although several specific social problems, such as bathing and education, received attention, particularly in regard to the immigrant poor, the question of their housing was paramount. Among the causes that pushed housing to the front, some were practical. Health hazards were especially fearsome; cholera and typhoid spread through the most congested and rundown areas of New York, bringing high death rates and endangering the city as a whole. Infant mortality figures were high. Other practical effects of slum areas were less immediate but no less dangerous.

Statistics, many quite exaggerated, demonstrated that the slums of the major cities produced the greatest percentages of criminals, beggars, and those who, physically or mentally crippled, became the wards of the city. Less demonstrable were the feared effects of slum-living on social and political morality. Not only crime but pauperism was predicted, the existence of a class of people who believed that they were owed a living. Darkly ominous as well was the threat of socialism or anarchism, of violence in the streets, of the destruction of property. America had begun as a democracy of property-holders; responsibility was most comfortably placed in the hands of citizens who held at least their own home. How could the democratic system be entrusted to those who rented bed space in filthy cellars? And what could the United States anticipate from the children of such an environment?

Being poor was one thing. While the nineteenth century American devoted most of his time and energy to acquiring money, he managed to continue to extol the benefits of decent poverty. Popular attitudes in America celebrated poverty for one's childhood and success for one's maturity. In fact, poverty was understood as a condition of flux, if not momentum. Therefore, in the popular mind poor people were just like middle-class people, in fact would become middle-class people given the requisite application of industry and thrift. But the road from rags to riches did not originate in the tenement house of the city slums, but in the village cottage or wilderness log cabin. The nineteenth century American success story moved not only from poverty to success, but from a rural to an urban environment. It was rural poverty and not urban pauperism that molded character.

> In our country, though all men are not 'created equal,' such is the influence of the sentiment of liberty and political equality, that
> "All thoughts, all passions, all delights,
> Whatever stirs this mortal frame,"
> may with as much probability be supposed to effect conduct and expectation in the log cabin as in the marble mansion.[2]

Decent poverty, in the farmlands and villages and workingmen's suburbs of America, consisted in the popular mind of hard, but dignified, labor, a life of care and saving without prodigality, and of a small cottage of three to five rooms, simple but scrupulously clean. From such homes came neither crime nor anarchism: "The worthy poor," pontificated a late nineteenth century churchman, "are generally the silent poor."[3] The worthy poor, moreover, did not create a menace to health and morals in the middle of the New York City, nor did they challenge by the very misery of their existence the social and economic premises of the nineteenth century. But the life of the tenements threatened to belie the American belief in the essential homogeneity of a society without impassable social and economic chasms. By the end of the nineteenth century the evidence of the slums mocked the theory of a classless society. A nation without fixed economic classes became a sentimental memory. In 1884 Wendell Phillips recalled, or created, such a world, describing the old New England town "with no rich man and no poor man in it, all mingling in the same society, every child at the same school, no poor-house, no beggar, opportunities equal."[4]

An alien population living in conditions of filth and degradation not only posed threats to the system, it created an insoluble paradox. Americans had fully accepted, by the middle of the nineteenth century, the concept of the power of the home in molding character. The home was the educating instrument, inculcating love, morality, economy, domestic virtue, and good citizenship. Jacob Riis, in his struggle against the slums and the tenements, frequently insisted on the essential work of the home: "Unsafest of all is any thing or deed that strikes at the home, for from the home proceeds citizen virtue, and nowhere else does it live. The slum is the enemy of the home."[5] Obviously, it was necessary to get the children of the tenements out of such an environment and into a real home, that is, a detached, private house. This solution, however, was unworkable. Not only was it too expensive, more importantly, such a solution would have defeated the very idea of a house by making it available as a gift rather than as a reward for and symbol of a man's honest labor and diligent thrift. Alfred T. White, a notable builder of model tenements in the 1870's and 1880's, warned that "The reception of a home as a species of charity is quite as harmful to the poor, quite as destructive of self-respect, quite as discouraging to the industrious, as is the direct receiving of alms without adequate return in labor."[6] The message of America was not that every man deserved a home, but that every man deserved the opportunity to work for a home. Robert Treat Paine, a social worker, summed it all up in 1882.

Surely the great end to aim at is that each family shall live in an independent home, with their children safe from the contagion of a crowded tenement house; and shall own a part of the soil of their country. To effect this, thrift must be promoted, not only by mere words and exhortation, but by wise and practical measures, by powerful influence and best of all, by close, constant and friendly contact so that the success of those who have already prospered in their thrift, may inspire a noble emulation, leading to like results among the far larger number of their fellow work-ingmen, who have not learned to save, and to whom a house and home seem an impossible dream, when they might and should before long be an accomplished fact.[7]

An investigation of the writing about American slums from the 1870's to the time of the Depression reveals the complexities wrought by the dilemma of property, and especially of the house as the most common species of property, in what had clearly become a class society. Except for the hazards to health, all the dangers feared from the tenement population and its children were crimes against property. Beggary and physical or mental feebleness took money from charitable citizens or from the city coffers. Theft and vandalism attacked private property, while socialism and anarchism threatened to redistribute it. Against these fears, the American system held out only one counter-measure: supply the dangerous classes with the opportunity to earn property of their own. The belief in the political efficacy of property appears not only in well-reasoned social essays, but even in casual comments in late nineteenth century novels. In *The House of the Merchant Prince* (1883), William Henry Bishop presented a conversation among a number of propertied gentlemen who discuss the recent threats of "socialistic revolt." With "no standing armies to put them down," one man asks, how can we defend our houses against a mob? Another replies, "The side that can pay is all right. . . . Your communists would rather take two dollars a day, any time, to defend property, than pull it down on speculation."[8]

Alongside the obvious sneer at socialism in Bishop's novel stands a belief in the ethical value of property, or to put it another way, an understanding of communism as an unreasonable response to property. Since theoretically, no property-holder would ally himself with a political movement that advocated the abolishment of property, the defense against the socialist threat was simply to encourage thrifty habits that would lead to the accumulation of savings toward the ultimate investment in a house. This ideal solution to the problem of the housing of the working class, however, was not so simply executed as it was conceived.

Where self-help failed, other sources of aid were necessary, either from private funds or public. The public sector entered the housing field in 1867 with New York's first Tenement House Law, enacting legislation against the most pernicious housing conditions. The role of legislation was limited, however, to setting standards for tenement houses; for example, New York laws made mandatory ventilation for every tenement house room and established requisite amounts of open space for every lot on which tenements were erected. Other legislation established minimal requirements for plumbing facilities. What government at any level, city, state, or federal, was not seen as responsible for was the construction and sale or rental of low-cost housing; this remained an area for private enterprise until emergency housing during the First World War set an example and the crisis of the Depression pushed the federal government into wide-spread action both in home-building and in home-financing.[9]

Two factors militated against government intrusion into housing: a general belief in non-interference with private enterprise and an equally wide-spread conception of the dangers of institutionalized charity. With government influence limited to legislation, the private sector was left the responsibility to alleviate and to improve housing conditions. Indeed, it had been a private group, The New York Association for Improving the Condition of the Poor, organized in 1843, that had been largely responsible for pushing the state into restrictive legislation in regard to tenements and slums, an effort that bore fruit in 1867 after a fearful outbreak of cholera.

The private sector acted not only through citizens' groups but also through capital investment. In the last quarter of the nineteenth century a good number of writers exhorted capitalists to invest in the construction of rental housing for the poor, not as charity but as a safe investment. Alfred T. White succeeded in building multiple and single dwellings for working men in Brooklyn, and he publicized his work, encouraging others to follow his model. The accomodations he provided were a great improvement over conditions in most tenements, offering light, air, privacy, and good sanitation. In 1879, he was housing one hundred and thirty-seven families of five hundred and thirty-nine people, at an average weekly rental of $1.48 for three rooms, and $1.93 for four. In 1885, his tenements and private houses had 1,059 tenants. The weekly rentals ran from $2.20 to $2.60 for three rooms, and from $2.40 to $2.95 for four (the bottom floors rented for the most money). The tenants received a dividend amounting to one month's rent after a full year of residence, if they paid their rent on time and complied "with the general obligations of Tenants." In 1885, one hundred and forty-one tenants received a total of $1225. Furthermore, payment of four weeks rent in advance entailed a rebate of ten cents per week, "a discount of five percent." The small houses White provided rented for $18.00 a month for six rooms and $24.00 for nine. As for the investing capitalists, they too were satisfied, having received in the first two years their six percent; in fact, White reported in 1879 that the properties had grossed twelve percent and netted seven.

Behind White's successful building and operation of his "improved Dwellings for the Laboring Classes," were a number of theories about housing, and about the poor. He viewed the tenements in the New York slums as a social menace; they were "nurseries of the epidemics . . . hiding places of the local banditti . . . cradles of the insane . . . and of the paupers." Worse, they produced children who were tainted in health and morals. Improved dwellings were essential, not only for the poor, but for the city as a whole, for "the enduring prosperity of any city depends to a great extent on the direct interests of all classes in the government thereof." However, these dwellings could not be donated as charity, which was "destructive of self-respect" and which provided unfair competition with honest landlords. Therefore, White felt it imperative to publicize his experience to show "that it is to the interest of capitalists to follow it." He went so far as to lay the blame for the current slum crisis on the "intelligent and wealthy," who have been content to blame greedy landlords and to accuse "the poorer classes of a fondness for dirt and bad air." The intelligent and wealthy must now respond, he argued; "Let the lawyers and sanitarians reform the laws, let capitalists build Improved Dwellings."[10]

Other late nineteenth century books and articles continued to cajole and threaten wealthy capitalists, while emphasizing the inappropriateness and even the danger of public or private charity. Helen Campbell, for example, published articles, collected in 1882 as *The Problem of the Poor*, emphasizing the responsibility of wealthy investors. One of her essays, "The Tenement House Question," presents a group of friends discussing the problem of housing the poor. The narrator, the most sympathetic and urgent of the group, articulates the threat emanating from the slums: "We pay over thirteen million dollars annual tax for the support of this army [of paupers and criminals], and then sit and shiver as we read of Pittsburgh riots, or the spread of German Socialism." With some irony, the bachelor member of the group suggests the solution of Proudhonian communism, but the narrator will have none of it. "Society has no right to absorb the individual any more than the individual has a right to *be* absorbed or supported." The only solutions available are remedial legislation and the positive contributions of private enterprise: "With Old World experiments in homes as a *charity* we have nothing to do."[11]

In 1896, the *Yale Review* printed E. R. L. Gould's "The Economics of Improved Housing." Gould formulated the problem along conventional lines. The solution to the housing question, he stated, "consists in discovering the means of housing the great mass of city dwellers with financial profit, and yet in such a manner that health, morality, sound family life, and social stability may be subserved."[12] A decade later, *The World's Work* presented a report on "Money-Making Model Tenements." Henry Phipps had invested a million dollars, anticipating a return of four percent. His ambition aimed at one hundred buildings housing 60,000 people; in 1908 he had one house with almost two thousand inhabitants. The accomodations ranged from two to five rooms, with bathing facilities, renting from $2.75 to $6.75 a week. The building also had rooms for rest and prayer, a rooftop playground and a basement nursery. Phipps claimed two major advantages for his housing: the building was doing well with a good financial return anticipated and the residents were undergoing uplift. "The erection of the buildings is business, not charity, and this fact makes them all the more effecting in pointing a way toward the betterment of tenement conditions. And they are appreciated." A small boy, the author tells us, pointed to the new building, where his family had an apartment, noting that there is "where they has baths."[13]

The history of capitalist benefaction in building low-rental housing was not always seen in such a rosy light. In some ways, in fact, the effect of tougher housing legislation was to deter investment, for the increasingly high standard of revised and newly-written tenement laws caused a corresponding increase in the cost of construction. In 1924, Frank Chouteau Brown wrote a series of articles for the *Architectural Record* insisting on

the "Economic Fallacy" of low-rental apartments. The most recent tenement law had "determined landlords to build no more;"
furthermore, "necessary improvements of standing buildings
were reflected in rent increases," making the situation worse
than it had been a decade earlier. No amelioration of this condition was possible, Brown argued, while America attempted to
compromise between the needs of the poor and the demands of
the rich investors.

> No permanent improvement can be expected until the same forces
> that united to obtain the legislation originally are willing to help
> modify these laws sufficiently to again place the matter of possible
> improvements in this class of realty in a more favorable light to the
> individual owner or investor, or until the City, State or national
> government enters the field, in some one of the various ways that
> have proved effective in European countries.

But Brown was no radical thinker. In searching for solutions to
what he saw as a deadlock, he also suggested lowering housing
costs by providing a cheap labor pool, and to that end advocated
raising immigrant quotas.[14]
   To whatever extent private investment alleviated the immediate problems of the housing of some of the poor, it did not
effect a real solution to the issue of making home-owners out
of slum-dwellers. Model tenements were better than slum tenements, and rented houses better than rented flats, but the ideal
remained the privately-owned, single-family, detached house.
One approach to this ideal came from an entirely different segment of the population, from the industrious and thrifty poor
who invested their small savings in building and loan associations. The concept of pooling together the small savings of a
large number of men and women originated before the Civil
War although it did not receive a great deal of public attention
until the latter part of the nineteenth century. As early as 1848
a pattern book addressed to the working man contained an
appendix on building and loan associations; the Articles of Association of the Brooklyn Accumulatory Fund Association and its
first Annual Report were printed. The organization had one
hundred and eighty-four members who paid $2.50 a month for
twelve months. Each $30.00 investment had grown to $62.78,
and the total capital of the fund was now $12,775.34. Consider-

ing that this book was addressed to the "industrious and frugal mechanic," providing designs for. houses that started as low as $250.00 (excluding foundation and land), it is clear that the relatively small amount of money held by the Brooklyn Association represented the possibility of a good number of working men's cottages.[15]

In 1875 *Scribner's Monthly* devoted a long article to building and loan associations. A number of advertisements from the Philadelphia papers were included. All announced meeting times and places, and invited new members and potential borrowers to attend. The general emphasis was on the independence to be earned by careful savings, most particularly in the form of a house.

> FOURTH OF JULY! INDEPENDENCE DAY!—Young man and Woman, stop and reflect! The money you fritter away uselessly will make you independent. To-day sign the magna charter of your independence, and, like your forefathers, in about eight years you will, in a great degree, be independent by saving only thirty-three cents each day. In that time you will realize $2,000, or have a home and be independent of the landlord. Let this, indeed, be your day of independence, by subscribing for shares in the new series, now issued, in the State Mutual Saving Fund, Loan and Building Association. One dollar per share each month. For shares or information, come to the meeting on Wesdnesday Evening, July 7, at 7½ o'clock, at the Pennsylvania Hall, Eighth street, below Green. The auditor's and director's reports will be distributed.

In this article, entitled "A Hundred Thousand Homes," the writer went into considerable detail about the workings of the building and loan associations, and along the way provided a good deal of moral advice about the home. An illustration of a Philadelphia dwelling was commented upon, "As a house it is not lovely; as a home it is charming and sensible, a hearthstone where the homely virtues flourish and grow strong. The paying for it, the winning it, is the most interesting part of the whole story." In Philadelphia, where such homes flourish, it is "small wonder . . . that her people are steady, thrifty, forehanded, and domestic in their habits." In Philadelphia, there are, he reported, six hundred such banking concerns, paying out "half a million dollars a month." "This is the seed from which sprang up her hundred thousand rooftrees."[16]

The building and loan associations had everything to appeal to the American mind. They inculcated thrift, they led to the purchase or construction of privately owned homes, they made property-owners out of renters, and capitalists out of working-men; and all of this was accomplished without charity or government aid. The popularity of the building and loan associations increased throughout the late nineteenth century. In 1890, "Co-operative Home Winning," in *Scribner's Magazine*, reported statistics from four thousand such organizations with total assets of $336,485,080. Equally impressive were individual examples of the rewards of thrift. A Pittsburgh blacksmith who had never earned over three dollars a day now "owns $75,000 of real estate," by having bought improved property and charging sufficient rent to cover both his own dues and the interest on his loans.[17]

In 1893, the *North American Review*, in a piece called "Hope of a Home," castigated New York state for its lack of progress in encouraging home ownership. New York savings banks held total assets of $375,000,000, but according to "the laws and the policy by which the savings-banks are regulated," this money, unlike that accumulated by the building and loan associations, could not be used to finance small homes. These laws and policies had kept New York behind other cities, the essay continued. Philadelphia, for example, had one house for every 1.1 families, and the ratio of people to houses was six per private house. New York had one house for every 3.8 families and an average of nineteen people per house. The housing situation that had developed in New York was individually and socially demoralizing and dangerous: "All other localities in this fair land, be they large or small, are intensely interested in the question of home-getting. No movement is more productive of the noblest and best efforts of human kind, and there is no greater safety for the republic than is founded on the universality of homes owned by the working people."[18]

Public enthusiasm for the building and loan associations depended on the popular morality celebrating thrift and hard work; the associations had the advantage of promoting these virtues and therefore of encouraging the poor to take on the characteristics of the middle class. Not only were positive activities encouraged, but negative behavior was discouraged; the individual was saved along with his money and society could relax its defenses against the dangers represented by the poor. In two sentences in an 1895 essay about Chicago's poor, Joseph Kirkland combined all these themes. "Membership in a building society, and the hope of a bit of ground all his own, are wonderful incentives to temperance in the man and economy in his wife. . . . A city of such homes is safe from anarchy."[19]

Building and loan associations, like private capital investment, answered only a small part of the housing problem. Slums and tenements remained, and the social and moral problems they raised continued to be blurred and complicated by a number of preconceptions and old ideals. The over-riding ideals for American housing were still those centered in the property-holding concept of Jeffersonian democracy. Of course, the suburban cottage on a small lot had replaced the farmhouse on its planted acres in this vision, but the moral, political, and economic efficacy of the home in the suburbs was counted as no less significant than that of the farmhouse. The family that owned its own private house represented both the societal nucleus and the societal microcosm. Furthermore, the acquisition of such a house indicated, as it had for generations, the serious, sober, hard-working life of the family—money had to be earned and to be saved. And finally, the fact of proprietorship itself was supposed to be the single most efficient conservatizing influence in the American experience.

Life in the tenements, conversely, lacked social and moral stability, and the tenement-dweller did not participate in the American experience. Depending on whether the tenement itself or the moral character of the poor was seen as causative, life in the tenements could be interpreted in one of two ways. From one point of view, tenement living was proof of the failure, or the refusal, of the family to engage in sufficient industry and thrift, and thereby, whether wilfully or not, to elude Americanization. Secondly, tenement life could be viewed not as the end result of failure, but as the cause of future failures; the environment of the slums bred characters who were inimical, hostile, and directly threatening to the American way of life. From either vantage point, substandard, multiple dwellings in city slums were antipathetic and dangerous to the American vision.

Poverty itself was not necessarily inimical. In the materials of the second half of the nineteenth century there are suggestions of a view of poverty as a condition of impermanence. On the upward side was membership in the middle class; on the downward side, pauperism. Morally, pauperism was conceived of as a state of torpor, a condition from which one no longer attempted to extricate himself. Alfred T. White, for all his sincere optimism about the effects of environment on character, believed in a class of poor who could not be reached even by his model tenements. "There is, of course, a class of people who prefer squalor and darkness to decency and light." This class could benefit, if at all, only from "moral reformation" which would have to precede their removal to improved housing.[20] A report of the New York Association for Improving the Condition of the Poor in 1896 admitted that there were some folk who did indeed "convert a palace into a pigsty," and saw help in these cases only from "moral suasion" and the "function of law."[21]

Sometimes the generalized belief in an unreachable class of slum dwellers blossomed into a vicious prejudice against one or another immigrant group; the Irish, the Germans, the Italians, and the Jews were all at different times dismissed as hopeless. Kirkland, in his piece about Chicago, turned his enmity against the Italians. He described a particularly vile hovel, and concluded, "What squalor, filth, crowding! The constant feeling of the visitor is, how dreadfully wretched these people—ought to be. Ought to be, but are not. They are chiefly the lower class of Italians."[22] An 1880 article in *Harper's* described the squatter shanties in New York, the population principally German. The tone of the author is that of a tourist, pointing out the picturesque contrast between these shanties and the palaces on Murray Hill and noting the interesting ways in which the effect of weathering had softened the color of the old boards, He tells the reader that "you cannot fail to be interested and amused at the unfamiliar sights and sounds of the neighborhood." Finally, however, he pointed out that even the examples of the flowers nearby, which should "be a constant stimulus to cleanliness," have no effect here. "The squatters are deplorably careless in their habits, eating and sleeping with no more decency than the goats, pigs, geese, and dogs that take 'pot-luck' with them."[23]

An article in the *American Magazine* castigated Poles, Russians, and Germans, but singled out the Italians as the worst of this "seething mass of humanity, so ignorant, so vicious, so depraved that they hardly seem to belong to our species." The housing of these people was an index to their depravity: "Men and women; yet living not like animals but like vermin!" Such immigrants had come expecting "affluence without work," and in their disappointment they freely expressed "Anarchist notions." Particularly offensive to this writer was the extension to such people of "the freedom of speech which is permitted by laws which were framed to govern a people of entirely different character to those who have been pouring in upon us from the slums of Europe."[24]

In effect, the general and the specific criticism of the poor worked to distinguish them from the rest of America by proving them lazy and anarchistic and by asserting that their unwholesome living conditions were the best such people could aspire to. Americans, on the other hand, worked hard and maintained decent houses. The implied conclusion was that the housing of the poor was no reflection on America but on the poor themselves who did not understand the meaning of the "Anglo-Saxon" home. To quote Kirkland again, "For depth of shadow in Chicago low life one must look to the foreign elements, the persons who are not only of alien birth but of unrelated blood—the Mongolian, the African, the Sclav, the semi-tropic Latin."[25]

A belief in the exclusively Anglo-Saxon recognition of the multiple meanings and values of the home emerges in other contexts as well, and may even have driven the native poor to assert a nativist superiority by struggling to maintain homes at the cost of terrible deprivation. Margaret Byington, who had been a member of the turn-of-the-century Pittsburgh Survey, wrote an article on "The Family in a Typical Mill Town," for the *American Journal of Sociology* in 1909. Since the average wages were low, $1.65 a day for an unskilled laborer and from $2.00 to $4.00 a day for a semi-skilled or skilled laborer, it was apparent that the establishment of a house was a difficult task. "In order to carry out the ideals of home life, such as having an attractive house, making due provisions for the future, or buying a house, certain absolute essentials must be gone without." However, different nationality groups in the Pittsburgh working-class suburb of Homewood met the problem in different ways. "Among the native white families a comfortable home is an essential proof of respectability." These families spent an average of 21.2% on rent, while the Slavs spent only 16.4%.

Furthermore, the native white workers were willing to cut down on their food budget to maintain the higher rent levels. They used 44.7% of their income on food; the Slavs, 54.3%.[26]

There is other evidence as well that the ability to live on as little food as possible, for children as well as adults, in order to save money for a house was seen as an indication of Americanization. In 1894 an article in *Lend a Hand* reported on the "Working Man's Model Home" displayed by New York at the 1893 Chicago Exposition. Without land, this house cost $1000 to build in New York state; it was 20 x 28 feet overall, with a parlor and a kitchen and bath downstairs, and three bedrooms on the second floor. Part of the display included the clothing for a family of five (one infant) and sample menus, all to prove what real thrift could accomplish. The menus gave examples of meals for two days. The first day totaled 52¢ for all five family members. Scrambled eggs for breakfast; codfish, potatoes, and oatmeal for the noon dinner; codfish balls and cornmeal mush for supper. Bread and butter with every meal. The second day totaled 54¢. Breakfast consisted of oatmeal and fried potatoes; dinner, of bean soup, fried ham, and potatoes; and supper, of cornmeal mush and more bean soup. Proof of the benefits of such a diet came with the information that the man of the family had gained four and a half pounds in one month.[27]

Many interested observers concentrated their attention on the younger generation among the tenement dwellers and found both a threat and a hope. The hope lay in educating and Americanizing the children of the slums, the threat in what appeared to be the greater aggressiveness of first generation Americans as compared with their parents. Statistics were cited to prove that the percentage of foreign-born among incarcerated criminals was greater than that of native-born, and that the percentage of first generation Americans was higher than that of immigrants. Furthermore, publicity was given to youth gangs in the city slums. In *The Dangerous Classes of New York* (1880), Charles Loring Brace warned that "the class of a large city most dangerous to its property, its morals and its political life, are the ignorant, destitute, untrained, and abandoned youth." The problem that bred such youth was "the overcrowding of our population," particularly in New York where tens of thousands swarmed in tenement houses.[28]

Where ominous threats proved ineffective, writers chose to

use sentiment. Jacob Riis, for example, printed dozens of stories of boys and girls. Some tenement children in Riis's narratives prospered through a combination of their own character and the help of some outsider; the others met an early death. A number of such stories were collected in *The Children of the Tenements* (1903). Where anecdote gave way to exposition, Riis, too, turned to dark prophecies about the children of the tenements as future citizens. Some would become thieves, victims of "the logic of the slums, that the world which gave him poverty and ignorance for his portion, 'owes him a living.'" Others would drift into pauperism; the pauper, like the thief, believed he was owed a living, but the thief was easier to deal with, "the very fact of his being a thief presupposes some bottom to the man."

Most ominous of all, however, was the inability of children brought up in such an environment to accommodate themselves to the democratic system.

> For, be it remembered, these children with the training they receive—or do not receive—with the instincts they inherit and absorb in their growing up, are to be our future rulers, if our theory of government is worth anything. More than a working majority of our voters now register from the tenements.[29]

A few years later, Riis wrote: "Put it this way: you cannot let men live like pigs when you need their votes as freemen; it is not safe."[30] Less melodramatically, Robert W. de Forest, in his "Foreword" to Lawrence Veiller's *Housing Reform* (1910) stated, "It is useless to expect a conservative point of view in the working man if his home is but three or four rooms in some huge building in which dwell from twenty to thirty other families."[31]

The economically disenfranchised voter, lacking the conservatizing influence of his own house, was seen as the easy prey of unscrupulous politicians. In 1878, when W. H. Tolman reported on the half century of work by the New York Association for Improving the Condition of the Poor, he observed that "The result of tenement house life was the existence of a proletarian class who had no interest in the permanent well-being of the community, with no sense of home, but lived without any deep root in the soil, the mere tools of demagogues and designing men."[32]

But the ignorant voter ensnared by the bosses of Tammany

was not the darkest shadow on American democracy. The greatest fear came from the threat of European radicalism imported to America. In 1880, Charles Loring Brace noted that to those who were "swarming in tenement-houses" capital was the tyrant.[33] Helen Campbell, in her piece for *Sunday Afternoon* pointed to the Pittsburgh strike and Haymarket riots as an evil foreshadowing of the future. Josiah Strong, a clergyman who wrote about the general problems of city life, remarked the increase in the socialist vote in national elections from 1888, when 2,068 socialist votes were recorded, to 1904, with 408,230 socialist votes. While the population had increased 30%, the socialist vote had gone up by 18,278%.

> As European peasants, many of the immigrants had already learned to sympathize with the proletariat. Its watchwords are already familiar, and the newcomers readily identify themselves with the same class here. To become Republicans or Democrats would imply some political education and a new point of view, but neither is required in order to oppose the 'capitalist class.'[34]

At his worst, the socialist was feared not as a voter but as a destroyer of property. The absence of a home, the environment of the tenement slums, could drive men to vengeance against the propertied classes. Jacob Riis declared that "the tenements had bred their nemesis, a proletariat ready and able to avenge the wrongs of their crowds." Such vengeance should never have been bred in America, vengeance that announced itself with "the danger cry of which we have lately heard the shout that never should have been raised on American soil—the shout of 'the masses against the classes.'—the solution of violence."[35] Again, E. R. L. Gould, in an essay for *Forum* in 1895, stressed the link between slums and unAmerican radicalism: "The genesis of 'isms most often takes place in the miserable tenements of a great modern city."[36]

In 1919 Edith Elmer Wood no longer warned of the political dangers from an ill-housed class; instead she proved the cost in American blood of slums left uncleared and tenements left unimproved.

> A large proportion of the people living in these rooms are Russians, and if the oft-repeated statement is true that Leon Trotsky derived his distrust of the United States from the housing conditions in

which he found his compatriots living in New York, and if the Bolsheviki peace with Germany was the result of Trotsky's distrust of America, then indeed our sons paid with their blood on the soil of France for the dark rooms of the Lower East Side, which it would have cost too much to lighten![37]

So strong was the connection in the popular imagination between slum living and socialism that William Dean Howells, in *A Hazard of New Fortunes* (1890), depicted a radical idealist, Lindau, as preferring to live in the slums. Indeed, Lindau needs to dwell among the desperately poor in order to keep his sympathetic imagination fired. March, Howell's protagonist, goes to visit Lindau and to bring him some work. He finds the old man in a cold and shabby room in a neighborhood that provided "abounding evidences of misery." But Lindau refuses the work; "I ton't needt any money just at bresent." He goes on to explain that he has not moved to his present room because he is "too boor to lif anywhere else." On the contrary, "I foundt I was begoming a lidtle too moch of an aristograt. I hadt a room oap in Creenvidge Willage, among dose pig pugs over on the West Side, and I foundt . . . that I was beginning to forget the boor!"[38]

Whether the poor were considered dangerous as potential socialists or anarchists, or whether their threat was seen in individual examples of criminality, pauperism, and drunkenness, the private home earned and maintained by individual labor was considered the single most effective deterrent. In 1877 the *Unitarian Magazine* echoed popular views on homeownership in stating that the "great aim [is] to increase the number of that class of workingmen which is frugal and independent and contented,—as contrasted with that class which is shiftless and migratory and complaining." The method by which this solution was to be effected was the encouragement of working men "to put their earnings into houses of their own," which will "promote economy and thrift, [and] strengthen self-respect. . . . Many a man who might otherwise drift into careless and dangerous ways of living— drinking and running into debt—is held in check and kept up to a better standard by the desire to own house and land."[39]

It was not, therefore, simply a case of providing more wholesome conditions in the multiple dwellings of the cities' most congested areas, but of establishing the ideal, a nation of home-owners. Before the Civil War, this ideal was accepted pretty much at face value. In his pattern book for workingmen's cottages in 1848, T. Thomas was simply echoing popular sentiment when he announced that "all social prosperity is infallibly enhanced by encouraging the working classes to be steady and persevering, and ultimately to enjoy A HOME OF THEIR OWN—sacred to the pure and noble affections, and cherishing a moral influence which will be as a strong castle to their children's children."[40]

But the course of events in the nineteenth century made the ideal more and more elusive, and rented homes replaced owned homes as a goal for working men. Thus, when Alfred T. White spoke of the benefits of the private home for the families of laboring men, he was reduced to the concept of the rented house, which at least provided "domestic privacy, the foundation of morality," even if it did not represent the ownership of property.[41] In 1896, E. R. L. Gould called for capitalists to invest in suburban houses for rental to workers. Like White, he stressed the importance of family privacy: "Home in a tenement building can never be what it is where a single roof covers an individual family."[42] In 1919, Edith Elmer Wood declared that "Good citizenship is a product of normal family life." Normal family life derived from suitable surroundings, and without distinguishing rented from owned property, she went on to define the most suitable environment for "normal family life." "The best opinion is strongly in favor of the single-family detached house with a yard around it, wherever such a type is practicable."[43]

Occasionally, a voice would be raised that questioned the sanctity of the conventional home-ideal. Jane Addams felt that "For a long time we have made a sort of fetich of the house, and have come to believe that a man has a sense of being at home only when he is within four walls standing alone upon one piece of ground." She recognized, however, that apartment-living did not provide the popular imagination with a substitute for the ideal: "we are timid and would rather be uncomfortable in a little house than start out in some reasonable way in building apartments." She added some practical data on the difficulties in the way of home-ownership for the laborer, whose job might be lost and whose house would inhibit his mobility. In a question and answer period following this address, Addams responded to a question that repeated the old values of diligence and stability, by remarking, "I think we have a way of relegating all the old-fashioned virtues to workingmen and reserving to ourselves the most interesting and adaptable virtues."[44]

Jane Addam's insight may appear paradoxical; how can America have relegated "the old-fashioned virtues" to the poor working man, and at the same time have suspected him of propensities to pauperism, crime, and anarchy? In fact, such a paradox existed in American thinking, and it depended upon the double view of the poor who were, on the one hand, worthy and silent, struggling to accommodate their lives to the standards of the middle class, and on the other hand, vicious, lazy, and criminal, beyond moral uplift. Furthermore, while the poor as a class might be conceived as dangerous and unwholesome, popular literature frequently depicted poor people as patient, hard-working, and virtuous. Narrative accounts of the lives of specific tenement-dwellers whether fiction or non-fiction, tended to sentimentalize the condition of the poor and to stress the love, brotherhood, charity, and strength of character to be discovered among these people.

Even Jacob Riis, who devoted vast reservoirs of energy to bringing the facts of slum life to the American public, fell easily into the sentimentalization of the poor. In *How the Other Half Lives* (1899), he noted "the readiness of the poor to share what little they have with those who have even less." Riis attributed this generosity not to a political or philosophical program, not to a "professed sentiment," but to "the instinct of self-preservation [that] impels them to make common cause against great misery."[45] Individual anecdotes collected in *The Children of the Tenements* (1903) and in *Neighbors* (1914) show Riis attempting to develop public sympathy through sentimental characterization. In one instance, Riis had been involved in searching for the three-year old daughter of the Lubinsky family. Going to visit them one evening in their slum tenement, he came upon their sabbath dinner where an empty high-chair marked the absence of their little girl. "I understood; and in the strength of domestic affection that burned with unquenched faith in the dark tenement . . . I read the history of this strange people that in every land and in every day has conquered even the slum with the hope of home."[46]

Paolo, another of Riis's slum children, lived in an "old and rickety and wretched" tenement, where "the whitewash was peeling from the walls, the stairs were patched, and the doorstep long since worn entirely away." But like the Lubinskys, Paolo's widowed mother maintained the decency of home in spite of this environment.

> On the shelf where the old clock stood, flanked by the best crockery, most of it cracked and yellow with age, there was red and green paper cut in scallops very nicely. Garlic and onions hung in strings over the stove, and the red peppers that grew in the starch-box at the window gave quite a cheerful appearance to the room. In the corner, under a cheap print of the Virgin Mary with the Child, a small night-light in a blue glass was always kept burning.[47]

Fiction, like Riis's anecdotes, frequently concentrated on the virtues of the slum family, bringing to these accounts the set of values once appropriate only to the native rural poor. Such a depiction of the life of the desperately poor was generally pointed toward a moralistic contrast with the lives of the rich or of the upper middle class. In part, this contrast implied the dangers inherent in the accumulation of money; in part, it merely enforced a general castigation of the rich by demonstrating the survival of virtue in people whose poverty made the exercise of virtue a strenuous activity. For example, Lily Bart, Edith Wharton's protagonist in *The House of Mirth* (1905), moves down the socio-economic ladder through a good number of upper and middle class houses. Late in the novel, when Lily is destitute, she has a chance meeting with Mrs. Nettie Struther, a poor working girl, who brings Lily to her little flat, where the kitchen "revealed itself to Lily as extraordinarily small and almost miraculously clean." For all the city and country homes of the very rich and of the comfortable middle class where Lily had lived, it is the memory of Nettie's kitchen that envelops her in the moments before her death. From that kitchen emerges the essential characteristics of "home."

> [Lily] herself had grown up without any one spot of earth being dearer to her than another: there was no center of early pieties, of grave endearing traditions, to which her heart could revert and from it would draw strength for itself and tenderness for others.

In these final moments of revelation, Lily realizes that "her first glimpse of the continuity of life had come to her that evening in Nettie Struther's kitchen."[48]

Jack London, unlike Wharton, had experienced poverty first hand, and as a result he was more circumstantial and less rhapsodic about slum-living. London relegated a sentimental view of poverty to the most ignorant and vicious of his middle class characters. In *Martin Eden* (1909), it is Eden's bourgeois fiancée Ruth who carries these attitudes.

> Poverty, to Ruth, was a word signifying a not nice condition of existence. That was her total knowledge on the subject. She knew Martin was poor, and his condition she associated in her mind with Abraham Lincoln . . . and of other men who had become successes. Also, while aware that poverty was anything but delectable, she had a comfortable middle-class feeling that poverty was salutary, that it was a sharp spur that urged on to success all men who were not degraded and hopeless drudges.

London describes the environment of poverty without sentiment, delineating the physical and psychological squalor of his sister's household. Furthermore, he establishes the intoxicating effect of the fine middle-class house of Ruth's parents on the innocent young ruffian, Eden. However, in the end, the fine house is the location of pretense and sham, while the miserable little house of Maria Silva, where Eden boards, provides a harbor. Maria Silva, a widow who supports her young children by taking in laundry, is presented as selfless and charitable. Unlike Ruth, who "never read hunger in Martin's face," Maria "read a different tale in the hollow cheeks and the burning eyes." When she can manage, Maria provides the starving Eden with a loaf of bread or a pitcher of soup, "debating inwardly all the while whether she was justified in taking it from the mouths of her own flesh and blood." When Eden falls sick, Maria unobtrusively nurses him.[49]

The solidarity among the poor, a solidarity capable even of crossing lines of religious prejudice, was another of the virtues discovered in tenement dwellers. Jacob Riis told anecdotes to this point, and they appear frequently in fiction. In Michael Gold's *Jews Without Money* (1930), the Irish family upstairs seems at first strange and brutal to Gold's Jewish parents. Sounds of the drunken husband beating his wife are particularly appalling. " 'It is worse than the whores,' said my mother, 'having Christians in a tenement is worse.' " But when the Irish woman's child chokes on a fishbone, "My mother, expert and brave in such emergencies," rushed upstairs, rescued the child, and then "had a long intimate talk with the Irish mother." At dinner that night, she tells her own husband "that Irish washerlady has so many misfortunes. . . . She is a good woman . . . even if she is Christian." Whatever narrow-mindedness had been forced on this Jewish woman by her training, she "was incapable of real hatred. . . . Her nature was made for universal sympathy, without thought of prejudice." [50]

In writers as different as Edith Wharton, Jack London, and Michael Gold, the housing of the virtuous poor may be shabby, but it is always clean. Like the Lubinskys and Paolo's mother in Riis's narratives, these characters consistently refuse to be beaten by their environment, and the fictionalized weapons of the war with the slums were brooms, mops, and washtubs. Significantly, even radical writers like London and Gold accepted the general bourgeois attitude about the housing of the poor: character emerged in the struggle against the wretchedness of one's environment. The corollary of that view, however, was a belief in the weakness, the moral torpor, of those who could not rise above the slums. In fact, the fictional strategy that permitted victory over poverty to the industrious poor was itself a celebration of conservative ideals.

In order for fiction to participate in any real battle against the slums, novelists had to be prepared to work with plots in which the protagonists were destroyed by their environment in spite of whatever struggle they were willing to mount against it. In Stephen Crane's *Maggie, a Girl of the Streets* (1893), Maggie's life moves inexorably from the squalid tenement, to the morally dangerous street corner and saloon, and finally to the pier from which she commits suicide. Both the tenement buildings and their inhabitants are depicted as wretched, filthy, and violent. Maggie grows up in a "dark region where, from the careening building, a dozen gruesome doorways gave up loads of babies to the street and gutter." Drying clothes hang from fire-escapes; corners and hallways are stacked with brooms and rags.

In the street infants played or fought with other infants or sat stupidly in the way of vehicles. Formidable women, with uncombed hair and disordered dress, gossiped while leaning on railings, or

screamed in frantic quarrels. Withered persons, in curious postures
of submission to something, sat smoking pipes in obscure corners.
A thousand odours of cooking food came forth to the street. The
building quivered and creaked from the weight of humanity stamp-
ing about in its bowels.

Unlike the tenement of *Jews without Money,* there is no relieving
charity or brotherhood, and in the apartment we enter, no noble
mother creating a home for her family. Instead, we find "a large
woman . . . rampant," in a room containing "a seething stove" and
"an unholy sink," Drunkenness numbs the pain for the parents;
nothing accomplishes this for the children.[51]

Richard Wright's *Native Son* (1940), in which racism exacer-
bates economic deprivation, outlines the same stages in personal
destruction: slum environment, crime, death. Wright begins his
novel with the Thomas family awakening; they live in one room,
the boys must turn their heads while their mother and sister dress.
Immediately, in the opening paragraphs, the family sees a huge
rat and start their day killing it. Before they eat breakfast, they
spread newspaper over the rat's bloodstain, the early morning
squabbling continues, and Bigger's mother complains that "We
wouldn't have to live in this garbage dump if you had any
manhood in you."[52]

Knock on any Door (1947), by Willard Motley, again develops
the chain from poverty to crime to death—specifically, as in *Native
Son,* to state execution for murder. However, the Romano family
in Motley's novel is at first mildly prosperous; in this period, their
son Nick is an altarboy, for whom the happiest day in his life is
his twelfth birthday, when he served at High Mass. He plans to
be a priest, and "some day he might be a saint too." But "then
they were poor." The family is forced to move to the other side
of town and Nick can no longer go to the same church. In the
miserable frame house on Rio Street, the family shares "four
dark rooms [which] were bare and sullen and dingy from having
been lived in by other poor people who had been unable to buy
paint or wallpaper to make them look any other way." In short
order, Nick meets some rougher kids and is soon sent to a re-
formatory, taking the rap for his friend Tony. Nick Romano ends
in the electric chair. Motley concludes his novel with a tour of
Chicago's South Side.

Over the jail the wind blows, sharp and cold. . . . North and
South runs Halsted, twenty miles long. Twelfth Street. Boys under
lampposts, shooting craps, learning. . . . Down Maxwell Street
where the prostitutes stand in the gloom-clustered doorways. Across
Twelfth Street either way on Peoria are the old houses. The sad
faces of the houses line the street, like old men and women sitting
along the veranda of an old folks' charity home. . . .
   Nick? Knock on any door down this street.[53]

In their novels, Wright and Motley advance more threatening
propositions than had Stephen Crane. Crane showed the reader
the ruin of one life, a ruin accomplished by environment. Wright
and Motley go further; Bigger Thomas and Nick Romano are
turned into predators, and society is menaced by their existence.
The menace of the tenements, pointed out by social workers
and reformers as early as 1880, reappears in the polemic Black
novels of the 1940's. The move from the tenements to the suburban
house had long been a moral and economic figure for the process
of Americanization. American blacks, cut off from this route of
assimilation into middle-class culture, articulate in novels like
Native Son and *Knock on any Door* the theme of disenfranchise-
ment and retaliation. In both novels the house is a major image.
Nick Romano's moral collapse follows the family's economic
collapse and its removal to substandard housing. Bigger Thomas
moves from his slum to the house of the wealthy slumlord Dalton,
and there commits murder.
   Housing reform in America underwent its most radical change
in the 1930's with the entry of the federal government into the
housing field. Precedent had been established during the housing
crisis of the First World War; subsequently, Herbert Hoover's
Conference on Home Building and Home Ownership in 1932 and
Franklin Roosevelt's New Deal, with the Home Owners Loan
Corporation, the National Housing Act, and the Federal Housing
Authority, made the alleviation of poor housing conditions a
public responsibility. From the restrictive legislation of the 1867
Tenement Law of New York, government has moved to increasingly broad measures, including the establishment of guaranteed
mortgage loans and, eventually, the provision of subsidized hous-
ing. Not all of these measures, however, serve the urban poor;
many are aimed at middle class Americans.
   Lawrence M. Friedman, in *Government and Slum Housing*

(1968), distinguishes between the real urban poor and the middle class with a reduced income. During the Depression, Friedman argues, "tremendous numbers of new and unwilling recruits joined the ranks of the unemployed, the underemployed, and the marginally employed." These men and women, "culturally members of the middle class who had fallen from economic grace after 1929," were "better equipped to demand measures of alleviation than the lowest group of urban poor before or since."[54] Friedman believes that New Deal housing programs, like Veterans Administration programs after the War, were a response to middle-class demands for houses, and were aimed at the provision of homes and mortgage-loans within the ideal American framework—the individually-owned, detached, private house.

A study of low-cost housing published in the *Architectural Record* for 1936 supports Friedman's assumptions. The statistical material in the article demonstrates the fact that at least one-third, and probably as many as one-half, of all urban families were financially unable to own homes in the 1930's. Nevertheless, the article concentrated on solving the problem of home construction to supply the relatively limited market of potential home owners. Hoover's Conference had established rough guide-lines for home-ownership: a family could afford a house the total cost of which equalled two years' salary. The *Architectural Record* adopted this guide-line and, figuring the minimum price for a decent house at $3000 (80% for the house, 20% for the lot), they determined that a family with an annual income of $1500 could afford such a house. Below $1500, home purchase was not possible. They quoted in support the statement of A. R. Clas, the Director of the Housing Division in Roosevelt's administration, who also set the minimal annual income for home-ownership at $1500. Also cited was the Financial Survey of Urban Housing, a 1934 CWA project, which showed the average family income in fifty-two cities. According to this survey, home-owners had an average annual income of $2269 in 1929, and $1478 in 1933. Tenants had averaged $1512 in 1929, but only $1052 in 1933. Following the statistical information, the Architectural Record published portfolios of low-cost houses that met the requisite standards: living-dining room, kitchen, laundry, three bedrooms, bath, and a garage, with a minimum of 10,000 cubic feet exclusive of the garage. These were not easy to build, although in Highland Park, near Chicago, Skidmore and Owings had built a five-room house of 11,100 cubic feet for $3,068.[55]

But even the development and construction of $3000 houses bought on mortgages sponsored by the National Housing Act could not alleviate the housing plight for urban families with an annual income below $1500. In Friedman's terms, federal programs were aimed at remedying the plight of a depressed, or a potential, middle class. The urban poor, on the other hand, would have to remain renters. In 1929, when the average income of tenants was $1512, the median urban rental was $32.06 a month, or nearly one-third of the total income. With so large a proportion of wages required for rent, it would take an inordinate amount of diligence and thrift to save money toward purchasing a house, even under the terms of the new federal mortgage laws requiring only 20% for a down payment (or $600 on a $3000 house).

For the urban tenant and especially for those who lived in slums, government assistance had to assume forms other than guaranteed mortgages. Public housing and direct subsidies, however, struck at deeply held American values about the house as contemporary attacks against federal housing programs reveal. For example, Blair Belles, in the *American Mercury* for 1936, attacked Roosevelt's resettlement programs. "The supposition is that, given a home, the occupant will find a source of income; which is in conflict with the old-fashioned human custom of developing a source of income first and building the home afterward."[56] Some writers were more fearful than angry. In 1939, Carol Aronovici dreaded the creation of "a separate class of citizenry who would become the 'housing wards' of the state." Like nineteenth century supporters of free enterprise, Aronovici hinted darkly at consequent "political, economic, and social dangers which I dare not contemplate."[57]

Conversely, Edith Elmer Wood, following up her 1919 study with *Recent Trends in American Housing* in 1931, reviewed the menace that bad housing posed for society and found more cause for alarm in the effect of the slums than in the inversion of old values. The housing problem, she insisted, was permanent as long as we operated under our present economic system. European cities had found solutions through large-scale government action in subsidizing housing. With an irony born of years of frustration, Wood declared that "we are still thanking God that we are not as other men and that we do not interfere with the sacred laws of supply and demand in the matter of providing homes for those who need them."[58]

In 1936, James Ford published *Slums and Housing*, an historical study of the housing of the poor in America. Like most Americans, Ford deplored the slum while maintaining the old ideal of the private house, earned by an individual's hard work and thrift. Ford could present reasonable arguments for the advantages of apartment living for those whose incomes made home ownership impossible without, as he added, prodigious thriftiness. He could even assert that it was "unwise for a family to undertake an investment in a house which it is not likely to be able to pay for." But in the same sentence he included the classic celebration of the American home: ". . . on the other hand, the families who are capable of such thrift and common enterprise make the backbone of citizenry and pass on the sturdy virtues of our forefathers to the coming generations." From the "owned home" came family pride, community responsibility, and "perhaps the chief training-ground for family and civic qualities which are the source and conservators of our republican institutions and our national progress." Ford recognized the fact that this ideal environment was beyond the reach of many, but he did not fully accept that fact. Like a nineteenth century moralist, he believed that hard work and thrift were sufficient, if strenuous, means to the realization of the "owned home."[59]

With each step in the symbolization of the American house, the tenement dweller, in fact the renter, was pushed further out of the mainstream of American life. Furthermore, to the extent that government-subsidized housing was considered as a subversion of American values, the urban poor were themselves seen as an alien population. In other words, the nineteenth century dilemma remained and, after the government's entry into housing, was intensified. Only occasionally was a voice raised to debate the premise that in the private home lay the source of individual civic virtue. Jane Addams had taken this position in 1902; in 1939 Aronovici mocked the sentiment adhering to the American house.

Much sentimentality has been developed around the idea of home ownership. Civic vrirtue, the sanctity of the family, the spiritual influence of the old homestead, the lasting value of the family council held around the fireside, seem to be the exclusive privilege of the home owner. Nothing is said by political orators, preachers, and crooners about the tragedy of mortgage foreclosures or overdue tax bills. Neither are the renters given a proper place on the roster of the solid citizenry, despite the fact that the majority of our people live in rented houses, while two-thirds of the alleged owners are merely custodians of other people's investment. The tenacity of the superstitions which have been built up around the 'ideals' of home ownership passes understanding.

But even this statement stands less as a philosophy than as a lead-in to a conclusion. "If home ownership is to be encouraged among our wage earners, we must first liberate it from the hazards and tragedies which characterize it today."[60]

Since the Second World War the government's role in housing has increased both in the maintaining of financial incentives to home ownership, as through the Veterans Administration, and in the development of subsidized public housing. Like the Improved Dwellings of Alfred T. White a century ago, public housing is intended as an alleviation of slum conditions in order to raise living standards, physically, socially, and morally. Government funding has replaced philanthropic capitalism, but the purpose remains the same: to rescue from the ranks of the poor potential members of the middle class. The essential problem, too, remains the same, for the American ideal is unrealized when home tenancy replaces home ownership. After a hundred years, we are caught in the same dilemma. The private home is the bulwark of democracy, but the provision of such homes to those who have not earned them subverts the conventional values of labor and reward and devalues the symbol of the house.

History, Myth and Nostalgia

Chapter Seven

The Log Cabin

*. . . trees are laid prostrate on the earth, one on
top of another, and a miserable log hut is the
only symptom of a man's residence.*
> Captain Basil Hall,
> *Travels in North America (1829)*

To bring back to the people, and through the
log cabin of the country, *the neglected and lost
Constitution.*
> John Sergeant of Pennsylvania,
> political speech,
> May, 1840.[1]

*One little hut among de bushes,
   One dat I love,
Still sadly to my memory rushes,
   No matter where I rove.*
> Stephen Foster, "Old Folks at Home"

The history of the humble rural home in America is a curious one.
Both the cottage and the cabin passed from a period of contempt-
uous tolerance into an era of sentimental celebration. The log
cabin, especially, took on a symbolic significance more and more
divorced from the reality of the rude discomfort of frontier housing. At the beginning of the nineteenth century the log cabin had
been understood as no more than the temporary housing of the
first stages of western settlement; but before the century ended,
it had come to stand as a symbol for the coming of civilization,
for the promise of an egalitarian society, and at last for the lost
innocence of the simple life in a younger, more vigorous, and
more virtuous America.

"Cottage" and "cabin" had both originated as terms for mean
dwellings. In Russell Sturgis's *Dictionary of Architecture and
Building, Biographical, Historical, and Descriptive* (1902), the

"cottage" entry maintains the older, pejorative value of the word by referring back to the original English cottage, a small, bare structure, of rough stone, with a thatched roof. "Cottages in this sense have hardly existed within the United States," Sturgis explains, "for the log cabin was admittedly a makeshift. . . ." In other words, an inferior dwelling of this type, from architect Sturgis's point of view, was not an American phenomenon, although, as he explains, the nineteenth century built country houses rather fancifully called "cottages" because they were "supposed to be simple as compared with the residences of the wealthy people in the neighborhood." As for the cabin, Sturgis defines it as "A residence smaller and more humble than a cottage. In the United States hardly used, except for the houses of slaves on a plantation. . . ." There is no entry for log cabin. Notably, Sturgis's general definition of "house" eliminates from consideration both humble rural dwellings as well as the housing of indigenous American tribes: "House: A dwelling, the term being usually restricted to those dwellings which have some elaboration; excluding Cabin, Cot, Cottage, in its original sense, Hut, Iglu, Shack, Shanty, Tipi, Wigwam, and the like."[2]

The voice of the architectural establishment may have dismissed cabin and cottage as types of houses, but in the myth-making process of American culture they had both, by 1900, become firmly established as typical house and archetypal home. The cottage achieved respectability first; we have seen that as early as 1815 the cottage was being sentimentalized as the dwelling of the virtuous and simple family, and that by 1832 the cottage had become associated with "true republican independence."[3] Even before the publication of Downing's *The Architecture of Country Houses* in 1850, the cottage was recognized as an important type of American house.

The log cabin was slower in achieving respectability, but its impact on the American imagination was finally much greater than that of the cottage. Despite H. R. Shurtleff's *The Log Cabin Myth*, published in 1939, many Americans continue to believe that the first settlers in Jamestown and Plymouth erected log cabins. Shurtleff's research proved that the log cabin was "a type of dwelling completely unknown to [the English] at home," and that "no evidence" of such houses "can be found in the sources."[4] He traced the infusion of the log cabin myth into history, finding the first suggestions of the possibilities of log cabins as the homes of New England settlers in an 1827 history of Dedham, Massachusetts, and in a footnote by Rev. Alexander Young in his 1841 *Chronicles*. By 1860, Washington Allston illustrated John Palfrey's *New England* with the "House of an Early Settler," a pictorial sentimentalization of the log cabin. As late as 1925, a Yale University Press history, *Pageant of America*, "produced an entirely new log-cabin picture of Jamestown."[5]

When the log cabin was introduced into America and during most of the period in which it was the nearly universal dwelling in frontier settlements, no romantic views sentimentalized this structure. The log cabin was a rude and uncomfortable house. It was intended as an impermanent dwelling, to be replaced by a more substantial structure of wood or brick as soon as frontier conditions permitted. Pattern books seldom included plans for log cabins and when a publication like Charles Dwyer's *The Immigrant Builder* (1872) did explain how to construct log cabins and other inexpensive frontier houses, of slabs or of rammed earth, the instructions were intended for the special audience of pioneer families. Dwyer hoped to make frontier living more comfortable, but he had no illusions about the permanence of the settler's log houses which, he explained were "predoomed to be the stable or the cow-house."[6]

In the eighteenth century, the attitude toward the log cabin reflected the national desire for the progress of civilization. Therefore, log cabins like any rough and temporary dwellings were an embarrassment; for, to the extent that the civilization of the colonies could be read by the houses the colonists built for themselves, log cabins were indices of a dismal lack of societal success. For the individual as well, make-shift housing strongly suggested a fairly low level of industry and thrift. By the early nineteenth century, however, a new element in the national consciousness altered the response to the log cabin. As the frontier was pushed westward and the log cabin appeared as the typical first shelter of the pioneer, it became possible to dignify the log cabin as an emblem of the march of civilization. In the pattern of progress, the respectable house of frame or brick soon replaced the log cabin, which then reappeared in the next area of wilderness. Through this pattern, the log cabin was absorbed into American mythology, but it was understood as ephemeral, merely a punctuation mark in the rhetoric of westward expansion.

European visitors as well as American writers commented on

the cabin as the herald of civilization, but for the Europeans the log cabin was witness as well to the personal independence of the American. Tocqueville marveled at the sense of dignity and proprietorship expressed by Americans he visited in frontier cabins; he noted their "air of rich folk who have temporarily gone to spend a season in a hunting lodge."[7] Mrs. Trollope, as well, commented on the independence communicated to her in visiting a house built of logs, consisting "of two rooms, besides a little shanty or lean-to, that was used as a kitchen." She found it "the best specimen I saw of the back-wood's independence, of which so much is said in America." The loneliness, which seemed to Mrs. Trollope "awful and almost unnatural," was mitigated perhaps by this independence: "But then they pay neither taxes nor tythes, are never expected to pull off a hat or to make a curtsy, and will live and die without hearing or uttering the dreadful words, 'God save the king.' "[8]

American writers in the first half of the nineteenth century put much less emphasis on independence. A sentimental point of view led a number of them to enhance the picture of log cabin life with intimations of gentility and even of sophistication. Catherine Stewart, an enthusiast for western life, wrote New Homes in the West in 1843 from material gathered in a series of western trips during the 1830's. Her picture of log cabin life is reminiscent of a somewhat decayed Renaissance pastoralism.

> One frequently feels agreeable surprise, on entering a cabin of simplest structure, to find that winning hospitality and intelligence that grace the fashionable saloons; more appreciated, in their humble garb, than when surrounded with ostentatious display.[9]

Another of Mrs. Stewart's themes was the pleasures of poverty, particularly in regard to those who have suffered a reversal of fortune. "To the mutability of fortune, these borders are indebted for the intellectual tone of character," she said, and added in another section of the book that in Michigan "In humble log cabins we may see remnants of families retired from that world they can no longer sway." Most didactically, in speaking of the settlement near the Fox River:

> . . . to those who have felt the chilling frowns of fortune, [the West] seems to say, come hither, and forget artificial wants in the

enjoyment of substantial blessings. Under your own vine, learn the philosophy so cheerfully inscribed in simple unadorned cabins, that however small the circle of human wishes may be drawn, comfort and peace may follow.[10]

Catherine Stewart's sentimental picture of log cabin life, however, did not come from the experiences of a frontier wife; she had viewed this world as a traveler. Mrs. Caroline Matilda Kirkland, on the other hand, tried log cabin life, and her viewpoint is refreshingly realistic. Mrs. Kirkland belonged to educated and aristocratic New York society, and her careers included teaching, writing, and editing. In 1836 she and her husband went to Detroit where he had a post as principal at the Detroit Female Seminary. After a year, they bought thirteen hundred acres in Pinckney, Michigan, sixty miles northwest of Detroit, and moved there with their five children. In 1843, they returned to New York. *A New Home, or Life in the Clearings*, was published anonymously in 1839. Other western books followed.[11]

The Kirklands arrived in Pinckney expecting to live in a loghouse already standing, but they had to wait for this "temporary home" "while the incumbent could build a framed one." Once the Kirklands took possession of the "loggery," they stayed there only until their new house was completed. Mrs. Kirkland had apparently read a good deal of contemporary sentimental literature about the log cabin, and in her book she pointed out the discrepancies between the romantic essay and the real experience.

> The circumstances of living all summer, in the same apartment with a cooking fire, I had never happened to see alluded to in any of the elegant sketches of western life which had fallen under my notice. It was not until I actually became the inmate of a log-dwelling in the wilds, that I realized fully what 'living all in one room' meant.[12]

Avoiding sentimentality, Mrs. Kirkland insisted nevertheless in inculcating a lesson. Civilized life was "apt to make us proud, selfish, and ungrateful," and for "the Sybarites, the puny exquisites, the world-worn and sated Epicureans of our cities," she recommended "a year's residence in the woods, or even in a Michigan village." On the other hand, she did not romanticize the inhabitants of Pinckney, whom she found rather overwhelmingly republican in spirit. Particularly, Mrs. Kirkland spoke of the open envy with which superior fortunes were regarded and the philosophy that insisted they should be shared. But she found an explanation for this point of view; on the frontier the differences in fortune were not revealed in luxuries and refinements, but in necessary commodities and comforts: ". . . the strength of their envy bear[s] a direct proportion to the *real* value of the objects of their desire."

> To the tenant of a log-cabin whose family, whatever be its numbers, must burrow in a single room, while a bed or two, a chest, a table, and a wretched handful of cooking utensils, form the chief materials of comfort, an ordinary house, small and plain it may be, yet amply supplied, looks like the very home of luxury.[13]

On the southwestern frontier, as in the north, the log cabin represented the first inroads of civilization, and with the progress of the settlement came finer houses. Early southern regionalists like Joseph G. Baldwin and A. B. Longstreet paid little attention to houses in their sketches of frontier life. High living in log cabins was, however, worth an ironic comment, and in *Georgia Scenes* (1825), Longstreet told of a dance in the squire's house: "The squire's dwelling consisted of but one room, which answered the three fold purpose of dining-room, bedroom, and kitchen."[14] In *The Flush Times of Alabama and Mississippi* (1853), Baldwin referred occasionally to houses to establish the pattern of progress. The "infancy" of a village is described: "A few log houses hastily erected and overcrowded with inmates, alone were to be seen." Fifteen years later, progress had brought its improvements: "—then the rude settlement, now the improved neighborhood, with its school-houses and churches; the log-cabin giving way to the mansion,—the wilderness giving way to the garden and the farm."[15] Similarly, Mrs. Kirkland in her chapter of farewell to her home in the clearing, wrote "Loggeries are becoming scarce within our limits, and many of our ladies wear silk dresses on Sunday."[16]

A few lonely cabins in the forest clearing, rather than a cluster of cabins in a village, created a particularly striking figure for the first stages of civilization. Settlers in these cabins confronted directly the terrors of nature and of Indians, and the comparison between the settlers and the Indians, frequently imaged in the houses of each, depended heavily on the inexorable, and obligatory, progress of civilization. William Gilmore Simms painted such a picture in *The Yemassee* (1835).

> A feeble colony of adventurers from a distant world had taken up its abode alongside of [the Indians]. The weaknesses of the intruder were, at first, his only sufficient protection with the unsophisticated savage.

The colony cleared its land and constructed its houses,

> . . . until at length, we behold the log-house of the white man, rising up amid the thinned clump of woodland foliage, within hailing distance of the squat clay hovel of the savage.[17]

With Simms, the references to houses go beyond the indication of the coming of civilization, however. In *The Yemassee*, savage Indians attempt an attack on young Elizabeth Matthews. The purity and virtue of the Matthews family enhance the melodrama and the sentimentality of the plot, and Simms used the Matthews' house as one symbol of that virtue. One way in which he established moral values through the house was to avoid the word "cabin," or even "log-house," in reference to the Matthews' home, and to call it a "cottage," for the cabin did not yet carry the strong sentimental values that already adhered to the cottage. But while Simms consistently used the word "cottage," he described a cabin: "The house itself was rude enough—like those of the region generally—having been built of logs . . . and affording only a couple of rooms in front, to which the additional shed contributed two more, employed as sleeping apartments." The superior qualities of the Matthews' house depended on its site, on the care with which the family had "improved the rude location," and on a white-washed veranda, with a porch supported by four columns made "of slender pines decapitated for the purpose." Most significant, however, was the evidence of the vines which covered the cottage.

> The clustering vines, too, hanging fantastically over the entrance, almost forbidding ingress, furnished proof enough of the presence and agency of that sweet nature, which, lovely of itself, has yet

added attraction when coupled with the beauty and purity of woman.[18]

In his book of short tales, *The Wigwam and the Cabin* (1845), Simms again used the image of the cabin for the initial stage of civilization. The title of the collection is itself symbolic, referring to the housing of Indian and white man and to the conflict between their cultures. The victory, of course, lies with the cabin, a forerunner of more respectable white man's houses. For example, in referring back from the present time to the period of first settlement, Simms talks of one Colonel Harris: "In place of the stately residence which now adorns his homestead, there was then but a miserable log-house, one of the most ordinary of the country." Although the word "cabin" served to carry ideas of progress and of the coming of civilization, Simms still did not find it adequate to express sentimental virtue. Therefore, in the tale about a simple and virtuous family, the vocabulary shifts. The narrator describes a cabin in a clearing, a common enough cabin, but one with an unusually "snug, trim, and tidy appearance." The grounds are swept, the trees are trimmed, and the interior "consisted happily with that without. Every thing was so neat, and snug, and comfortable." As in *The Yemassee*, this dwelling is called a "cottage."[19]

Simm's use of the log cabin is unusual for pre-Civil War America, insofar as he romanticizes it, using it as a metaphor for its inhabitants. Given the setting of *The Yemassee* and the stories in *The Wigwam and the Cabin*, Simms could not employ more conventional dwellings for his young and virtuous protagonists; therefore, it was necessary for him to elevate the domestic settings available to him. In this context, it is particularly noteworthy to see that the terms "log-house" and "log-cabin" could not carry the proper sentimental weight, and that Simms turned to the safer word "cottage."

One factor that slowed the elevation of the word "cabin" was the association of this word in the South with the housing of plantation slaves, a connection maintained by Sturgis in his *Dictionary*. Evidence can be found as well in southern novels, for example in John Pendleton Kennedy's *Swallow Barn* (1832). Kennedy created a northern narrator, through whose eyes the reader learns about plantation life. In one chapter, the narrator viewed The Quarter: "These hovels, with their appurtenances, formed an exceedingly picturesque landscape." While "some few were built after the fashion of the better sort of cottages . . . the more lowly of these structures, and the most numerous, were nothing more than plain log-cabins."[20]

The log cabin of the white frontiersman differed from the cabin of the plantation slave in two exceptionally significant ways. In the first place, the white man theoretically built his own cabin, and, of course, he owned it. Secondly, his cabin was merely temporary shelter. For the slaves, conversely, the cabin was a permanent part of the plantation and it was the residence of any particular slave family at the pleasure of the owner of the plantation. Despite the fact that a slave's tenancy of a cabin depended on the disposition of the plantation owner, literary allusions to slave cabins typically stressed the unusually strong attachment a slave felt for his cabin. Implicit here is the contrast between the energy and self-interest of the hard-working white man and the indolence of the happy slave. Kennedy explains the "inhabitiveness" of plantation slaves in a passage from *Swallow Barn*.

> It is a trait in the dispositions of the negroes on the old plantations, to cling with more than a freeman's interest to the spot of their nativity. They have a strong attachment to the places connected with their earlier associations,—what in phrenology is called inhabitiveness;—and the pride of remaining in one family of masters, and of being transmitted to its posterity with all their own generations, is one of the most remarkable features in these negro clans.[21]

Constance Fenimore Woolson repeated this theme in 1874 in a *Harper's* essay about a visit to St. Augustine. Woolson spoke with the new owner of an old mansion, which he has sold in order to build a home for aged blacks. He took Woolson to visit Uncle Jack's Cabin, a hovel which would be replaced by "a picturesque porter's lodge." But, the benefactor said, "I doubt whether the old man will be as comfortable there as in this old cabin where he has lived so long."[22]

Already established as a symbol for the march of civilization, the log cabin was further enhanced by the election campaign of 1840, when the cabin became a fully developed symbol for the egalitarian promise of America. The cabin had already been associated with personal independence, as we have seen, but now its associations were enlarged; the child of the log cabin would become the president of the nation.

C. A. Weslager's *The Log Cabin* (1969) traces the log cabin campaign of 1840, a campaign which took its symbol from an unfriendly comment by a newspaper writer. John de Ziska had attacked Whig candidate William Henry Harrison, with the lines:

> Give him a barrel of hard cider, and settle a pension of $2000 a year on him, and our word for it, he will sit the remainder of his days in his log cabin by the side of the 'sea-coal fire' and study moral philosophy![23]

By May of 1840, the log cabin furor had become intense enough so that a Baltimore parade featured banners with log cabins on them and even a number of real log cabins drawn on wheels. One delegation had transplanted a gum tree on to the roof of its cabin with a live possom clinging to one of its branches. The campaign elicited, as well, songs and speeches celebrating the cabin. One such speech included the now-famous remarks of Daniel Webster in which he confessed that he was *not* born in a log cabin.

> I was not myself born in one, but my elder brothers and sisters were—in the cabin in which at the close of the Revolutionary War, in the perils and suffering of which he bore his part, my father erected on the extreme frontiers of New Hampshire, where, beyond the smoke which curled from its chimney, not another stood between it and the walls of Quebec. In this humble cabin amid the snow-drifts of New England, that father strove, by honest labor, to acquire the means for giving to his children a better education, and elevating them to a higher condition than his own.[24]

William Henry Harrison, of course, had not been born in a log cabin either; on the contrary, he had been born at "Berkeley" on the James River in Virginia, built in the early eighteenth century for one of King Carter's daughters.[25] The only log cabin Harrison had any association with had once stood on a one hundred sixty acre property he bought on the Ohio River in 1796, shortly after he was married; on these acres was a four-room house built around an original one-room cabin. Harrison made additions to this house, so that it eventually had six-teen rooms. In 1894, he built another house, "Grouselands," a twenty-six room mansion in Vincennes, Indiana, costing $20,000.[26] The Harrison family settled, finally, on their Ohio property, where Harrison's grandson, Benjamin, was born in a newer brick mansion that had replaced the older house. Benjamin Harrison, in his own campaign for president, liked to refer to his grandfather's log cabin on the Ohio property.[27]

The Lincoln campaign of 1860 fixed the log cabin permanently in the minds of Americans as the symbol of the hardy and rugged life lived by honorable, self-sufficient, and courageous men. The route from the log cabin to the White House marked out the road of ambitious young men, for whom the promise of an egalitarian America was now confirmed. At its most intense, the log cabin symbol not only represented one nursery for the energy and the moral fiber of America, but it stood for the most advantageous such nursery. To have been born in a log cabin was to offer proof of one's virtue and vitality. In 1926, when Chesla Sherlock of *Better Homes and Gardens* published his *Homes of Famous Americans*, he included a chapter on Ulysses S. Grant's cabin "Hardscrabble." Sherlock's remarks honor the log cabin with its most extreme celebration.

> There is something reassuring about a log-cabin set in a knoll of trees about a winding creek. The very ruggedness of the place is suggestive of the strength of those departed souls who once wrought shelter and hearthstone out of the naked woods.[28]

The cabin represented "the simple life," that of "home-makers and home-builders," from whose ranks will come "Other Grants . . . to save the day for us." In fact, the security of America depends on the life symbolized by "Hardscrabble" and other rude cabins: "So long as the moral fiber exists among the majority of the rank and file which produced our Lincolns and Grants, just so long will we, indeed, be secure."[29] It takes an iconoclast like Weslager to point out what Sherlock could never have mentioned—that the list of Americans born in log cabins also includes Jesse James and John Wilkes Booth.

The final stage in the canonization of the log cabin came in the latter half of the nineteenth century, when the cabin became the symbol not only of the life of fortitude and hardship that breeds leaders but more generally of the vanished life of simple virtue and rural innocence. The increasing complexities of American life in the years following the Civil War bred nostalgia for a lost Edenic America, one without city slums, a growing immigrant population, or a class of millionaires developed out of new businesses and technologies. In the past that Americans recreated, the world was simpler and men were purer. Contemporary man had lost his Adamic simplicity, his strength and competence, and above all his innocence.

The role of the log cabin in the nostalgia of post-Civil War America is apparent even in material that is intended for comic irony rather than sentimental expression. A *Lippincott's* article in 1883, called "The Vagaries of Western Architecture," is a comic history of "Joinwater," now the eleventh largest city in the United States. The author traces the population growth by decades, for the period from 1790 to 1880; from three people to 160,146. Similarly he traces, with illustrations supplied, the architectural style of each decade, and in so doing he mocks the pretensions of the townspeople: "To live in a cheap house in Joinwater was as great a crime as to eat cheap food in Connecticut." Log cabins, or as the author calls them, "log shanties," are the architectural type for the first decade. After describing the simple log cabin life and the meagre possessions of the early citizens of Joinwater, population eighteen, he adds "Happy people! and happy Joinwater! a 'truly rural' democracy!" But the cabins are replaced, in one case with "a genuine New-England farmhouse," which is an improvement in comfort though not necessarily in symbolic value. After that, the history of Joinwater, architectural and morally, is all downhill.[30]

More serious essays and reminiscences described the log cabin and the life lived in it with an extravagant sentimentality. John Burroughs, who wrote about houses for over thirty years, frequently included material on the log cabin. In an essay in *Scribner's Monthly* from 1875-1876, Burroughs established his philosophy of houses, one developed directly from Downing. Expressiveness and organic intimacy between a man and his house are basic to Burroughs' thought: "It is not the snails and shell-fish alone that excrete their tenements, but man as well. When you seriously build a house, you make public proclamation of your taste and manners, or your want of these." The natural instinct to build houses, however, becomes corrupted with the coming of wealth and pride. Burroughs' purpose in the essay was to talk of houses in general and of specific house plans in particular which have not sacrificed the qualities of innocence and naturalness found in the log cabin.

When father or grandfather, beginning at the stump, set out to build his house, filled with this impulse alone,—the desire for shelter, safety, and simple comfort, —and the log cabin arose under cover of the dark forest, the result was beautiful to the true eye.

The subsequent clapboard dwelling was still natural and good, for it preceded the period of the large white house that "marks the end of . . . rural settlement," and "the end of the spirit of friendliness and social interchange between neighbors. It inaugurates the period of jealousy, of coldness, of back-biting." Burroughs expresses at this point the full equivalence between the log cabin and the virtues of the simple life.

While the people yet lived in their log huts, and the battle went hard with them, they had things more in common; there was sympathy and hearty good-will between them; hard work and hard times made all the world akin; the people were drawn together and their humble abodes were scenes of sweet domestic life and neighborly interchanges.[31]

The association of the cabin with a life in which pure and generous men lived in social harmony depends on a view of the past that is more wishful than historical. Similarly, the writers who idealized the log cabin life were typically not the men and women who had lived in them; instead they created out of the memories of others the content of their own domestic dreams. Burroughs, for example, recreated the experience of his grandparents.

My grandmother said the happiest day of her life was when she found herself mistress of a little log house in the woods. Grandfather and she had built it mainly with their own hands, and doubtless with as much eagerness and solicitude as the birds build their nests. . . . it was home and fireside, a few square feet of the great

wild, inclement, inhospitable out-of-doors subdued and set about
by four walls and made warm and redolent of human hearts.[32]

One need only compare this prose with the even-handed reportage
of Caroline Kirkland to grasp the effects of distance.

In the popular imagination, decent poverty and dignified
labor, in a rural environment, were the virtues especially connected to the sentimentalized log cabin. From the vantage point
of the late nineteenth century, the dangers of wealth and of urban
life were very striking to a romantic like Burroughs. The mansion,
emblemizing both city life and great riches, was the antithesis
of the log cabin. In 1906, for *Cosmopolitan*, Burroughs wrote a
piece called "The Vanity of Big Houses," in which he insisted
again on the blessings of the simple life. In this short essay, he
concentrated on the dangers inherent in the houses built by
riches; the cabin was a safer dwelling for the soul.

> A man can fill and warm a cabin, he is not swallowed up by it; he
> can make it a part of himself—he can make it fit him like his
> old shoes, and be as expressive of his daily life. But the moment
> he goes beyond the simplest structures . . . and begins to build for
> looks, for position, or from the pride of a full purse, that moment
> there is danger that the gentler divinities will forsake him.[33]

The glamor of log cabin life, for those who were not forced to
live it, was strong enough to capture not only romantics like Burroughs, but realists like William Dean Howells as well. Howells
had lived one year in a log cabin, in Xenia, Ohio, when he was
twelve or thirteen years old. As an adult, Howells experienced
great pleasure in his own house "on the water side of Beacon,"
but he was capable of an indulgent nostalgia about that log cabin.

> It was all that could be asked for by the most romantic of pioneer
> families. . . . [The fireplace] was six feet wide and a yard deep, its
> cavernous jaw would easily swallow a back-log eighteen inches
> through, and we could pile in front sticks of hickory cordwood
> as high as we liked. We made a perfect trial of it when we came
> out to put the cabin in readiness for the family, and when the
> hickory had dropped into a mass of tinkling, snapping, bristling
> embers, we laid our rashers of bacon and our slices of steak upon
> them and tasted with the appetite of tired youth the flavors of the
> camp and the wildwood in the captured juices.[34]

The sentimentalization of the log cabin is particularly striking when the nostalgia of Burroughs or Howells is compared with the writings of men who actually lived a number of years under frontier conditions. For example, William Nowlin wrote a memoir in 1876, one of a group of such reminiscences encouraged by the centennial celebrations. Nowlin's book, *The Bark Covered House, or Back in the Woods Again,* is a sentimental recall of the family's migration to Dearborn, Michigan in 1834, but the sentiment does not extend far enough to include the log cabin they built for their first shelter. Two years after their arrival in Dearborn, Nowlin's father built their second house, and eventually was able to "buy a farm, build a large brick house, and end his days, in peace and plenty." The sentiment of the literati not withstanding, the point of westward migration and of backbreaking labor was the acquisition and cultivation of the land and the construction of a solid family house. There is no regret in Nowlin's book for that original cabin.

> I was pleased to think that Father had so good a house and was so well situated. He built him a very strong house and located it upon a commanding eminence overlooking the country in every direction. From its very solid appearance, shortly after it was built it was called "Nowlin Castle," it is now known to many by that name.[35]

The nostalgia of the later nineteenth century touched both urban and rural Americans, but only the sophisticated chose to extend this nostalgia to the log cabin. Their error was to confuse the cabin with the homestead, which was generally an object of veneration. The typical log cabin dweller, however, never considered the cabin as his homestead. Hamlin Garland, for example, was capable of greatly idealizing the family home, but not the log cabin he was born in. In 1893, after a decade in the East, Garland returned to the middle west and bought a home for his mother in Wisconsin. The newly purchased house in West Salem, "the little village from which we had all adventured some thirty years before," had never been in the Garland family; nevertheless, it became "a family homestead." Garland explains, in *A Daughter of the Middle Border* (1929), that the homestead "was not the building in which my life began—I should like to say it was, but it was not." His birthplace, he continues, "was a cabin, part logs

and part lumber—on the opposite side of the town. Originally a
squatter's cabin, it was now empty and forlorn, a dreary monument of the pioneer days, which I did not take the trouble to
enter."[36]

At one point, Garland and his father returned to the town in
Iowa where they had once lived, and Garland again expressed
disgust at the squalor he confronted. "The yard was attractive
but the house (infested by the family of a poor renter) was
repulsive. The upstairs chamber in which I had slept for so many
years presented a filthy clutter of chicken feathers, cast-off furniture and musty clothing." The purchased "homestead" in West
Salem was a defense against the return to squalor, and on that
simple house Garland squandered his time, affection, and money,
widening the front porch, throwing out a bay window, adding a
fireplace. An advance of fifty dollars from *McClure's* went for
a "new set of dinner china and a piano." Later a dining room, a
new porch, and a bathroom were added.[37]

Far from discovering a pastoral glamor in the log cabin, Garland threw himself into creating a house at once homestead and
up-to-date suburban cottage, but the continuing descriptions of
the house in *A Daughter of the Middle Border* reveal an unas-
suageable discomfort in Garland about the success of his house.
After his marriage he visited Boston, where he found things
apparently smaller and drabber than he had remembered them.
"Dr. Holmes' mansion on 'the water side of Beacon Street' and
the palaces of Copley Square left me calm, their glamor had
utterly vanished with my youth. . . ." Disparaging Boston, however, did not allay his envy; he found it hard after this trip to
take his wife "back to a shabby farm house." He even bought
three hundred and twenty acres in Oklahoma and dreamt of
buying more Oklahoma land: "In imagination I saw myself in
a wide-rimmed hat and white linen suit sitting at ease on the
porch of a broad-roofed house (built in the Mexican style with
a patio) looking out over my thousand acres." And later still,
when he had a house in the city as well as the homestead in
Wisconsin, he talked of himself as having a "country place" and
noted that he "did not explain to all my friends that it was
merely an ugly old farmhouse on the edge of a commonplace
village."[38]

Garland is an interesting example of the victim of America's
confused values. Unable to believe in the log cabin, he was still

at once imbued with the romanticism of the "home place" and infected with the desire for ever more grandiose houses, the American reward for success. In a passage confessing his restless desire for a better home, he explained this need as "perfectly natural" given his "close association with several of the most successful writers and artists of my day. It was inevitable that while contrasting my home with theirs, I should occasionally fall into moods of self-disparagement, almost of despair."[39]

The lure of the homestead is apparent as well in an interview Garland did for *McClure's* with James Whitcomb Riley, for a series called, "Real Conversations." Riley had purchased back the old family house, and the interview took place on the porch "of the old homestead." Garland explained that "In this house his childhood passed. . . . He bought it because of old-time associations." A photograph of the house is labeled "Griggsby's Station—The Old Riley House and Present Summer Residence;" below, the following lines are quoted from Riley's "Griggsby's Station."

> Le's go a-visitin' back to Griggsby's Station—
> Back where the latch-string's a-hangin' from the door,
> And ever' neighbor round the place is dear as a relation—
> Back where we ust to be so happy and so pore!

To Garland's question: "Did you actually ever live on a farm?" Riley unabashedly declared, "No. All I got of farm life I picked up right from this distance—this town—this old homestead."[40]

The books of other midwestern writers illustrate the same point as Garland: sentiment for the land and for the homestead, but none for the cabin. Willa Cather's *O Pioneers!* (1918) paints a grim picture of the log cabins on the Nebraska prairie.

> One January day, thirty years ago, the little town of Hanover, anchored on a windy Nebraska tableland, was trying not to be blown away. . . . The dwelling-houses were set about haphazard on the tough prairie sod; some of them looked as if they had been moved in overnight, and others as if they were straying off by themselves, headed straight for the open plain. None of them had any appearance of permanence.

Log cabins and sod houses alike failed to dispel the sense of "the absence of human landmarks," although they were the forerunners of civilization against "the great fact [of] the land itself, which seemed to overwhelm the little beginnings of human society that struggled in its sombre wastes." The novel, the history of the Bergstrom family and especially of the daughter Alexandra, recounts the success of civilization. The early picture of the prairie's desolation is contrasted with the view sixteen years later, when "From the graveyard gate one can count a dozen gaily painted farmhouses." It is this later rural landscape, the life expressed in Alexandra's big house on a hill, that is celebrated, particularly in contrast with the city, a place of anonymity, where one paid "the exorbitant rent one has to pay for a few square feet of space near the heart of things." Against this is displayed the fact of Alexandra's world, her large and simple house, proof of the victory over nature and an emblem of the great labor that turned the "windy Nebraska tableland," into "the beauty and fruitfulness of the outlying fields."[41]

Although first-hand accounts in memoirs or fiction failed to encourage the sentimentalized portrayal of the log cabin, other, more naive enthusiasts successfully accomplished its idealization. Given the nostalgic search for a vanished Edenic America that so possessed the minds of Americans after the Civil War, it was not surprising that the rudest domestic shelter in the national experience should have received the attention it did. Furthermore, the egalitarian promise of American society incorporated the log cabin into its mythic structure. The qualities of independence and resourcefulness popularly associated with the frontier man came together with the pietistic belief in the advantages of poverty in building character to create a sentimental myth that made a log-cabin birth one prerequisite in the American myth of the birth of the hero. As Elbert Hubbard put it in connection with Daniel Webster's father and the log cabin in which two of his children were born and one conceived, "It seems that biting poverty and sore deprivation are about as good prenatal influences as a soul can well ask."[42]

Chapter Eight

George Washington Slept Here

HISTORICAL JESSE JAMES HOME

Jesse James, the famous outlaw, lived in this home with his family, under the name of Howard, and was shot and killed here on April 3, 1882, by Robert Ford, to win the $10,000 reward offered by the State for the body of Jesse. He died at the age of 34 after a lawless career of 16 years. The home, now a museum and open to the public, is located at St. Joseph, Missouri, on East Belt Highway U.S. 71, 169, 59.

From a postcard of the house "Where JESSE JAMES was killed."

Seeing a new market in the European tourists drawn to America by the Chicago Exposition of 1893, Baedeker published a guide book to the United States. The first one hundred pages were devoted, in leisurely nineteenth century fashion, to general information, to essays on American politics, the Constitution, the "aborigines," geology, climate, arts, education, and even penology. Informed so broadly, the traveler was also warned of some peculiarly American characteristics, such as the non-submissiveness of those menials with whom he was likely to come in contact.

Baedeker took the potential tourist carefully through American towns and cities, pointing out landmarks of interest, but he had little to say to the pilgrim from England or France brought face to face with a famous American house. For the Craigie House he supplied only the building date, the name of the builder, and the dates of Washington's occupancy, with a casual reference to its significance as Longfellow's residence: "It contains many interesting relics of the poet." Paul Revere's house was passed over completely, although the tourist was guided to the Copp's Hill Burial Ground and to Christ Church. In Salem, Baedeker mentioned that "the quaint gambrel-roofed house in which [Hawthorne] was born is no. 21 Union St., a narrow side-street extending from Essex St. to Derby St." "The Turner House, 34 Turner St.," is pointed out as the "House of the Seven Gables." And Mount Vernon, the visitor was told, contained an "abundance of interesting relics" of which the key to the Bastille was perhaps the "most notable."[1]

These dry observations in no way echo those of American visitors to houses so marked by tradition and "association." Notable houses have, in America, become shrines to visit, to sketch and later photograph, and to set as the subjects of books and articles that, from the middle of the nineteenth century, have been published in such number as to constitute a minor literary genre: the historical house essay.

The Craigie House, the House of the Seven Gables, and Mount Vernon are not dismissed in a few cool sentences in these essays. And as the subject of notable homes gained in popularity, the essayist turned to the discovery and celebration of more obscure houses: the log cabin where a statesman was said to have been born, the cottage in which a poet was raised, the old house at the corner of some derelict city street where a future novelist once rented a room. The popular market for pictorial essays about famous houses continues to flourish, as does the popular fascination for visiting houses with an historic or romantic appeal.

For only in America could the tourist be directed to a crumbling log cabin because Jesse James grew up there. (A side trip to the house in which he was shot is also available.) On a desolate country road in western Missouri, a fairly large, faded and soiled sign at once advertises 7-Up and, with a minatory arrow, points the tourist to THE HOUSE OF JESSE JAMES. The house itself is the conjunction of a sagging cabin (it cannot be entered; age and the devastation of the famous Pinkerton bomb have made it unsafe) and a turn-of-the-century frame cottage. The two structures, the non-descript cottage and the collapsed cabin, meet to form a "T". Nearby, not hidden from view, is the pink mobile home in which a tour-director awaits the visitor. Within the house, there are memorabilia and mementos, the latter for sale. One peers through the single doorway connecting the newer and older structures, down a foot or more to the floor of the old cabin, to be erroneously, if doggedly, assured that the two were built at one time and as one structure.

In the summer of 1973 this sordid relic was offered for sale; for the house, exclusive of the land, the owner was asking $365,000. Americana, under the right operation, is good business.

American houses, whether Jesse James' cabin or Jefferson's Monticello, have not always been good investments, nor always the goal of sentimental journeys or the subjects of romantic prose. Even Monticello, when Jefferson died impoverished, was sold for $7,000 to be inhabited by the new owner; houses were maintained as residences, not as museums. Not until 1923 did the federal government purchase and restore Monticello; in the later nineteenth century it had been used in part for grain storage. Less elegant homes and homes with less significant associations were permitted to decay, particularly in sparsely populated areas; while houses in urban areas passed from family to family down the socio-economic ladder. In crowded cities, older homes, frequently substantial and even fine residences, were turned into boarding houses and tenements, in some cases converted into shops or insurance offices or funeral homes. Booth Tarkington expressed the metamorphosis from mansion to mortuary with a good deal of bitterness in *The Magnificent Ambersons.*

> Other houses had become boarding-houses too genteel for signs, but many were franker, some offering "board by the day, week, or meal," and some, more laconic, contenting themselves with the label: "Rooms." One, having torn out part of an old stone-trimmed bay window for purposes of commerical display, showed forth two suspended petticoats and a pair of oyster-coloured flannel trousers to prove the claims of its black-and-gilt sign: "French Cleaning and Dye House." Its next neighbour also sported a remodelled front and permitted no doubt that its mission in life was to attend cosily upon death: "J. M. Rolsener. Caskets. The Funeral Home."[2]

The preservation of historical American homes is a relatively recent phenomenon; Mount Vernon was not purchased for the purpose of historical preservation until 1859 and this unusually early date reflects not so much the interest in historical homes themselves as a tribute to Washington's status as a culture hero. To buy and restore a home requires financial support either from public or private sources, and financial support depends upon popular interest in the houses or in what they represent. The recent history of preservation attempts in New York and particularly in Chicago demonstrates the difficulty of saving older buildings, no matter what their architectural value, standing in what is determined to be the path of urban progress. Preservation is less difficult, of course, where soaring land values do not play a part and where historic association invests the structure with sentimental value; public outcry could be expected to unleash more fury at the projected demolition of the Betsy Ross house in Philadelphia than of Louis Sullivan's Auditorium in Chicago.

Architectural value is commonly insufficient to engage public sympathy; it certainly counts for a good deal less than age and romantic traditions. It is the connection of a house with an historical character or event that constitutes the "story" of that house, and it is the "story" that has always made the deepest impression on Americans either as tourists or as readers of the historical house essay. In tracing the development of this special literary form invented to describe the visits to famous homes, one can discover a great deal about the popular attitudes toward historic houses in America.

An unusually early report of such a visit, one that predates by half a century the literary house essay, is preserved in a letter that Samuel Eliot Morison has printed in his biography of Harrison Gray Otis. In 1801 Otis' wife Sally wrote her sister a long description of the trip they had made from Washington to Mount Vernon. The journey culminated when, "at half past two [we] surmounted all perils by land & by water and had the satisfaction to see on a beautiful eminence the Mansion of the great *Washington* and here description fails me." Her account is highly colored by her sense of the presence of the great man. It is all "we, in our most romantic moments have imagined of grandeur taste and beauty." "The house is antique like the inhabitant: capacious and substantial. . . ." They visit all the rooms with the gracious widow, and one notes the *frisson* typical of generations of Americans in scores of other such houses in her remarking "his own particular apartments his chamber where he died. . . ."[3]

Even more marked is Mrs. Otis' response to the grave:

> At the distance of a quarter of a mile is seen the Humble tomb of
> the illustrious Washington known only by the little willows &

cyprus that wave their melancholy branches over it. I walked down with a solemn and awful sensation to this sacred spot.[4]

Remembering that the Otises were acquainted with the first president, the reader may be struck by the solemn distance between Sally Otis and "the illustrious Washington." The emotions are not personal but institutional. Nevertheless, there is no concept at all of visiting a public shrine in the sense that we understand that today. This is a private house; after visiting the grave, the party takes breakfast with Mrs. Washington whose hospitality they have enjoyed. ". . . I assure you it was very difficult to get away. She urged us in the most flattering manner to remain a few days with her. . . ."[5] I am sure that Sally Otis could not have conceived of this private house becoming a public museum and monument.

A quarter of a century later, James Fenimore Cooper included a Mount Vernon pilgrimage in his *Notions of the Americans* (1828). His description opens with a detailed view of the mansion, and a detached tone is maintained. "The house of Mount Vernon is constructed of a framework, whose interstices, I am informed, are filled with bricks." Emphasis is laid on the overall simplicity of the residence. "Most of the furniture was of the time of the hero. It was exceedingly simple, though I thought it quite good enough, in fashion and in form, for a country residence." But Cooper soon succumbed to the emotional atmosphere: "More than once, as my hand touched a lock to open some door, I felt the blood stealing up my arm, as the sudden conviction flashed on my mind that the member rested on a place where the hand of Washington had probably been laid a thousand times." When he caught sight of a "leathern fire bucket" with "the words 'Geo. Washington' . . . legibly written on it in white paint," he was so moved as momentarily to see in his friend, Cadwallader, the spectre of Washington; "I felt the blood creeping near my heart with awe."

But the mystique of Mount Vernon rests not only on the fact of its having been Washington's home. In Cooper's description, association breeds resemblance; Mount Vernon reflects Washington, typifies and symbolizes his character. Cooper's encomium to house and man is particularly remarkable in view of the fact that Cooper belonged to a generation that had abandoned Greek Revival architecture in favor of Gothic.

The character of Washington was Doric, in all its proportions. Its beauty is the beauty of harmony between purpose and means, and its grandeur is owing to its chaste simplicity. Like the order of architecture to which I have ventured to ascribe a resemblance, it is not liable to the details of criticism. You see it in its majesty of outline, in its durability, and in its admirable adaptation to usefulness; but it rests on a foundation too firm, and it upholds a superstructure too severe, to be familiarly dissected. . . . Truth, bold, clear, and radiant, is the basis of his renown.[6]

An interest in houses and their stories first became marketable just before the Civil War. In 1853 Putnam's published *Homes of American Authors*, essays and sketches by various hands; this was soon followed by *Homes of American Statesmen*. The volume on authors focuses on the major writers of the day from Miss Sedgwick to Ralph Waldo Emerson. The essays are written by people of distinction, suggesting that there were bright hopes for this new literary form. After this period, very few books of house essays boasted such well-known authors as Henry Tuckerman, Rufus Griswold, Parke Godwin, E. E. Hale, and Mrs. Caroline Kirkwood, with William Cullen Bryant apparently warming up here for his editorship of a similar volume two decades later; the enterprise had all the aura of respectability. The review in *Putnam's Monthly* coyly noted that the title of the book would amaze as "It implies . . . that the ambiguous class of men called authors, may be in possession of *Homes,*—consequently of wealth, social position, and respectability."[7]

The Putnam's volume establishes the basic attitude and tone taken in the very numerous books of famous houses that would succeed it. The only significant change that occurs in the house essay form as it develops is a general increase in sentimentality and facile emotionalism. While the writers for Putnam's were capable of relative restraint, their essays revealed the major characteristics of the form: avoidance of architectural description of any sophistication and the employment of a narrative line which, wherever possible, connected the house under discussion to history and biography. The essay on the Craigie House is representative; furthermore, it provides a useful reference point, for no general volume could omit it. The perfect house, this beautiful eighteenth century mansion served as the headquarters of Washington and later as Longfellow's home. Age and beauty are provided with all the "association" one could desire. Built by Major Vassal some twenty years before the Revolution, it was abandoned when the Tory major decamped. After Washington's use of the mansion for his headquarters, a series of owners held it, the last of these Dr. Andrew Craigie, whose widow was forced to let out rooms. One boarder was the young Longfellow, recently appointed Professor of Modern Languages at Harvard. Long-fellow used Washington's room and bought the house soon after.

The narrative line developed in the Putnam's essay depicts the young Longfellow looking at the house, at the knocker on the door, at the paths in the garden and brooding on the romantic and historic past of the house. As he walked the paths, "Imaginary ladies of a state and dignity only possible in the era of periwigs, advanced in all the solemnity of mob-caps to welcome the stranger." Longfellow was next accosted by the acerbic land-lady, who did not rent to students; nevertheless, she bent so far as to place the young professor in "General Washington's chamber," a remark she made with a "slight sadness in her voice."[8]

The Craigie House is treated again in Mrs. Martha J. Lamb's *The Homes of America* (1879). Quotations from Longfellow's poetry supported the description of the house. For instance, in reference to Washington's occupation, Mrs. Lamb led the reader to the rooms most closely associated with the General and then added Longfellow's words, which "embalmed with dainty verse . . . historic memories."

> Once—ah once! within these walls,
> One whom memory oft recalls,
>   The Father of his Country dwelt,
> . . . .
> Up and Down these echoing stairs,
> Heavy with the weight of cares,
>   Sounded his majestic tread;
> Yes, within this very room,
> Sat he in those hours of gloom,
>   Weary both in heart and head.[9]

Mrs. Lamb concluded with a brief history of the mansion.

The Homes of America differs in significant ways from the *Putnam's* volumes. The quarter century between the two publications had witnessed the Civil War and the Centennial, both of which had their effect on the treatment of American houses. The Civil War prompted a profound nostalgia; the Centennial encouraged an historical sense. In the seventies, what can best be called a nostalgia-ridden sense of American history, spurred the writing of historical house essays. Some of these essays concentrated on the sentimental and personal associations of houses; others focused more closely on the houses themselves. In some cases, writers dealt generally with a type of domestic architecture found in one particular place or representative of one specific time period. At the same time, running counter to the celebration of the past, a belief in national progress led some writers of house essays to denigrate Colonial and early Republican architecture and to praise the "modern."

Although it is organized historically, Mrs. Lamb's study is primarily a celebration of progress. The book is divided into three parts: Colonial, Later, and Modern. In the first two sections, historical and architectural material outweighs the sentimental and romantic interests so typical of the earlier Putnam's volumes. Mount Vernon, for example, was introduced with the briefest allusion to its associational value: "Mount Vernon, reposing peacefully upon the Virginia shore of the beautiful river, is more tenderly familiar to the public eye than any other of the Colonial homes of America." After this single sentence, Mrs. Lamb turned to a brief history of the building of the house, a short account of Washington's life on the estate, and a single-paragraph description of its appearance."[10]

The houses of the modern period were placed within an altogether different frame of reference. Mrs. Lamb's thesis was the progress evidenced in American domestic architecture; therefore, modern houses, with their eclectic romanticism, were seen as an architectural and an ideological improvement over the homes of Colonial and Republican America. Early American houses, she determined, were interesting as a reflection of character and of early American society, but they "were neither notable nor typical of any peculiar moral, religious, social, or intellectual idea." In all these qualities modern houses excelled, for during "the present half century domestic architecture has been running a race with the general development and prosperity of America."

Cottages and villas now combined "the beautiful with the practical and useful" and revealed the "idiosyncrasies of the human character." Many of the modern houses "are in themselves the expression of sentiment, self-respect, and artistic culture."[11]

Mrs. Lamb's premise was reflected in nearly every house she treated in the Modern section. The "newer and more castle-like abode" of John Quincy Adams, for example, was held up in contrast with the old "ancestral residence of the Adamses." The ancestral house, whose old-fashioned simplicity apparently displeased Mrs. Lamb, seemed to call for every visitor "to don a powdered periwig, laced coat, and silk stockings, in order that the prevailing idea may not be disturbed." The new house made no such demands; furthermore, it had the advantage of being "elegant and showy," as well as being decorated "in accordance with the most approved modern taste and notions." Modernity won the contest: "Architecturally the two houses of the Adamses eloquently portray the contrast between the venerable past and the bright and cheerful present."[12]

Over all, romantic architecture and large expenditures were interesting to Mrs. Lamb. "Armsmear," the bizarre Moorish mansion of Samuel Colt near Hartford, Connecticut, was described as carrying "out no decided principles of architecture: like the mind of its originator it is bold and unusual in its combinations." Armsmear, generally considered to be one of the sillier pieces of domestic architecture in America, was considered here as a reflection of "the fine taste of Colonel Colt [which] is revealed in all the details and appointments of his mansion." "Ogantz," once the home of Jay Cooke, was noted as "one of the most expensive private residences ever projected in this country by an American citizen." 172 feet long, containing seventy rooms, "It is grand and impressive in its immensity," we are told, along with the fact that it cost over two million dollars and required $60,000 annually for upkeep.[13]

Mrs. Lamb closed her book with a statement of her aim.

. . . to show that domestic architecture as an art is eminently progressive in America; that its manifest destiny is to triumph over obstacles, and strike the perfect balance between a beautiful idea and the material form in which it is conveyed to the eye; that force of expression springing from strength of character in the inhabitant leads to the highest degree of symmetry between the dwelling and its surroundings, as well as to dignity of detail and permanent elegance in the building itself; and that with its historical and its personal associations it becomes a monumental language as impressive as it is suggestive and singularly interesting.[14]

The Homes of America stressed the significance of the house as an expression of individual character and historical association. The achievement of architectural beauty was evidence of American progress, even of "manifest destiny." For Mrs. Lamb, houses were neither incidental points of interest in the landscape nor convenient pegs on which to hang biographical sketches. They were the real and not the incidental focus of her book.

Picturesque America; or The Land We Live In, a work contemporary with *The Homes of America,* also celebrated the American past and announced American progress, but in *Picturesque America* there was no special concentration on the house as a unique emblem of either past or present. In this two-volume centennial work by various writers and illustrators under the general editorship of William Cullen Bryant, the contributors seem to come upon houses at random and then to work them into the general texture of national sentiment and national pride. In essays that constitute visits to cities or towns, for example, contemporary houses were noted for the social and economic progress they represented. Stamford, Connecticut, received praise; once "a simple and unattractive hamlet," it had become a "favorite resort of New York merchants many of whom have embellished its heights and knolls with elegant mansions and villas." Newport was admired for the splendid "cottages" now being constructed there, particularly when one recalled that only fifty years before it had been "a torpid, quiet place," a "forlorn, delapidated village."[15]

More impressive to the authors of the essays in *Picturesque America* were the new houses of Boston and New York. The domestic architecture of the rich was cause for patriotic pride. The suburbs of Boston boasted "estates which would far from shame an English duke who dated from the Conquest." In New York, Fifth Avenue was remarkable for its individual houses and for the fact that such houses stretched out over two and a half miles of the famous street.

. . . every city has as handsome a street as Fifth Avenue . . . but
no city has an avenue of such length given over exclusively to
wealth and elegance. From its southern extremity at Washington
Park to the entrance of Central Park at Fifty-ninth Street, the distance is two miles and a half, and, with the exception of the short
space at Madison Square, it presents through this long extent one
unbroken line of costly and luxurious mansions.[16]

The writers in *Picturesque America*, like Mrs. Lamb, found
Colonial and early Republican architecture disappointing, even
embarrassing. Mrs. Lamb, however, had placed these houses in
an historical setting and thereby developed some interest in them.
But in *Picturesque America*, not even historic sentiment can excuse such architecture. Providence, Rhode Island, was particularly
unattractive, having a great number of Greek Revival houses, and
"more *wooden* buildings . . . than can be found in any other place
in the United States." "The humbler sort of dwellings," found in
Providence, "were constructed after a very uniform model, and
that an exceedingly commonplace design. The same thing may
be said of most of our older New England towns."

Although in general, progress outweighed nostalgia in *Picturesque America*, under special circumstances these values could
be reversed. When a house could be connected with a particular
personality, and when that personality himself evoked sentimental emotions, standards of progress as well as standards of architectural interest went by the boards. Cooper had submerged his
dislike of Greek architecture in his emotional response to Mount
Vernon as the home of George Washington. But enthusiasm like
Cooper's that depended on personality rather than on architecture had previously been limited to the homes of national heroes
or major American writers. Furthermore, the houses in question
had an architectural value, even if an outdated one; at the very
least they had an antique charm. But in one essay in *Picturesque
America*, these attitudes are extended to embrace a run-down
farmhouse with no architectural value whatsoever. Sentiment
triumphs in "Scenes in Eastern Long Island," which takes us to
the home of John Howard Payne, the composer of "Home, Sweet
Home." To accompany the text, the illustrator provided two
sketches, one of the house itself and one of the kitchen with its
colonial hearth, massive fireplace, and old wooden rocker, the

symbolic American interior. The exterior sketch shows a common-place, fairly ramshackle farmhouse; if it is not precisely a "lowly thatched cottage," it can surely be seen as Payne's "sweet, sweet home."[17]

Payne left the homestead as a young man and spent his life abroad, in "homeless wanderings over the world." The standard story relates that in a period of deep depression following a series of failures in the musical world, Payne found himself leaving his dismal London garret on Christmas Eve to walk the streets. The sight of the Christmas crowds, of lighted windows and yule logs and wassail bowls of a highly Dickensian cast, moved Payne to return to his attic room and pour out his feelings in the song, "Home, Sweet Home." Actually, the song was composed for the score for Payne's opera *Clari, or the Maid of Milan.*

Whatever the provenance of the song, it swept America and left a trail of sentiment of which the comments in *Picturesque America* are only one example.

> It was truly a homely home; but, no doubt, many a happy hour was passed in the family circle around the bright blaze on the hearth, the simple joys of which were well calculated to inspire one of the best-known and best-loved lyrics in our language. Let no sacrilegious hand touch the old timbers of the precious relic! In a land where simple, happy homes are so abundant, it is specially fit that we should preserve the roof which sheltered one who has expressed the memories that cling around the hearthstone in words that thrill the hearts of millions.[18]

Threaded through this passage are scraps of the rich fabric that Americans had come to weave about the idea of the house: the joys of family communion around the hearth, joys which served to motivate the later lives of Americans once their destinies had removed them from that hearth; the ubiquitousness of such homes as well as their particularly American character; the yearning to preserve, even through such simple cottages, some material proof of the national past. In the rush of such national emotion, progress as a theme was altogether abandoned.

Although sentimental nostalgia was most easily brought to a house that had specific associations with a personality or an event, some writers in the seventies were capable of applying this tone to whole towns or to the older sections of large cities. For these writers, old houses in general expressed the quality of "association," a quality evocative of a vanished America whose values of stability and gentility had been lost. Thomas Bailey Aldrich wrote about Portsmouth, New Hampshire, for *Harper's* in 1874, showing that houses which had once appeared "commonplace," now possessed the glamor lent them by "association." "Many of these buildings were new and undoubtedly commonplace enough at the time of Washington's visit; time and association have given them a quaintness and a significance which now make their architecture a question of secondary importance." In fact, Aldrich approved this architecture declaring these homes the "solid and dignified abodes which our great-grandsires had the sense to build." Solidity and dignity have vanished, however; "The art of their construction seems to have been a lost art these fifty years."[19]

Again in *Harper's* (1874), John W. Chadwick wrote of Marblehead, Massachusetts. He did comment favorably on the improvement of the town in recent years, but added that while the new houses were handsomer than the old, the old had "a history" and "associations."[20] In 1879, a *Harper's* piece on Baltimore conceded even the greater beauty of simpler old houses. In Baltimore the "homes were those of old English merchants, blooming with the added grace of a warmer sun and sharper shadows. They were panelled and tiled, and spacious and secure, honestly built." The older houses stood for an older life-style, without architectural or financial pretenses; they were "not weighed down by extravagant excrescences either in the way of cupola or mortgage.[21]

The most popular form of house essay, however, did not treat houses in clusters or look for the appeal of generalized house-types. Americans were primarily interested in houses with specific personal associations and in essays that linked houses with romantic or historic biography. No eighteenth century mansion could compete, after all, with the house of John Howard Payne's childhood. House essays, therefore, abandoned architectural for associational values.

An index to the popularity to which the biographical house essay had risen in the early twentieth century is Elbert Hubbard's series, *Little Journeys to the Homes of Great Men*, which ran to fourteen volumes. Hubbard selected his subjects for biographical and moralistic interest. The first volume had focused on contemporary British figures whom he visited when abroad and interviewed. Subsequently, he developed each volume around one type of personality—American Heroes, Famous Orators, Great Business Men, and even Great Lovers, So insignificant was the house itself, that Hubbard included visits to the homes of heroes from Classical Greece.

Hubbard's overriding message was the goodness of the simple life, a message he included in nearly all his essays, from those concerned with national heroes to those focused on robber barons. John Hancock, for example, grew up in simple circumstances, a fact convenient for Hubbard's purposes. However, the son of a minister was also the nephew of the wealthy Thomas Hancock. John inherited his uncle's splendid mansion where, one assumes, he was delighted to live; certainly he enjoyed the life of a rich Bostonian and entertained magnificently. Hubbard could not deny Hancock's delight; therefore he turned his attention to Hancock's less affluent neighbors, whose relative poverty assumed a proper moral posture. "The Puritan neighbors were shocked, and held up their hands in horror to think that the son of a minister should so affront the staid and sober customs of his ancestors."[22]

Other writers concentrated on Mount Vernon when they came to a consideration of Washington; not so Hubbard, who established his purpose "not to show the superhuman Washington, the Washington set apart, but to give a glimpse of the man Washington who aspired, feared, hoped, loved, and bravely died." Therefore, he takes us in his imaginary journey to the house where George was born: "The Washingtons were plain, hardworking people—land-poor. They lived in a small house that had three rooms downstairs and an attic where the children slept, and bumped their heads against the rafters if they sat up quickly in bed." And when he came to Jefferson and Monticello, Hubbard shifted his focus away from the mansion to Jefferson's wife: "In laying out the grounds and beautifying that home on Monticello mountain, she took much more than a passive interest. It was 'Our Home,' and to make it a home in very sooth for her beloved husband was her highest ambition." To an extent, in the American imagination, "home" will take the sting out of almost any elegant mansion. Thus, Henry Clay's mother, whose second marriage united her with a wealthy man, was excused for such material considerations on the grounds of her seven children: "surely one cannot blame the widow for 'marrying for a home' when opportunity offered."[23]

However, the earnest morality of Hubbard's treatment of American Heroes did not take much sleight-of-hand; after all, many of these heroes had been dead a century and the popular imagination had already woven about them the tapestry of romance. A much more remarkable set of difficulties appeared when Hubbard turned to Great Businessmen like Philip D. Armour and James J. Hill. The most readily available technique turned on the morality inherent in the Horatio Alger myth, the assurance that hard work was a positive good and that its rewards were the manifestations of that good.

When these Horatio Algers could be demonstrated to have been born in poverty, or at least to a family with only a marginal income, Hubbard had found his material. H. H. Rogers' birthplace, already one hundred and fifty years old when Rogers was born in 1840, and where Hubbard went to take tea with the present inhabitants, did not fully qualify, but at least it was old and the rafters in the garret were hand-hewn. And Hill, about whom even Hubbard cannot be altogether enthusiastic, "has one credential, at least, to greatness—he was born in a log house." Other figures in this volume started their independent lives hard up; John Jacob Astor "lived over his store in Water Street," and James Oliver, the inventor of the chilled plow, who came to America from Scotland at eleven, lived with his wife in "a well-built cottage—not very large, but big enough for two. It was a slab house, with a mud chimney and a nice floor of pounded blue clay," for which he paid eighteen dollars. We are informed that it "was love in a cottage all right" when Rogers and his wife, following the oil strike in Pennsylvania, dashed to the oil-fields with enough hope or greed to live in "a one-roomed shack on the banks of Oil Creek."[24]

Hubbard took as his text for this romantic treatment of the self-made millionaire the words of Andrew Carnegie himself: "I congratulate poor young men upon being born to that ancient and honorable degree which renders it necessary that they should devote themselves to hard work."[25] Enthusiasm carried Hubbard through most of these pages permitting him to feel sure that no Homestead Strike would have occurred had Andrew Carnegie been in the country, and that H. H. Rogers, having been castigated by Ida Tarbell and Upton Sinclair, will be described as he really is in this sketch, the man whose life expressed "the complete American romance." Astor was congratulated for his generous patronage of Washington Irving, and A. T. Stewart, the New York merchant, accorded the nobility of soul that came with having earned his $40,000,000 by "legitimate trade" rather than through real estate or by inheritance.

But Hubbard was cautious, perhaps unwittingly, for with all the attention lavished on the early homes of these men, where descriptions of hardship could establish the conditions for greatness of character, the later mansions of these millionaires are, with one exception not treated at all, but simply ignored. The one exception is the St. Paul, Minnesota, home of James J. Hill. In the passage describing this house, the tone is strained and irony is neither clearly sustained nor altogether dispensed with.

> Mr. Hill's mansion on Summit Avenue, Saint Paul, was built to last a thousand years. The bronze girder that supports the staircase is strong enough to hold up a locomotive.
>
> Nothing but the best will do for Hill. The tallest flagpole that can pass the curves of the mountains between Puget Sound and Saint Paul graces the yard. The kitchen is lined with glazed brick, so that a hose could be turned on the walls; the laundry-room has immense drawers for indoor drying of clothes; no need to open a single window for ventilation, as air from above is forced inside over ice-chambers in Summer and over hot-water pipes in Winter.

Hubbard's comments are almost entirely restricted to such "marvels." Of the overall impression of the mansion we learn only that it is nearly two hundred feet long, "but looks proportionate. . . ." and that "It is of brownstone—the real Fifth Avenue stuff. Fond du Lac stone is cheaper and perhaps just as good, but it has the objectionable light-colored spots."[26]

It is apparent that the homes visited by Hubbard had in themselves little or no interest for him. Why then concentrate at all on the homes of these men; why not write biography in a more straight-forward fashion? The answer lies deeper than the mere availability of a popular literary genre. For one thing, the houses were a concrete and visual symbol of the American past, of the particular traditions that these thumb-nail biographies were based upon. For another, Americans had developed a strong metaphoric connection between a man and the house in which he was born, in which he lived or that he finally constructed for himself. Says Hubbard, "The clothes that a man wears, the house that he builds for his family, and the furnishings that he places therein, are all an index of his character."[27]

A belief in the organic relationship between a house and the man who had once lived in it is nowhere more emotionally expressed than in the house essays of Chesla Sherlock, the editor of *Better Homes and Gardens*, who published *Homes of Famous Americans* in 1926. Sherlock's criteria for the selection of material were, like Hubbard's, sentimental and moralistic. His overall theme, repeated in nearly every essay, was one of frantic patriotism. The houses of national heroes elicited particularly emotional responses from Sherlock. Lincoln's house in Springfield, Illinois, provided the best example. Sherlock first introduced the simple and unpretentious Abe: "He was a man, something of an average man, who lived in a house down on a corner lot five squares from the courthouse; a man who had a 'back-yard' just like thousands of other folks." In this vein, Sherlock retailed the anecdote of Lincoln's inability to find his own house when he returned from a trip, for during his absence Mrs. Lincoln had added another story—the poor fellow walked all over town asking directions to the Lincoln home.[28]

But the tragedy of Lincoln's death surpassed the narrative value of such downhome humor. We are taken to the museum room and there "see that bit of flowered-silk dress, *with Lincoln's blood-stains on it,* [that] comes as the great climax of your pilgrimage." Startling in this context is the next remark, so indicative is it of the fierce link between sentiment and property: "Through your tears, you realize that the man is secure in his place, and the homes of America are safe so long as we are willing to approach our problems in his unselfish spirit." Sherlock quoted Lincoln a few pages before this emotional end to his essay; the man who failed to recognize his altered house, this careless good fellow, becomes suddenly the very voice of property.

Property is the fruit of labor; property is desirable, is a positive good in the world. That some should be rich shows that others may be rich, and hence is just encouragement to industry and enterprise. Let not him who is houseless pull down the house of another, but let him work diligently and build one for himself, thus by example assuring that his own shall be safe when built.[29]

Not surprisingly, Sherlock had only antipathy for Benedict Arnold; his hatred for the traitor was so intense that it prevented him from finding any beauty in the fine mansion "Mount Pleasant" which appeared to him a "cursed thing." But the mansion provided a moral; the young Arnold bought it "in order to win" Miss Shippen, whose father was "the richest merchant in the colony." Such overreaching, social and financial, led to a desperate need for money; the original house had cost him, so it was said, $100,000. As Sherlock reasoned, "this house played a large part in causing his treason." So minimal are architectural considerations in *The Homes of Famous Americans*, that Sherlock can close the Benedict Arnold essay on the note of the victory of moral over aesthetic considerations: "We cannot appreciate its beauty or thrill at its architecture; we hurry as if pursued by its insidious spell. We would that we might sing its praises, and honor the man who once dwelt within its halls; but the challenge of his perfidy everywhere stares us in the face."[30]

Very few house essays adopt so negative a tone. The passage of time softens most American crimes and relegates most criminals more to folklore than to history. Mount Pleasant is open to the public and Jesse James' wretched cabin is a tourist stop; similarly, the great palaces of America's nineteenth century millionaires are treated within a special context that omits ruthlessness and develops in its place the American myth of success. Hubbard had treated his great American business man in this framework, creating biographies that closely resembled the forms of conventional fiction in delineating the rise from rags to riches. That convention is not defunct in the mid-twentieth century, when house essays continue to feature the houses of nineteenth century millionaires and to interpret these houses as fitting monuments to the success of the self-made man.

Cyrus Hall McCormick might well have felt some pride in contemplating the contrast between his luxurious mansion and the humble dwelling in Virginia where he was reared. [1941]

James Jerome Hill was born in a crude log house not far from Toronto, Canada, in September, 1838, of hard-working father and mother, both of whose parents were Irish immigrants. [1947]

Colonel Jonathan Hamilton became rich through retail trade "selling salt-fish, molasses, rum, sugar and tea to farmers in exchange for wood, timber, poultry, butter and eggs." He resolved to build the finest house in Berwick [Maine]. [1966][31]

Thus, up to the present time, the house essay has continued to work with the conventional forms of the American success story and to support a cluster of powerful American traditions.

By popularizing the traditional stories of famous houses and by emphasizing the belief in the organic relationship between a man and his house, the house essay has played an important role in creating an audience for historic houses in America. This audience provides a market for attractive and expensive books about historic houses; furthermore, from this audience come the great numbers of tourists who visit America's famous, and not-so-famous, houses. Once the house-as-shrine became a fact of American culture, it was possible for the category of "notable houses" to be enlarged to include not only the houses of great national heroes and of well-loved novelists and poets, but also houses of minor and even of unknown figures about whose homes stories could be shaped, stories that continued to enforce basic American traditions of diligence and its rewards.

An unusual example of this process can be found on Puget Sound where a whole town has become an historic house museum. Port Townsend on the Olympic Peninsula in Washington State looked in the latter part of the nineteenth century like the boom city of tomorrow. Not only was there an active shipping industry but the town was also under consideration as the terminal point of the Northern Pacific Railway in the early 1870's. That plan fell through, but in the 80's it appeared that Port Townsend would be linked by rail to Portland, Oregon. Land boomed all over the Northwest at this time and fabulous prices were paid for property in Port Townsend. When the bubble burst, Port Townsend was not even left with its illusions. All that remained were the ambitious houses of the late years of the century, some particularly grand, some smaller but extravagantly ornamented, all of them bearing the gaudy signs of optimism. "Adieu," wrote the author of *Canoe and Saddle,* "Adeiu, Port Townsend, town of one house on a grand bluff, and one sawmill in a black ravine."[32]

Today Port Townsend is a pleasant town in a resort area. Manresa Castle, the house on the bluff, built in 1890 for Charles Eisenbeis as an enormous tribute to his belief in the town, and in himself, now offers a "Royal Vacation" in its guest rooms, dining room, cocktail lounge, or ice cream parlor. The less overwhelming but far from modest Starrett House provides luncheon. Some houses of a more moderate size have been made into museums or antique shops, while the owners of other middle-class homes have been carefully restoring them. Local artists make sketches of these houses, and small stores sell notecards with reproductions of the sketches. The town is indeed pictur-esque, and it presents a pleasant irony, surviving today on the vanity of yesterday. If no one house has much of a "story," the town as a whole surely provides a tale: probably not a tale whose moral is the vanity of a vanished prosperity, but one in which the hero rises from defeat and through thrift and industry brings himself from rags to (modest) riches.

> This is the saga of Port Townsend. It is a history of the town and its people. But more than that, it is a case record. . . . the tale of this city symbolizes an American epic. . . . It delineates the spirit that founded, settled and advanced America. Values of independence, courage, hope and strength are found in abundance as this saga unfolds. These were the resources that settled and welded the United States. They are the culture and heritage that have been given to us.[33]

The House as Property
and the House as Home

> ... *Home ownership, by its encouragement of common family ideals and cooperation, by its development of family pride and self-respect and of community responsibility and active interest in neighborhood and community problems, provides, perhaps the chief training ground for family and civic qualities which are the source and conservators of our republican institutions and our national progress.*
>
> James Ford, *Slums and Housing* (1936)

> *No man who owns his own house and lot can be a communist . . . he has too much to do.*
>
> William Levitt, quoted by Eric Larrabee (1948)

For well over a century, Americans have developed and extended the metaphor of the house. The greatest attention, however, has been paid to houses that lie outside the range of experience for most Americans, to Fifth Avenue mansions and lower East Side tenements, to Southern manor houses and frontier cabins. In the manipulation of these stereotypes, writers have been able to isolate and express the specific sets of values important to them. Thus, the mansion frequently served as a symbol warning against the excesses of materialism, while the eighteenth century manor house came to represent tradition, history, and a lost world of elegance and refinement. Nevertheless, for most Americans, neither rich nor poor, the houses they have dreamed of and, perhaps, achieved lie somewhere well between the palace and the poorhouse. And in that dream house of what may be roughly termed the American middle-class, the values, the paradoxes, the contradictions carried in the symbol of the American house have all met.

Max Lerner has called the home "the most lyrical of American symbols." He catalogues the types of houses that lie at the extremes of the American imagination, but asserts the greater metaphoric potency of the typical suburban or small-town house.

> It may mean a sharecropper's hut, a tumbledown shack near the railroad tracks, an estate at Newport or on Long Island or the east coast of Maryland, a company house in a mining or steel town in West Virginia, a government housing project in Detroit, a Lake Shore Drive mansion near Chicago, a movie star's estate-cum-swimming-pool in Beverley Hills. But generally the image is that of the middle-class suburban or small-town home, with memories of pies eaten in the kitchen, a radio or TV set in the living room, a tool shed, a bicycle to ride to school, perhaps (in the earlier days) a swimming hole and sand-lot baseball games.

Lerner continues, "the fact that America has been so mobile makes this home idyl the more evocative," and adds that "It is not nostalgia alone that moves Americans but the longing for a social unity to stand firm in the wrack of a dissolving world."[1]

Lerner is correct in seeing that something beyond nostalgia informs and vitalizes the "home idyl." The idea of home in the American consciousness is a complex network of attitudes. In a man's house lies the evidence of his labor and thrift. There his family is raised in an environment that is, at least theoretically, created as an expression of that family's unique individuality. Beyond such personal and family values, the American house also represents the individual's link to his community and to the traditions of the past. Furthermore, both as an objectification of tradition and as the realization of property, the house has been a bulwark against threats to political stability and, therefore, a profoundly conservative institution in America.

But the conditions of American life have greatly complicated the meaning of the house as property, loading heavier burdens of symbolism on the family home. Traditionally, the conservative influence of property depended largely on inheritance. In America, where the house became the chief metaphor for property, conservative values were most naturally associated with ancestral homes, from the great manor house to the simple homestead. But the facts of the American experience have militated against the ancestral house. Furthermore, from the time of A. J. Downing a belief in the special meaning of the individual house, built by one man's labor to express one family's unique life-style, has successfully competed against the multigenerational homestead to become the typical, and the ideal, American house. Since it has not commonly been the physical house that passed from father to son, in its place a symbolic inheritance developed. In the family home, the son learns the virtues of industry and thrift, virtues for which the house itself is the tangible reward. The American inheritance, then, is the house as a model, a lesson, an incentive. A set of abstract values to be realized in whatever physical dwelling the son may acquire.

Nevertheless, Americans have continued to feel a longing for ancestral homes. Certainly the nostalgia that developed around old American houses, particularly the homes of national heroes, reveals a need for tradition. The Colonial Revival in domestic architecture, beginning in the 1870's, served a similar function, offering Americans new houses designed to suggest the old homes of the Colonial and early Republican past. Colonial Revival architecture, like the Colonial ranch house of contemporary suburbia, is an attempt to compromise between individual self-expression and historic tradition. But more is at stake in these architectural compromises than the need to supply Americans with spurious homesteads. For the great majority of American home-owners, there has long been an uncomfortable dilemma about the form and the degree of self-expression their houses might appropriately display. In a culture that reads houses as texts on character, taste, goals, and success, the purchase or construction of one's own home is an act of self-revelation.

Some critics of American houses have reacted strongly against the excess and vulgarity they have observed in domestic architecture. Behind their complaints lie strong elitist notions about the message a house conveys. A costly house built with new money is a kind of false witness, at least a form of hypocrisy. American houses, they argue, reveal only a man's economic status; furthermore, the new rich have been capable of disguising themselves architecturally, and of looking like the aristocracy of old family and old money. Ancestral homes would have prevented this situation, but America has few ancestral homes.

In 1889, Charles Eliot Norton wrote an essay called "The Lack of Old Homes in America." He lamented that "we have already lived to see the day when scarcely a man builds his house for his own posterity." In Boston and New York, "scarcely a house remains that was a home at the beginning of the century," and even those few remaining homes are not "occupied by persons of the same social situation." According to Norton, the "lack of hereditary homes—homes of one family for more than one generation—is a novel and significant feature of American society." This condition weakened social sentiment and loosened the bonds of genuine community. The individualism fostered by our egalitarian society, argued Norton, has caused the lack of old homes, for men choose to express their new success in the houses they build. Money would "buy the finest of new houses," he granted, "but it cannot buy the associations and memories by which life is elevated and enriched." In Norton's words, "we suffer as a result of the spirit of equality, and the practices, especially in regard to the disposition of property, that have resulted from it."[2]

Norton's essay is no simple exercise in nostalgia; it is a profound attack on the values of the individual house as A. J. Downing had expressed them. He believes that the construction of individual houses, replacing the ancestral homes of America, undermined the domestic and political strength of the nation, for he restricted to ancestral houses the values of moral and political stability. Without these attributes the individual house was symbolically devalued, and at the most extreme could be seen as no more than the raw assertion of a man's economic and social aggression. Those who viewed the fluid class structure of America with distaste, if not alarm, were affronted by the houses of men who had earned their way into the middle class.

As early as 1857, J. Elliot Cabot attacked the chaos of domestic architecture in America, a chaos Cabot attributed directly to the absence of fixed social classes. "Were our society composed of few classes, widely and permanently distinct, a fitting style for each would naturally arise and become established and perfected." Cabot wanted the American house to express not the individual character of its inhabitant, but the fixed social class to which he belonged. Ancestral houses and homesteads were, of course, a clear index to hereditary social position; new houses in America were not. Cabot pointed out that in a less fluid society "there would be fewer occasions for new houses."[3]

In 1876, Wilson Flagg wrote an essay on rural architecture in which he argued for the suitability of humble homes for humble people. He opened his essay with a sentimental description of a simple cottage and its inhabitants. The house is "homely," at best "picturesque," but it suits "this honest couple." The same couple, in "an ornate residence in the villa style," would be "ridiculous;" even the villa itself, because it was inappropriate for its inhabitants, would be "a false object on the landscape." The humble cottager, as Flagg describes him, can never rise to the villa; all the routes to social betterment are closed. The acquisition of wealth makes him vulgar: "Conscious that wealth alone can distinguish him above his equals, he seizes the first opportunity to gain distinction by building a costly house." Even aesthetic self-improvement is unavailing, for were this man to be "elevated . . . in refinement and taste" so as to suit his new house, there is still no guarantee that he would be similarly elevated "as a moral and intelligent being." At base, Flagg was arguing for the stabilization of social classes in America. The poor are different from the rich and ought not, therefore, build houses that confuse this distinction.

> An educated poor man in such a house might not seem out of place to one who is not aware of his poverty. But an ignorant man with clownish manners cannot live in a palace without making his personal defects both conspicuous and ludicrous. Yet how often do we observe that the most ostentatious house in a village belongs to some unlettered clown who has by a blind turn of Fortune's wheel become rich.[4]

Although Flagg's essay is atypical in its direct attack on the poor and its open avowal of the desirability of fixed social classes, his premises about the relationship between a man and his house, and his discomfort with conditions of free architectural self-expression, are not unique. Flagg's anti-egalitarian ideas can be found implicit in much American thinking, for essentially the problem raised by the individual house was one of suitability. If a man who had earned sufficient money could build whatever kind of house he wanted, what guarantee was there that his house was an honest expression of his class, his background, and his character? Ancestral houses made statements that could be trusted; new houses might well bear false testimony. However, the position taken by Flagg, his blatant distrust of egalitarianism, was one avoided by most American writers. Therefore, the question of the relationship between a man and his house was not generally raised in terms of social class, but rather in terms of moral or intellectual or aesthetic suitability. In such a framework, substituting moral and aesthetic values for socio-economic standards, a number of American novelists addressed the issue of the man and his house.

The classic American study is William Dean Howells's *The Rise of Silas Lapham*. Having made a fortune in paint manufacturing, Silas Lapham has left the old family farmhouse and moved to Boston's Nankeen Square with his wife Persis and their two daughters. When the novel opens, Lapham has raised his architectural sights and is engaged in a house-building adventure. He has hired an architect and purchased property on the "water side of Beacon," in Boston's prestigious Back Bay. The three houses emblemize Lapham's economic progress and his moral decline. Once a simple and unpretentious man, he lived in the old family house. With economic success came the respectable, but tasteless and unpretentious, house on Nankeen Square. But success has forced Lapham into ethical compromise; his fortune rests in part on manipulations that brought economic failure to his former partner. Success, furthermore, has introduced social vanity and tempted him with the vision of the house on Beacon Street.

Lapham does not deserve the new house. The money that pays for it is morally tainted. When Persis learns of the plight of her husband's former partner, she says, "Don't ask me to go to that house with you any more. You can sell it, for all me. I shan't live in it. There's blood on it." Furthermore, Silas does not deserve the new house aesthetically. His taste is vulgar and, in Wilson Flagg's terms, "an ignorant man cannot live in a palace without making his personal defects both conspicuous and ludicrous." On the farm and in Nankeen Square, Lapham's aesthetic vulgarity is comical but harmless ."The standard family photograph" of the Laphams shows them "in front of an old farmhouse, whose original ugliness had been smartened up with a coat of Lapham's own paint, and heightened with an incongruous piazza." In Nankeen Square, the household appointments are ridiculous, notably the statues of Prayer and Faith.

But in these houses, the natural habitats of the species Lapham, incongruous piazzas and sentimental sculpture are innocuous. On Beacon Street they represent a threat.

Once Lapham is bitten by social ambition, he attempts to plant himself, and his aesthetic standards, in an inappropriate locale. The architect whom Silas hires tried to educate his client away from his love of black walnut and "Ongpeer," but a tutorial in taste is no more effective than new money in turning the aesthetically "clownish" Lapham into a suitable resident of the Back Bay. Howells points up Lapham's unsuitability by contrasting him to the members of the Corey family, aristocratic, intellectual and refined in their Georgian house on "the handsome, quiet old street," where "the dwellings are stately and tall, and the whole place wears an air of aristocratic seclusion."

> [The house] has a wooden portico, with slender fluted columns, which have always been painted white, and which with the delicate mouldings of the cornice, form the sole and sufficient decoration of the street front; nothing could be simpler, and nothing could be better. Within, the architect has again indulged his preference for the classic; the roof of the vestibule, wide and low, rests on marble columns, slim and fluted like the wooden columns without, and an ample staircase climbs in a graceful, easy curve from the tesselated pavement. Some carved Venetian *scrigni* stretched along the wall; a rug lay at the foot of the stairs; but otherwise the simple adequacy of the architectural intention had been respected.

The Laphams can never achieve this; they cannot even recognize its value: "the place looked bare to the eyes of the Laphams."

Lapham's aesthetic vulgarity is more than an ironic enrichment of character. Howells raises the aesthetic problem as seriously as he does the ethical question, and in the crucial scene in the novel the distinction between aesthetic and ethical values is blurred. Business reverses cause a financial crisis for Lapham and only two solutions are available. He must either sell the still uncompleted house or accept a shady business proposition offered by a group of Englishmen. On the critical evening, Silas walks through his house. He tries to bring himself to the decision to sell, but the sacrifice is too great. Even the lamps along Beacon Street seem a "part of his pride and glory, his success, his triumphant life's work which was falling into failure in his helpless hands." At this point, the house is no more than a poster advertising Lapham's success. But suddenly he looks at the house as if with new eyes, and he approves "the satisfying simplicity of the whole design." Instinctively, as if some finer moral and aesthetic character were momentarily released in him, Silas sees the house anew. "It appealed to him as an exquisite bit of harmony appeals to an unlearned ear, and he recognized the difference between this fine work and the obstreperous pretentiousness of the many overloaded house-fronts which [the architect] had had him notice."

That night a fire destroys the house, a fire started by Silas's own cigar. Moreover, the insurance has lapsed. Silas is left without his house and without the money to begin it again. Nevertheless, in the face of this disaster, he finds the courage to turn down the Englishmen's "deep game" and for "standing firm for right and justice to his own destruction." Moral reform has been possible. It may well be that the momentary aesthetic vision permitted to Silas, the fleeting apprehension of "the satisfying simplicity," was the catalyst of ethical change. However, that vision was but momentary, and even a morally reborn Silas Lapham cannot be aesthetically recreated. In the plain house to which Silas and Persis now must move, a house with "all the necessaries, but no luxuries," Howells lets us know that the statues of Prayer and Faith are still to be found.[5]

Although the comparison of fictional characters with their creators is a dangerous business, in the case of Silas Lapham and William Dean Howells the comparison is worth exploring if for no other reason than the fact that the house on the "water side of Beacon," denied to Silas Lapham, was Howell's own new house. Howells, no more than Lapham, was a member of the Corey aristocracy with hereditary rights to Boston's Back Bay. His new house was his assertion of membership in a world far different from that to which he was born. On the other hand, Howells was no Silas Lapham. An editor and author, this midwesterner had earned the right to intrude upon eastern society. He had earned it not only with money, but with aesthetic cultivation and intellectual superiority. To an extent, *The Rise of Silas Lapham* is William Dean Howells's assertion of his right to a house on the water side of Beacon.

Among Howells's letters are three, written within twelve days, which report to different correspondents the news of his recently acquired house. For each letter, Howells struck a different posture, as if he were trying on modes of relationship to his new property. On August 10, 1884, he wrote to his father. The letter, later incorporated into *The Rise of Silas Lapham* as a social worker's comment on economic inequities, takes a moralistic view of the unfairness of class differences.

> There are miles of empty houses around me. And how unequally things are divided in this world. While these beautiful, airy, wholesome houses are uninhabited, thousands upon thousands of poor creatures are stifling in the wretched barracks in the city here, whole families in one room. I wonder that men are so patient with society as they are.

The same night, Howells wrote to Mark Twain. In this letter, the social critic made no appearance; instead, the hearty, masculine host took over. "I've got a mighty pretty house here on the water side of Beacon Street, and Mrs. Howells wants Mrs. Clemens and you to consider yourself engaged for a visit to us when my opera comes out in November."

On the 22nd of August, Howells was in Maine where he had gone to join his family. From there he wrote to Henry James, and a new character emerged, one who took an urbane and witty delight in the experience of tasteful living.

> It is a pretty house and an extremely fine situation . . . I have spent some desolate weeks in it already, putting my books on their shelves, while my family were away at mountainside and seaside, and I can speak authoritatively of the sunsets from the library window. The sun goes down over Cambridge with as much apparent interest as if he were a Harvard undergraduate; possibly he is; and he spreads a glory over the Back Bay that is not to be equalled by the blush of a Boston Independent for such of us Republicans as are going to vote for Blaine. —Sometimes I feel it an extraordinary thing that I should have been able to buy a house on Beacon Str.[6]

The Rise of Silas Lapham is not only a novel profoundly concerned with the problem of how fine houses are earned, morally and aesthetically, it is as well an indication of the insecurity felt by upwardly mobile Americans, even upwardly mobile editors and novelists, about the houses with which they expressed their success. It was not only a question of looking at the houses of others and suspecting them to be shams; it was also a problem of achieving a belief in one's own house as an honest projection of character. Because some novelists provide both fictional representations of this problem and personal histories of economic success, their double vision is a valuable insight into the insecurities raised by the individually-expressive house in a land without ancestral homes. In this context, the comment of Hamlin Garland is particularly poignant, as he explained his desire for a better house as "perfectly natural" in consideration of his "close association with several of the most successful writers and artists of my day. It was inevitable that while contrasting my home with theirs, I should occasionally fall into moods of self-disparagement, almost of despair."[7]

Mark Twain provides another example. Rather like Thoreau, Twain developed an idyllic metaphor for houselessness in Huck Finn's raft. On a raft, one is freed of the conventions of society; in the houses on the banks of the Mississippi, one gets civilized, and civilization means not only the piling up of sham amenities, but the explosions of deception, violence, and brutality that occur ashore. Twain could level cruel irony at the vulgarity that, in the American west, passed for gentility. To that end, he permits us to see the household of the Grangerfords, through the innocent eyes of Huck Finn.

> On the table in the middle of the room was a kind of a lovely crockery basket that had apples and oranges and peaches and grapes piled up in it which was much redder and yellower and prettier than real ones is, but they warn't real because you could see where pieces had got chipped off and showed the white chalk, or whatever it was, underneath.

But Twain had himself fallen under the spell of a more refined version of gentility. In 1874, he had his personal expression of the American house built in Hartford. Land, house, and furnishings cost over $120,000 in a Victorian extravaganza of bedrooms, guestrooms, billiard room, schoolroom, library, and the famous steamboat porch. If the Hartford house appears excessive to the modern eye, it did not appear so to Twain, who found it the perfect expression of domestic intimacy and home atmosphere. In the period of his bankruptcy and despair, he returned to the Hartford house and from there wrote to his wife Livy .

> How ugly, tasteless, repulsive, are all the domestic interiors I have ever seen in Europe compared with the perfect taste of this ground floor, with its delicious dream of harmonious color, & its all pervading spirit of peace & serenity & deep contentment. . . . It is the loveliest home that ever was. . . . when I stepped in at the front door —I was suddenly confronted by all its richness & beauty. . . . it almost took my breath away . . . the place was bewitchingly bright & splendid & homelike & natural.[8]

Twain and Garland and Howells were men without ancestral homes. For each of them, as for Silas Lapham, the individual house was the only possible expression of personal achievement.

The ownership of a house has, however, another profound cultural significance beyond that associated with economic success and the acquisition of property. In the privately-owned house exists the American home. The concept of the home has an extraordinary potency in American culture. To maintain the spirit of home is, in fact, to legitimize one's house. In a home the traditional family and community functions of the ancestral house can be carried out, whatever the physical nature of the structure. In part, the power of the home derives from its ambiguity; unlike the house, the home need not assume any particular architectural shape. A man's house may be tasteless, shabby, out-of-date, vulgar, too large or too small; his home is always above reproach, having only to be homey, home-like, and filled with home atmosphere. So abstract and sentimental is the concept of home, that apologetic millionaires have claimed it to describe their mansions, and a sweated laborer in New York's lower East Side could once have been flattered by having the term applied to his wretched tenement. Nevertheless, for the vast majority of Americans, house and home coexist; home flourishes most successfully in the privately owned, detached, single-family dwelling.

For over a century, Americans have accorded honorific labels to the term "home," calling it the "Christian home" and "the Anglo-Saxon home," with overtones both of historic association and racial exclusivity. In 1861 *The Monthly Religious Magazine* located the Anglo-Saxon home in New England. The writer asserted that the New Englander, "a man of special qualities," was the product of his home; in fact, "his Anglo-Saxon blood would have availed him little, but for his Anglo-Saxon home." The New Englander might be "cosmopolitan" in his maturity, but find him where you would, "his strongest instinct is his love for home."[9] Harriet Beecher Stowe was willing to extend the sentiment of Anglo-Saxon home feeling beyond New England to America as a whole and, of course, to England; no other people understood it. "Let any try to render the song, '[Home] Sweet Home,' into French, and one finds how Anglo-Saxon is the very genius of the word."[10] In 1892, Mariana Van Rensselaer asserted that "In their homes men of so-called Anglo-Saxon blood need comfort in a much more detailed, complicated, and varied sense of the word than is understood by men of Latin blood."[11] At the turn of the century, Joy Wheeler Dow contrasted Colonial Revival architecture with more modern styles in terms of the amount of "Anglo-Saxon Home Feeling" in each.[12]

Generally speaking, the American house can be seen as the physical architectural entity, and the home as the interior experience, including the decoration, the furniture, the atmosphere, and the domestic activities. Largely, though not exclusively, the house has been symbolically associated with the man who has earned it; while the home has been sentimentally associated with the woman who operates it. There has never been any careful attempt in American writing to distinguish so carefully between "house" and "home" as these generalizations might imply; nevertheless, an investigation of American materials over the last century and a quarter supports the overriding distinction between the man's house and the woman's home. In the mid-nineteenth century, when changes in the patterns of American work made it increasingly typical for men to spend their working hours away from the home, particularly from the suburban home, the full responsibility for the home fell more and more into the hands of women. With increasing attention paid to the experience of the home came a fairly rigid codification of the woman's role as home-maker. By 1869, Catherine Beecher and Harriet Beecher Stowe could call their domestic handbook,*The American Woman's Home*, and could dedicate it to women as home-makers.

TO
THE WOMEN OF AMERICA,
IN WHOSE HANDS REST
THE REAL DESTINIES OF THE REPUBLIC
MOULDED BY THE EARLY TRAINING AND PRESERVED
AMID THE MATURER INFLUENCES OF HOME,
THIS VOLUME IS
AFFECTIONATELY INSCRIBED.[13]

To create and maintain a home has been seen for over a century as a complex set of responsibilities. The Beecher sisters' book covers a wide range of subjects from material on the Christian family to chapters on scientific domestic ventilation, the proper construction and treatment of "earth-closets," and information about stoves, furnaces, and flues. An important section of the book presented detailed plans for a house that was convenient, healthful, and easy to care for, with particular attention paid to the plans for a workable, efficient kitchen. Homemaking was a serious and difficult occupation, and Catherine Beecher pioneered in designing an education to prepare women to carry out their domestic responsibilities efficiently and intelligently.

Because of the intimate connection between the home and the domestic role of women, the turn-of-the-century feminist movement appeared to a number of observers to pose a serious threat to the survival of the American home, and therefore, of the American family. A feminist like Charlotte Perkins Gilman perceived the home as a fatal trap for women. In 1903 she published *The Home, its Work and Influence* and made herself the enemy of every home-traditionalist. The cherished attributes of home, its privacy and sancity, she exploded as "domestic myths." The economy of home she called a fallacy, as was "that pretty fiction about 'the traces of a woman's hand.'" As for motherhood:

Our eyes grow moist with emotion as we speak of our mothers—and what they have done for us. Our voices thrill and tremble with pathos and veneration as we speak of 'the mothers of great men'—Mother of Abraham Lincoln! Mother of George Washington! and so on. Had Wilkes Booth no mother? Was Benedict Arnold an orphan?

Since Mrs. Gilman's goal was to free women from the house in order to pursue other careers, she had to demonstrate that both the house and the home could survive the woman's absence. Household chores, she argued, could be virtually eliminated if the residual household industries of laundry and food-preparation were turned over to professionals outside the home. This change would leave a woman free to work, and both husband and wife could return in the evening to "a clean, pretty, quiet home—not full of smell and steam and various messy industries." The home, too, could endure the absence of the woman, for a house with a woman waiting in it all day did not constitute a home. "It is a home *while the family are in it*. When the family are out of it it is only a house; and a house will stand up quite solidly for some eight hours of the family's absence. Incessant occupation is not essential to a home."

Charlotte Gilman denied, furthermore, the pious claim that the house was the center of moral learning and the seat of good citizenship. It was nonsense to conceive "that the ethical progress of man is a steady stream flowing out of the home." She argued that the first duty of women, like men, was owed not to the home but to humanity; in fact, "the true human home, is the round world." The truth was that in the name of home man plucked what he could of the fruits of civilization in order to carry them back to "the woman, content to receive." To grant dignity and honor to a man on the grounds of his being a "good family man" was to make heroes out of "burglars, meat-packers, and scabs."[14]

Charlotte Gilman was unquestionably astute in perceiving that the sentimental moralistic conception of the American home was the major obstacle to feminism. But in attacking this stereotype she brought on a storm of hostile criticism. In 1906 Mrs. L. H. Harris, identified only as "a Southerner," called Mrs. Gilman's theories "The Monstrous Altruism," and insisted that the true human home was not the round world at all, but "the cave, tent, tenement room or house where a married man and woman live and bring up children if they have them."[15] A 1909 essay, "The Home at the Basis of Civic, Social, and Moral Uplift," asserted the urgency of saving the home through the house and home functions of American women. "God himself founded the home when he created man and woman, each with different qualities but neither complete without the other." Therefore, "whatever places before a woman another sphere as preferable, whatever diverts her ideals to business or a literary or political career apart from the home is in the line of descent from what is highest."[16]

The celebration of the American woman as home-maker had its obverse side: the denigration of the American female as inept and extravagant householder. Both points of view indicate the increasing degree to which the house had moved into the woman's sphere. The facts of domestic experience in America did not diminish the significance of the house as an emblem of a man's economic achievement, but throughout the nineteenth century, evidence can be found to demonstrate that particular aspects of house-symbolism were becoming specifically connected with women. The middle-class wife or daughter, for example, was frequently portrayed as a demanding and foolish spendthrift, using her house as a means of social-climbing. Such women are parallels to Silas Lapham, but comic scolding, sometimes a rueful experience, generally solves the problem.

The stereotype of the vain and giddy woman, ambitious for a fashionable house, appears as early as the 1840's. Mrs. Tiffany in Cora Mowatt's *Fashion* is such a figure. In 1843 *Godey's* published a didactic story about the difficulties of Mr. Disney, beseiged by the pleas of his wife and daughter to acquire a country seat. The poor man had been pushed from house to house over the years of his marriage, and this latest request elicits the following complaint.

> There is no limiting the wishes of you women. When we first went to housekeeping, it was in a snug two-story house, twenty feet front, where I was quite as comfortable as I have been ever since; then, in a couple of years, I was argued into going to one of twenty-five feet . . . because your mother thought it would be more genteel. Next . . . I had to build a story, because the other girls lived in three-story houses; and at last . . . you wheedled me into putting up this [house], which is too large by half, and which cost three times as much as a reasonable and prudent man in business ought to have in dead capital.

Still, the country-house is rented, and there the Disney daughters run into some bad experiences, all of them laid to the house itself. The women learn that father was right after all.[17]

Harriet Beecher Stowe preaches much the same sermon in

her pseudonymous "House and Home Papers" for the *Atlantic* in 1864. The Crowfields have always had a pleasant house with a livable parlor. But the adolescent daughters now despair of that parlor, which according to one of them "has always been a sort of log-cabin, -library, study, nursery, greenhouse, all combined." The purchase of a new carpet begins the destruction of the friendly old room. New furniture must be added to suit the elegance of the carpet, and consequently many family activities are curtailed to spare the furniture. Mr. Crowfield moves to another room with his comfortable and shabby old furniture and before long the rest of the family follows him. Again, the women have been taught a gentle lesson.[18]

The popular notion, then as now, held that men like rather messy, comfortable houses and that women preferred to put on airs, an activity that not only undermined the cozy warmth of the house but cost money as well. The facts, of course, supported this assumption to the extent that men had certainly left the interior decoration of their houses to their wives, a situation with important ramifications. As more and more houses were built by contractors, in the cities and in the suburbs, both rented and owned houses tended to lack any real individuality. Hence, the unique character of a house was expressed in its interor décor, and the woman of the house chose the décor. The house that had been described from 1850 on as the expression of the character of its owner, the man who built or purchased it, gradually became an expression of the woman who decorated it.

By the end of the nineteenth century, female control of the house was seen as an American phenomenon. William Dean Howells mentioned it in his *Letters of an Altrurian Traveller* (1893-1894), and intruded a typical note of masculine tolerance for feminine willfulness. "In fine, the American house as it is, the American household, is what the American woman makes it, and wills it to be, whether she wishes it to be so or not; for I often find that the American woman wills things that she in nowise wishes."[19] In 1894, Price Collier addressed the issue of the woman and the house directly and without tolerance. In an article for *Forum* he compared the English and American home, Americans, he said, find that England is a country of men, while "Englishmen in America are struck by the fact that America is

the country of women." Women express themselves through
their houses here, but "it is the husband rather than the wife
who is supposed to advertise the family prosperity in England."
Furthermore, American men are discommoded and made uncomfortable by their houses because women use them solely for
their own benefits and pleasures. Compare England, where
"domestic economy . . . is devised for, and directed to, the aim
of making the men as capable as possible of doing their work.
The home is not a play-house for women, but a place of rest in
which the men renew their strength."[20]

While men grumbled, women became increasingly earnest
about their home-responsibilities, from domestic economy to interior decoration. Books were published on home decoration,
asserting the same domestic and civic effects from properly furnished houses that the pattern books had argued for properly
designed houses. In 1898 Edith Wharton, in collaboration with
Ogden Codman, Jr., published *The Decoration of Houses*. The
book was not intended as an aid to the selection of colors and
fabrics, but as a well-researched study on matters of consequence. The authors had consulted more than sixty books in
English, French, German, and Italian, dating from 1700 to 1895.
Decoration, they asserted, was a significant matter, the expression of one's intelligence and breeding. Tasteful decoration was
intrinsic to the creation of the effective family home. Beautiful
houses, furthermore, produced finer children.

> The child's visible surroundings form the basis of the best, because
> of the most unconscious, cultivation: and not of the aesthetic
> cultivation only, since, as has been pointed out, the development
> of any artistic taste, if the child's general training is of the right
> sort, indirectly broadens the whole view of life.[21]

The claims of Edith Wharton and Ogden Codman may seem
excessive, but they indicate the seriousness with which home-
decoration could be viewed. As a means of self-expression
imposed upon common-place, contractor-built houses, interior decoration permitted the middle-income home-owner a degree of
individuality otherwise unavailable. Furthermore, as serial homes
became more and more the norm for families in American
cities and suburbs, the furniture and ornaments collected by a

family were frequently a more permanent part of their life than was the physical house. An essay for the *Atlantic* in 1906 suggested that the intense preoccupation of Americans with both architectural style and interior decoration was an attempt to assuage the "strange homesickness . . . of those who have no background in the landscape of the world."[22]

The preoccupation with style and decoration is nowhere so pronounced as in Emily Post's *The Personality of a House* (1930). Originally published in the *Ladies' Home Journal, The Personality of a House* was a book for women, an audience recognized in even the most casual metaphor.

> A high-porticoed white-painted Colonial house on a windswept crag jutting out into the ocean is as unsuitable as an organdie dress worn out in a snowstorm. A low-flung building of massive boulders in a warm and tranquil valley is like a coonskin coat in July.

The American house, as Downing had described it, declared to the public at large the character of the man who built it. Emily Post's house now murmured to intimates the personality of the woman who might have built it, may well have purchased it, but who certainly had it decorated to suit herself.

Emily Post analyzed all styles of architecture and decoration in relation to the personality of the women who would "wear" them. "Formally balanced design" is suitable for women who "never glue or cut out or spread things about." But, if "you sit on the center of your spine, 'wear' a cigarette in the corner of your mouth, and dress in the latest exaggeration of fashion . . . then modern French or Viennese or American monolith is obviously yours." Miss Post was cognizant, if grudgingly, of the presence of men and children in houses; certain concessions had to be granted them. Men, for example, needed rooms not "easily spoilable" although this did not mean they had to be furnished with a room that expressed "solidity suitable for caging a grizzly bear."

The Personality of a House is a vulgar reduction of the idealistic belief in the subtle and intimate relationship between the house and its owner. Downing, articulating this ideal, spoke of character in the deepest sense. Emily Post devoted pages to cataloguing the color schemes most flattering to each of the three types of women, "blondes, brunettes, and mediums," and for the subdivisions of each type, "for instance, four types of blondes—the noonday blonde, the moon blonde, the drab blonde, and the red-haired blonde." The moon blonde, "one whose coloring is porcelain fine," must be very careful about the colors with which she surrounds herself.

> . . . robin's-egg blue at high light, apple-green, white, black and steel with emerald and lemon. But she must avoid strong values, which would wash her out. Feminine rooms suit her—French ones and certain very modified modern ones that are carried out in pale blues or greens or mauves and silver. Colonial, French, or not too imposing Georgian houses suit her best; or very little cottages furnished fragilely. In fact, so feminine should her own surroundings be that her husband should have a plain wood-lined room to counterbalance the rooms that are too obviously hers. But let him not have heavy Tudor or Jacobean furniture if she is to be admitted —ever.[23]

In spite of the frivolous and self-serving aspects of *The Personality of a House* and in spite of the petty reductionism apparent in Emily Post's concept of the house, the cultural belief in the value of the American house persists. "Every normal person," she asserted, "longs for a home." That longing had taken on a new dimension in the first third of the twentieth century, particularly after the First World War. The late nineteenth century belief in the power of the house to make middle-class property owners out of poor tenement-dwellers and to make Americans out of immigrants began to weaken. Those hostile to changes in American culture frequently discovered the cause of change in alien influence. What had once been a homogenous society was now a potpourri of different nationalities, and American values were struggling to prevail.

Some writers discovered the American house as a useful symbol in that struggle, specifically the ancestral house. Voices of conservative reaction turned to old houses, emblems of the traditional American experience, and deployed them as part of a nativist artillery against anti-American attitudes and theories. Didactic patriots hoped to use these houses to inculcate lessons in Americanism.

An example is provided by *The Homes of our Ancestors*, a

guide book to the American Wing of the Metropolitan Museum in New York, opened in 1924. To visit the American wing, devoted largely to rooms from old houses, was not only to admire Colonial and Federal architecture and decoration, but to be moved to a profound patriotism.

> Traditions are one of the integral assets of a nation. Much of America today has lost sight of its traditions. . . . Many of our people are not cognizant of our traditions and the principles for which our fathers struggled and died. The tremendous changes in the character of our nation, and the influx of foreign ideas utterly at variance with those held by the men who gave us the Republic, threaten and, unless checked, may shake its foundations.

The power of old American houses is such that, even viewed piecemeal inside a museum, they are capable of encouraging political and social assimilation and of protecting American ideals. "Any study of the American Wing cannot fail to revive those memories, for here for the first time is a comprehensive, realistic setting for the traditions so dear to us and so valuable in the Americanization of our people, to whom much of our history is not known."[24]

Seen in this context, Chesla Sherlock's *Homes of Famous Americans* (1926) is more than a series of sentimental tours of architectural shrines. When Sherlock promises that the continued security of America, threatened only by "dissolution . . . from within," will be assured "so long as the integrity of the home is preserved," he is asserting the political power of the home. Since the houses that he visits are shrines, he is implying that this political power resides most intensely in the old homestead and the ancestral house. Like the authors of *The Homes of our Ancestors*, Sherlock knew his enemy, the ideologically unAmericanized citizen. On visiting Paul Revere's house, he confronted this enemy in person. The route to the Revere house is "a pilgrimage in patriotism, a rededication to the ideals which have made this nation great, and which we must cling to if we are to continue on the journey toward our high destiny." But when he reached the street in Boston's North End, his mood of patriotic reverie was smashed.

> For North Square has long since ceased to be the residential center of Boston, or even the business place of native sons. It is in the

very heart of the little Italy, reeking with the odor of decayed vegetables and fruits, and alone and silent among the babble of alien tongues, I had literally to fight off the street urchins, jabbing an unintelligible tongue, as I took a picture of the house, and at one time they almost wrecked my camera.[25]

The concept of the ancestral, sometimes the historical, house as a bulwark of American values was also treated in fiction where the concept of the alien was somewhat more ambiguous, referring not only to immigrants or first-generation Americans, but to anyone outside a particular societal microcosm. Silas Lapham is alien to the culture of Boston's Back Bay; similarly, the Snopes family is an alien element intruded into the decaying aristocracy of Faulkner's Yoknapatawpha County. As ownership of a house signalled membership in middle-class culture, so American novels of house-acquisition often played with the theme of alienation and intrusion. But in the 1930's a new element appeared in these novels, reflecting the grim fact of dispossession in the Depression years. In Louis Bromfield's *The Farm* (1933) and Mary Ellen Chase's *Silas Crockett* (1935) old houses, old families, are sacrificed to progress, until at last the old family home is lost to aliens, and the traditional values of American society suffer a fatal blow.

Bromfield's work is obliquely autobiographical. Beginning with the settlement of the Ohio wilderness, the novel traces the history of a family and its home, known as "The Farm." The Farm is more an organic than an architectural entity, growing around the original log cabin by a process of gradual accretion. For the needs created by marriages and births, new space is created, or in the language of Bromfield, the new wing, "like the other wings, joined itself to the cabin." By the time that Johnny, the young protagonist of the novel, becomes aware of the Farm, it is described as "the rambling low white house [that] spread over the top of the hill and [was] enveloped by big trees, as if it had grown there and not been built at all." Although Johnny lives in town, he attaches himself to the Farm, "with a strange tenacity," as if it were "really his home." Toward the end of the novel, when Johnny's family moves out to the Farm, Bromfield states that it was "after all, the home of all of them. . . . It was from the Farm that they derived their inexhaustible vitality and their physical strength. From the Farm came the hunger for freedom and space which was in all of them."

The Farm is not the only house in Bromfield's novel. Houses
are placed like milestones throughout the work. In the town,
as it appears in the middle of the nineteenth century, the houses
create an atmosphere of "home." Some are of clapboard "in the
New England manner with bow windows on the second story;"
some of "brick, flat, retiring, and discreet, with shallow steps
of white scoured stone;" "there were even log houses." All three
types declare their allegiance to American tradition. One great
house, its architecture extravagant and individualistic, adorns
the town at this time; but although its Gothic styling has earned
it the name of Trefusis Castle or Trefusis Folly, it eventually
attains a "romantic and literary" charm.

However, the town changes under the pressures of the
modern world. Now Trefusis Folly stands between "sordid
streets lined with humble houses. . . . All round it were the
houses of the mill-workers, abandoned respectable houses belonging to another day, used now as rookeries and falling into
ruin, or cheap new dwellings surrounded by patches of yellow
clay." Another rich man has built another great house, but unlike the Trefusis house, it is "uncompromisingly ugly," as befits
the house of a man who made his fortune "during the looting of
New Orleans." Even the old New England-style houses, with
"a look of having been there forever," seem old, with "cold . . .
grim facades. . . . And the people who lived in them seemed
all to be old women who were widows." The houses in the
newer sections of town are even less satisfactory, "the bastard
offspring of strange matings of styles." Unlike the older houses,
they had no "air of belonging to the earth," but were instead
"monuments to the era of McKinley and Hanna, Aldrich and
Foraker. The strange mongrel fortresses were the strong-holds
of men who lived by the faith that any man was a fool not to
make as much money as possible."

These houses, and the world they represent, are the survivors
in modern America; the old houses, like the old world, are
doomed. Trefusis Castle is torn down and not long after the
Farm is sold "to a man who bought it as speculation because
now it was within the sound of the mills." Progress appropriates
the ancestral home of Johnny's family, and Johnny's inheritance
is no more than the knowledge of what tradition means, how
it has, "in other countries . . . kept generation after generation

living upon the same land." But "such a continuity was impossible in the country in which he had been born." In Johnny's world "nothing was allowed to grow old, because it was always being overtaken by change and progress. There was no room for old houses, for old customs, or for old habits of mind."

The Farm is a cry of despair for a world Bromfield, like Johnny, knew only in its death throes. Only the Farm has remained from that older world: an organic house, growing on and out of the land, sheltering its family. It is homestead, the center of family strength and solidarity through a number of generations. In the last scene of the novel, Johnny returns after a dozen years to see the Farm. The speculator has continued to lease it to tenants, and now Johnny finds "a flat-faced woman with a cotton handkerchief tied over her head. She only spoke Polish." Johnny does not stay long to witness the alienation of his family homestead. "There was too much of desolation," and even the garden has fallen to ruin, "filled now with nettles and Spanish needles and beggar's-lice."[26]

In Mary Ellen Chase's *Silas Crockett*, as in Bromfield's book, the ancestral home is a victim of progress, a prize for the alien. The novel deals with four or five generations of the Crockett family but concentrates on Reuben in whose old age the family house is sold. Through the eyes of the young Reuben we first see the Crockett house.

> Built and furnished by Amos Crockett as a wedding gift for his son in the last years of the seventeen hundreds from the profits and products of foreign voyages . . . it was now suffering the inroads of time and the reverses of fortune.

> And since Reuben had never known the house as it had been in his grandfather's boyhood and even in his father's, it seemed to him the most satisfying of houses. He conceived, in fact, a premature affection for it, seeing in it far more than the place of warmth and protection accepted by most children when they think of home . . . feeling a surge of pride throughout his body, not only because it was his home but because it was stately and beautiful.

The Crockett house, unlike the Farm, is no organic accident of time and family growth; rather, it is the careful architectural construction of the eighteenth century and the product of economic success. With the end of the great shipping fortunes, came the end of the era of "great white houses, which voyages to the Far East had built," and now these houses "passed one by one through the lawyer's hands to men from Philadelphia and Boston and New York." These city people are themselves aliens, but in Chase's world there are degrees of alienation. Reuben's grandmother, Solace Winship Crockett, is forced to sell her father's house, but she does not sell it to "a man from St. Paul, who had offered her a larger price," but to "two maiden ladies from Boston," who were New England people and appreciated the home. In time, the Winship house is sold again, at auction, "passing to the local manager of the Atlantic and Pacific Tea Company, who was slowly paying back his borrowed capital by renting rooms to the chauffeurs and gardeners of neighboring estates."

As the "neighboring estates" imply, money is being made in the world of the Crockett family, but not by the old members of this traditional society. The Crocketts themselves descend into ever deeper poverty. The house, once refurbished with the money from the sale of the Winship home, falls again into disrepair. Reuben is forced to find money where he can and little by little he sells off his heritage. First the family portraits, sold to a Mr. Schwartz whose city origins and Jewish name mark him as an alien. The furniture from the front bedroom follows. Eventually the house itself is sold. Like Bromfield, Chase closes her novel with the visit of Reuben's son Silas to the old house. Unlike the Farm, the Crockett house has not fallen into ruin and decay. On the contrary, a new elegance has been superimposed on its antique dignity, but this very elegance demeans the house and cuts it off from its past. The fields around the house have been graded and turned to lawn, the meadows transformed into a small golf course. The old woodbine and lilac at the front door are gone, replaced by sophisticated cedars and evergreen shrubs. As for the interior of the house, whatever changes have been made remain a secret. A servant comes to the door and Silas explains that "my father owned this house and all my family. Would it be possible for us just to come into the house and see if it's as it used to be?" He is denied entrance.[27]

The Farm and *Silas Crockett* can be seen as responses to the specific insecurities of the 1930's, to the foreclosures and evictions that created a newly homeless population. However, these works do not deal with the social and economic crisis of the loss of shelter; they specifically rehearse the tragedy of the loss of the ancestral home, the center of family tradition and the emblem of the tie with the past. In a time of cultural instability and fear, it is not surprising that the house symbol should have taken the particular shape of the ancestral home and that despair should have been expressed in the metaphor of the loss of the homestead. Nevertheless, the ancestral home has never been the typical American house, which has been, and remains, the house earned by one man's work and built to shelter his wife and children. The sense of tradition and stability provided by the ancestral home cannot compete with the meaning of the earned, individual house.

In 1931, President Herbert Hoover told the Conference on Home Building and Home Ownership: "That our people should live in their own homes is a sentiment deep in the heart of our race and of American life." In his address to the Conference, Hoover went on to celebrate the great benefits that home-ownership brought to individuals and to the society as a whole.

> Every one of you here is impelled by the high ideal and aspiration that each family may pass their days in the home which they own; that they may nurture it as theirs; that it may be their castle in all that exquisite sentiment which it surrounds with the sweetness of family life. This aspiration penetrates the heart of our national well-being. It makes for happier married life, it makes for better children, it makes for confidence and security, it makes for the courage to meet the battle of life, it makes for better citizenship. There can be no fear for a democracy or for self-government or for liberty and freedom from home owners no matter how humble they may be.[28]

Nowhere did Hoover allude to the ancestral home; on the contrary, all the functions of the homestead are here ascribed to the individual house. In fact, it is specifically and uniquely the individual house than can attain the character of home. As the report of the conference expresses it, "A 'home' . . . must have personality; it must symbolize the group that occupies it."

One avowed purpose of the Conference on Home Building

and Home Ownership was to encourage more Americans to purchase their own houses. Although "a family usually has a natural desire to own such a home," incentives for home-owner- ship needed to be developed and extended to more and more American families. The promotion of home-ownership promised significant advantages. The home-owner, of course, would bene- fit in his family life, his economic stability, and his self-image. But there were advantages as well for the community as a whole and these were political.

> Probably nothing creates greater stability in government than a wide distribution of property ownership on the part of the people interested in that government.

> It is doubtful whether democracy is possible where tenants over- whelmingly outnumber home owners. For democracy is not a privilege; it is a responsibility, and human nature rarely volunteers to shoulder responsibility, but has to be driven by the whip of necessity. The need to protect and guard the home is the whip that has proved, beyond all others, efficacious in driving men to dis- charge the duties of self-government.[29]

Property is the great conservative influence, and in America the house is property. The home-owner is proof against the sub- version of American values and is, therefore, the defense of democracy.

In its rhetoric Hoover's Conference reenforced all the values associated with the American house, but the Depression and the Second World War prevented any major implementation of its programs. In the 1950's, however, the construction of small, suburban homes became a major industry and Levittown a pro- totype of the new American domestic environment. Levittown and similar suburban developments, with the aid of FHA financing, made the ideal of the privately-owned, detached, single-family house a reality for millions of Americans. Critics protested, however; suburbia became a new menace to American culture, for it sacrificed individuality to the economic advantages of mass-production. What Herbert Gans has called the "myth of suburbia" threatened a new conformity and sterility, of which the symbol was the small, private house on a street of many small, private houses whose minor variations in decoration could not disguise their mass-produced similarity.

Sociologists, social critics, and novelists attacked the mass-produced life of the mass-produced suburb. Gans' study, *The Levittowners* (1967), set out to correct the prejudice and error inherent in this view of the American suburb. Gans proved that for most of the Levittowners their lives provided pleasure and contentment. Not the suburb itself, but the owned house in which the family lived, supplied the principal source of this contentment. The benefits and pleasures enjoyed in these houses were essentially the benefits and pleasures American houses had provided for well over a century; they were property and they were home.

Contentment results principally from home-ownership, however, particularly among men. Aside from the acquisition of property and its monetary value, ownership brings the freedom to do as one pleases and to indulge in forms of self-expression inside and outside the house that are not available to a tenant; it permits or encourages familial 'settling down' and provides a public symbol of achievement, 'something to show for all your years of living,' as one Levittowner pointed out.[30]

William Levitt's use of modern technology made Levittown possible, but modern technology strikes no chords of tradition and association. Therefore, in the styling of Levitt's houses, contemporary technology was masked with imagery that served the American idea of home. Three basic house types made up Levittown. One of these, "The Rancher," harked back to the turn of the century Bungalow, though with modern touches. The other two types echoed Colonial American styles; one was a story-and-a-half Cape Cod, the other a two-story Colonial. In these houses, Levitt offered buyers a symbolic link with the past and the ancestral home. Like the houses inspired by the Colonial Revival of the 1870's, the Cape Cods and Colonials of Levittown have an aura of tradition and association. Although a family may buy such a house planning to inhabit it for as few as five years, the historical styling politely ignores their transience and provides an architectural symbolism that speaks of stability and permanence.

Like the Colonials and Cape Cods of Levittown, most American houses today use their architectural and incidental iconography[31] to signal a complex personal and social message, for in many ways the American house has become more symbol than reality. The individual house is often no more than one in a series of houses; yet it assumes to itself the values once accorded only the ancestral house, establishing itself as the temporary representation of the ideal permanent home. These houses, furthermore, stand for property, despite the fact that most are held by banks to whom the residents pay mortgages. These serially-owned, bank-held houses are, with increasing frequency, the unindividualized results of mass-production and design. Yet, a man's house is still considered the expression of his own taste and character, and men and women find in their homes the greatest opportunity to express their personal taste. The activities of the house, as well, have changed. Home industries have long since vanished and home functions of child-rearing, education, and care for the sick and elderly have passed to public institutions. Only laundry and food preparation remain, and should they disappear as Gilman suggested over seventy years ago, the home would survive their departure.

In the last century and a half a great many changes have occurred in the physical house. Once fashionable styles are now quaint survivals, and technology has altered techniques of construction. But the symbolic house in America remains virtually unchanged. The aspirations and satisfactions experienced by the man who lived in one of A. J. Downing's Gothic cottages are the aspirations and satisfactions of today's suburban householder, whose house remains the evidence of property and the emblem of home.

❖   ❖   ❖

It is not within the compass of this book to examine the house, real or ideal, in the 1970's; however, it seems appropriate to look briefly at houses and housing in contemporary America in order to indicate how powerfully our cultural ideals about the house continue to operate. Styles of architecture and methods of construction may change, technology or radical politics may offer physical or social alternatives to the traditional house, but the cultural conventions attached to the American house remain unchanged. Mobile homes and condominiums, communes and subsidized housing may appear to undermine the ideal of the privately-owned, single-family, detached dwelling; in fact, such contemporary solutions to the dilemma of housing in America are in themselves either reflections of or responses to the values and the contradictions inherent in American ideas about houses for over a century.

The concept of the home, profoundly associated with the idea of the family, is obviously threatened by the commune. Just as clearly, the commune subverts the idea of private property. It is probably the most radical solution to the need for shelter, both in the sense of its romantic recall of simple, primitive society and in its disavowal of property-ownership and family ties. But the commune is no new concept in America. Such experiments have been conducted for over a century and a half and have consistently been condemned by conservative Americans who overtly deplored the break-up of the family and covertly feared for the sanctity of property. In the 1970's, as in previous periods in our history, communal living provides a corrective to materialism and individualism, but it is extremely unlikely that communes will have any more significant an impact on the values of house and home in contemporary America than they have had in the past.

"Commune," with its overtones of political radicalism and social unity, may be contrasted with "condominium," a word heavy with legal and Latinate burdens. In a condominium, one property is not held in common by a group, but divided in such a way that each portion may be privately held. The "cubicles in rows or shelves on shelves," rental flats at which Frank Lloyd Wright leveled his contempt, are now available for ownership. Such rectangles, may not supply the requisite sentimental association, but they serve a hard economic purpose. To own a condominium is to enjoy all the tax benefits that accrue to home-owners in America, and from which renters are excluded. It is legally property-ownership, and as such it affords its owners all the real and the subtle privileges once connected with the holding of "real" property. The house supplanted the land in America as a symbol of property; now the "house" may lie poised tens, even hundreds, of feet above the land, land which is itself probably not owned at all, but leased for ninety-nine years.

The condominium is one solution to the ambivalence Americans have felt about apartments from the time in the nineteenth century when "French flats" were first introduced to this country. Flats were an improvement, of course, over the boarding house in which there was no hope whatever of preserving the qualities of family life. At least in an apartment, the family food could be prepared and eaten in family privacy. But many Americans doubted that childrearing was possible in a flat, and as late as 1930 Herbert Hoover denied that such fine old American songs as "Home on the Range" and "Home, Sweet Home" could have been written about apartments or tenements. Americans have always been conservative about the physical shape of the ideal house, and apartment flats failed to supply the qualities associated either with home or with property.

While apartment-living has gained respectability since the end of the nineteenth century, the renter has never been afforded the full status of the owner. At the bottom of the social scale of renters are those who live in subsidized flats. More has been done in the second half of the twentieth century than in any previous period in American history to alleviate substandard housing conditions for the urban poor; nevertheless, the prejudices of the nineteenth century have not been eradicated. A hundred years ago, men feared that industry and thrift would disappear if housing were provided to those unable to earn it. Under the threat of social disorder, the twentieth century has learned to provide shelter without status, to deny the residents of subsidized housing the special values and meaning of home-occupancy. Any number of architects and social critics have pointed out the drab mediocrity of public housing, which seems to have been designed as a public denial of individuality either in achievement or in expression. The necessities are provided: air, light, plumbing; but subsidized housing never looks quite like other high-rise buildings where the tenant, in compliance with our cultural system of values, bolsters his marginal respectability by paying the rent.

Urban living is not altogether restricted to high-rise buildings. Some cities have preserved elite neighborhoods of fine town houses, although even in Boston's Back Bay, Chicago's near North Side, and San Francisco's Telegraph Hill, older homes are remodeled as multiple-family dwellings. Elsewhere, reconstruction has rescued the decayed residences of the past.

Philadelphia's Society Hill is a remarkable example of the recreation of a chic neighborhood; behind the chaste facades of eighteenth century town houses, the well-to-do enjoy all the benefits of twentieth century technology. The interest in old urban areas has been spurred by historic as well as economic interests; furthermore, the lack of urban space and the high cost of new construction have been influential, as has America's continuing nostalgia for its own past. That nostalgia has influenced not only the resurrection of such unique areas as Society Hill. In older suburbs, once unfashionably close to the city center, turn-of-the-century houses are being purchased by families who remodel them in arduous weekends of plastering and painting. These rambling graceful structures are a recent object of sentimental admiration, their casual spaciousness now evocative of a more genteel and gracious era.

For the would-be owner with a limited amount of money, technology has provided another possibility—the mobile home. Prefabricated and streamlined, the mobile home is a remarkable example of the ability of Americans to create new forms of shelter and to bedeck them with symbolic trappings. Like other prefabricated, mass-produced houses, the mobile home is decorated with the imagery appropriate to the American house: aluminum siding that resembles frame, non-functional shutters, perhaps a picture window and an awning stretched out to describe a porch. Parked in a small settlement resembling a miniature suburb, and set on a tiny plot of grass, the mobile home becomes a perfect replica of the suburban house. For it is the suburban house that remains for the great majority of American families the closest approximation to the ideal house.

Over all, the symbol of the house has played a beneficial role in American culture. To invest the house with the values once associated only with real property was to make available to a very great percentage of the population the status of property-owner, and thereby to establish a rough egalitarianism supportive of the democratic ideals of America. Furthermore, although the full achievement of the goal of home-ownership, the possession of a single-family, privately-owned, detached house, may elude a number of Americans, the extension of the symbolic values associated with home-ownership to the mobile home or the condominium or the heavily-mortgaged ranch house, has meant the extension of the concept of property-ownership and, hence, of full membership in the society. Moreover, for many American families the ideal house represents a future possibility, one worth working for, one they intend to achieve. Since that achievement is far from unlikely, the symbolism of the house has significance even for those who have not yet enjoyed their own home.

However, because the significance of home-ownership depends on the economic self-sufficiency of the home-owner, Americans have never solved the problem of the housing of the poor. As if to preserve the potency of a primitive totem, Americans have insisted that the privilege of home-ownership be earned. Grudgingly, we have admitted that "home" may exist in any shack or tenement, and gracelessly we have extended the necessities of shelter to those economically disqualified from ownership. But shelter unearned and unowned fails to carry the cultural values associated with the house in America; for at the very roots of the symbol of the American house lies the fact of property.

Notes

Chapter One

1. William Bradford, *Of Plymouth Plantation,* ed. Harvey Wish (New York, 1962), pp. 59-60.

2. Edward Johnson, *A History of New England [Johnson's Wonder-Working Providence: 1628-1651* (1654)], ed. J. Franklin Jameson (New York, 1910), pp. 113-14. For a thorough study of shelter in the early settlements see Fiske Kimball, *Domestic Architecture of the American Colonies and of the Early Republic* [1922] (New York, 1966).

3. *Travels and Works of Captain John Smith,* ed. Edward Arber, rev. ed., by A. B. Bradley, 2 vols. (New York, n.d.), I, 95. Arber glosses "castles in the air" to mean that the settlers lived in trees; such an unfounded assumption is seriously undercut by Bradford's use of the same expression to mean, as in the modern cliche, that there were no houses at all. See *supra,* p. 10.

4. *John Winthrop's Journal,* ed. James Kendall Hosmer, 2 vols. (New York, 1908), p. 58.

5. *Records of the Governor and Company of the Massachusetts Bay,* ed., N. B. Shurtleff (Boston, 1853-1854), I, 74; quoted in Harold Robert Shurtleff, *The Log Cabin Myth,* ed. Samuel Eliot Morison (Cambridge, Mass., 1939), pp. 47-48.

6. Shurtleff, *The Log Cabin Myth,* pp. 16, 20.

7. *A State of the Province of Georgia* (London, 1742), pp. 4, 5; in Peter Force, *Tracts and Other Papers. . . . ,* 4 vols. [1836] (Gloucester, Mass., 1963), Vol. I.

8. Johnson, p. 210.

9. William Wood, *Description of Massachusetts* [1633], in Alexander Young, *Chronicles of the First Planters of the Colony of Massachusetts Bay, from 1623 to 1636* (Boston, 1846), p. 412.

10. Johnson, p. 68.

11. Smith, I, 82-83, 154.

12. John Hammon, *Leah and Rachel, or the Two Fruitfull Sisters, Virginia, and Mary-land* [London, 1656], p. 7; in Force, Vol. III.

13. Smith, I, 96(repeated II, 392), I, 121.

14. Winthrop, p. 77.

15. Bradford, pp. 48-49.

16. Bradford, p. 94.

17. William Hubbard, *History of New England, Collections of the Massachusetts Historical Society,* 2nd series, VI (1815), 334; quoted in Fiske Kimball, *Domestic Architecture,* p. 12; and in his "Architecture of the Colonies and Early Republic," *American Historical Review,* XXVII (1921), 48.

18. Norman M. Isham and Albert F. Brown, *Early Connecticut*

Houses [1900] (New York, 1965), p. 95; Kimball, however, asserts that the "fragmentary and sometimes inconsistent data concerning these houses . . . do not permit reliable conclusions regarding their form," *Domestic Architecture*, p. 12.

19. *The New Life of Virginea* [1612], p. 10; in Force, Vol. I.

20. Smith, II, 507.

21. Hammon, p. 7.

22. Robert Beverley, *The History and Present State of Virginia* [London, 1705; 1722], ed. Louis B. Wright (Chapel Hill, North Carolina, 1947), p. 48 .

23. Bradford, pp. 90-91.

24. *Mourt's Relation. A Relation or Journall of the beginning and and proceedings of the English Plantation settled at Plimoth in New England* [London, 1622] (Ann Arbor, Mich., 1966), p. 26.

25. Cotton Mather, *Magnalia Christi Americana; or, The Ecclesiastical History of New England* (Hartford, Conn., 1855), p. 80.

26. Robert Beverley, *The History and Present State of Virginia* [London, 1705; 1722], ed. Louis B. Wright (Chapel Hill, N. C., 1947), pp. 289-90.

27. William Byrd, *The Prose Works of William Byrd of Westover*, ed. Louis B. Wright (Cambridge, Mass., 1966), pp. 23, 143, 147, 175.

28. Byrd, pp. 143, 311.

29. Byrd, p. 173.

30. Timothy Dwight, *Travels in New England and New York* [1821], ed. Barbara Miller Solomon (Cambridge, Mass., 1969), p. 155.

31. Samuel Sewall, *Samuel Sewall's Diary*, ed. Mark Van Doren (New York, 1963), p. 106.

32. Cotton Mather, *Diary of Cotton Mather, Vol. I: 1681-1709, Vol. II: 1709-1724*, ed. Worthington Chauncey Frod (New York, 1957), I, 266, 343; II, 124.

33. Mather, II, 630.

34. James Truslow Adams, *Provincial Society, 1690-1703*, Vol. III of *A History of American Life*, eds. Arthur M. Schlesinger and Dixon Ryan Fox, 12 vols. (New York, 1928), pp. 19-20.

35. Vincent Scully, "American Houses: Thomas Jefferson to Frank Lloyd Wright," in *The Rise of an American Architecture*, ed. Edgar Kauffmann, Jr. (New York, 1970), p. 165.

36. This information, as well as other biographical data to follow, is taken from the *Dictionary of American Biography (DAB)*, unless otherwise noted.

37. Arthur Gilman, "The Hancock House and its Founder," *Atlantic Monthly*, XI (1863), 692-707.

38. Quoted in Gilman, pp. 699, 703, and in Fiske Kimball, *Domestic Architecture of the American Colonies and of the Early Republic* (New York, 1966), p. 268.

39. "Description of the Seat of John Hancock," *Massachusetts Magazine*, I (July, 1789).

40. See Samuel Eliot Morison, *Harrison Gray Otis, 1765-1848: The Urbane Federalist* (Boston, 1969), pp. 75-79.

41. *Collections of the Massachusetts Historical Society*, LXXI, (1914), 131-37; quoted in Kimball, pp. 98-99.

42. Henry Bradshaw Fearon, *A Narrative of a Journey of 5000 Miles. . . .* (London, 1818), p. 113.

43. Henry Adams, *The Education of Henry Adams* (New York, 1931), pp. 10-11.

44. *DAB*, and see Kimball, p. 285; Kimball believes Derby house was not begun until after the death of Elias Hasket Derby, but was undertaken immediately after his death by his son, Ezekiel Hersey Derby.

45. Carter Letters vii-viii, 60-61, 63-64; quoted in R. V. Coleman, *Liberty and Property* (New York, 1959), p. 284.

46. Coleman, pp. 391-94; and see Kimball, p. 284.

47. Lorenzo Sabine, *Biographical Sketches of Loyalists of the American Revolution*, 2 vols. (Boston, 1864).

48. *Documents, post.*, IV, 251; quoted in *DAB*.

49. Charles Woodmason, in *Gentleman's Magazine* (1753); quoted in Wayne Andrews, *Architecture, Ambition and Americans* (New York, 1964), p. 25.

50. Quoted in Andrews, p. 33.

51. Alexis de Tocqueville, *Journey to America* (New Haven, Conn., 1960), pp. 19-20.

52. Ellen Susan Bulfinch, *Life and Letters of Charles Bulfinch* (Boston, 1896), pp. 75-76; quoted in Harold Kirker, *The Architecture of Charles Bulfinch* (Cambridge, Mass., 1969), p. 119.

Chapter Two

1. *New York Magazine*, II (1791), 246-47.

2. *Massachusetts Magazine*, IV (1792), 594-95.

3. *Massachusetts Magazine*, IV (1792), 650-51.

4. Shubael Bell, "An Account of the Town of Boston Written in 1817," *Bostonian Society Publications*, III (1919), 24-25; quoted in Charles Kirker, *The Architecture of Charles Bulfinch* (Cambridge, Mass., 1969), p. 49.

5. Anna Ticknor, *Memoir of Samuel Eliot* (Boston, 1869), p. 15; "Diary of Nathaniel Cutting," p. 63; both quoted in Kirker, p. 45.

6. "Reflections: *On Viewing the Seat of* Jos. Barrell, *Esq.*," *Massachusetts Magazine*, VI (1794), 693-94.

7. "The Progress of the Arts," *Massachusetts Magazine*, I (1789), 240.

8. Thomas Jefferson, *Notes on the State of Virginia* [1781-1782] (New York, 1964), pp. 146-47.

9. *Voyages de M. le Marquis de Chastellux dans l'Amérique septentroniale*, 2 vols., Paris, 1784; quoted in Merrill D. Peterson, ed., *Thomas Jefferson, A Profile* (New York, 1967), p. 223.

10. "Remarks on the Progress and Present State of the Fine Arts in the United States," *Analectic Magazine*, VI (1815), 369, 373-74.

11. James Fenimore Cooper, *The Pioneers*, [1823] (New York, n.d.), pp. 31-34.

12. James Fenimore Cooper, *Home as Found* [1838] (New York, 1893?), pp. 128-29, 151.

13. Timothy Dwight, *Travels in New England and New York* [1821], ed. Barbara Miller Solomon (Cambridge, Mass., 1969), Volume I of 4, p. 82.

14. Dwight, pp. 163, 266.
15. Dwight, pp. 155-56.
16. Dwight, pp. 307, 323-24.
17. Dwight, pp. 317-18.
18. Dwight, pp. 335-36.
19. Dwight, pp. 346-47.
20. Dwight, p. 333.
21. "Remarks on the Progress. . . .", p. 373.
22. "Domestic Architecture," *New England Magazine*, II (1832), 34-35.
23. Michel-Guillaume [Hector St. John] de Crevecoeur, *Letters from an American Farmer* [1782] (New York, 1951), pp. 23, 34-35.
24. Crevecoeur, pp. 24-25, 40.
25. Crevecoeur, p. 47.
26. James Fenimore Cooper, *Notions of the Americans*, 2 vols. (Philadelphia, 1828), I, 117.
27. From the *Mémoires* of the Marshal Count de Rochambeau; included in Rufus Wilmot Griswold, *The Republican Court* [1854] (New York, 1867), p. 433.
28. Alexis de Tocqueville, *Journey to America* [1835] (New Haven, Conn., 1960), pp. 332, 136.
29. David Thomas, *Travels through the Western Country in the Summer of 1816.* . . . (Auburn, New York, 1819), pp. 5, 82, 143.
30. Washington Irving, *A History of New York . . . by Diedrich Knickerbocker* [1809] (New York, 1884), pp. 123-34.
31. "Domestic Architecture," pp. 32-33.
32. Michel-Guillaume de Crevecoeur, *Eighteenth Century Travels in Pennsylvania and New York*, Percy G. Adams, trans. and ed., (Lexington, Ky., 1961), pp. 5-6.
33. Washington Irving, et. al., *Salmagundi* [1807] (Philadelphia, 1871), pp. 127-28.
34. Cooper, *Notions*, II, 149.
35. Irving, *Salmagundi*, p. 269.
36. Tocqueville, p. 182.
37. Cooper, *Pioneers*, p. 401.
38. Charles Brockden Brown, *Arthur Mervyn, or Memoirs of the Year 1793*, Vol. II of *Charles Brockden Brown's Novels*, reprint of David McKay edition of 1887 (Port Washington, N.Y., 1963), pp. 47-48.
39. Griswold, p. 166.
40. Griswold, p. 115.
41. Griswold, p. 255.
42. Henry David Thoreau, *Walden and Civil Disobedience*, ed. Owen Thomas (New York, 1966), p. 7.
43. Thoreau, pp. 26-27.
44. Thoreau, pp. 23, 31.
45. Thoreau, pp. 31-32.
46. Thoreau, pp. 30-31.
47. Thoreau, pp. 19-21.
48. Nathaniel Hawthorne, *The House of the Seven Gables*, ed. Seymour Gross (New York, 1967), p. 27.
49. Hawthorne, pp. 263, 261, 260.
50. Hawthorne, pp. 183-84.

51. Hawthorne, pp. 72, 136, 141.
52. Hawthorne, pp. 307, 314-15.
53. Thoreau, p. 20.

Chapter Three

1. Asher Benjamin, *The American Builder's Companion; or a System of Architecture.* . . . [1806], reprint of the 6th ed. (New York, 1969), p. 24.
2. Minard Lafever, *The Modern Builder's Guide* [1833] (New York, 1969), pp. 80-81.
3. A. J. Downing, *The Architecture of Country Houses* [1850] (New York, 1969), p. 23.
4. Downing, pp. xix-xx.
5. Downing, pp. 1, 3.
6. Downing, pp. 22-23.
7. Downing, pp. 25, 35, 26.
8. Downing, p. 27.
9. Downing, p. 264.
10. Downing, p. 35.
11. Downing, p. 40.
12. Downing, p. 71.
13. Downing, p. 97.
14. Downing, pp. 136-37.
15. Downing, pp. 138-39.
16. Downing, p. 138.
17. Downing, pp. 257-58.
18. Downing, p. 259.
19. Downing, p. 263.
20. Downing, pp. 266-67.
21. Downing, p. 268.
22. Downing, pp. 269-70.
23. Downing, pp. 270-279.
24. Downing, pp. 353-63.
25. Downing, pp. 72-78.
26. Downing, pp. 333-38.
27. Calvert Vaux, "Hints for Country House Builders," *Harper's Monthly*, XI (1855), 763-778; reprinted in *Villas and Cottages* [1864] (New York, 1970), pp. 346-48.
28. Vaux, pp. 123-28.
29. Vaux, p. ix.
30. Vaux, pp. xi-xii.
31. Vaux, pp. 28-29.
32. Vaux, pp. 39-40.
33. Vaux, pp. 47-48.
34. Vaux, pp. 37.
35. Lewis F. Allen, *Rural Architecture.* . . . (New York, 1852), pp. 189-90.
36. Allen, p. xii.
37. Allen, p. xii.
38. Allen, p. 111.
39. Allen, p. 24.

40. Allen, pp. 167-68.
41. Allen, p. 133.
42. O. S. Fowler, *A Home for All; or, the Gravel Wall and Octagon Mode of Building* (New York, 1854), p. 1.
43. Fowler, pp. 11, 8.
44. Fowler, p. 9.
45. Fowler, p. 184.
46. Fowler, pp. 184-85.
47. Fowler, pp. 11-12.
48. Fowler, pp. 12-13.
49. Fowler, p. 13.
50. Fowler, p. iii.

Chapter Four

1. George L. Hersey, "Godey's Choice," *Journal of the Society of Architectural Historians*, XVIII (1959), 104-11.
2. *Godey's Ladies' Book*, XXXIV (1847), 307; XL (1850), 1; XXXIV (1847), 44-46.
3. *Godey's Ladies' Book*, LXXXVI (1873), 193, 288, 473; LXXXIX (1874), 382.
4. H. Hudson Holly, "Modern Dwellings: Their Construction Decoration, and Furniture," *Harper's Monthly*, LII (1875), 856, 859.
5. Holly, p. 864.
6. Henry Hudson Holly, *Modern Dwellings in Town and Country* (New York, 1875), p. 27.
7. Holly, "Modern Dwellings," *Harper's Monthly*, LIII (1876), 56; *Modern Dwellings*, pp. 129-33.
8. Bruce Price, "The Suburban House," *Scribner's Magazine*, VIII (1890), 18, 19.
9. John W. Root, "The City House in the West," *Scribner's Magazine*, VIII (1890), 433, 434.
10. "A Successful Boston Residence," *Architectural Record*, XVIII (1901), 173.
11. Harriet Sisson Gillespie, "The Practical Farmhouse of a Country Gentleman," *Architectural Record*, XXXVI (1914), 49, 50, 54.
12. John Beverley Robinson, "Architects' Houses," *Architectural Record*, III (1893-1894), 188.
13. Robinson, pp. 191, 192, 205.
14. Harold D. Eberlein, "Five Phases of the American Country House," *Architectural Record*, XXXVI (1914), 340.
15. Joy Wheeler Dow, *American Renaissance: A Review of Domestic Architecture* (New York, 1904), Plates VII & VIII.
16. Dow, p. 41.
17. Dow, p. 29.
18. Dow, pp. 18-19.
19. Dow, pp. 135, 167.
20. George E. Woodward and F. W. Woodward, *Woodward's Country Homes* (New York, 1865), pp. 24, 17-18.
21. *Frank Lloyd Wright, On Architecture*, ed. Frederick Gutheim (New York, 1941), p. 10.
22. Henry L. Wilson, *The Bungalow Book* (Los Angeles, Calif., 1908), pp. 22, 50, 81.

23. Gustav Stickley, *Craftsman Homes* (New York, 1909), p. 6.

24. Stickley, pp. 194-97.

25. Louis Sullivan, *Kindergarten Chats,* originally printed in fifty-two issues of *Interstate Architect and Builder,* 1901 (n. p., 1934), p. 134.

26. *The Testament of Stone: Themes of Idealism and Indignation, Writings of Louis Sullivan,* ed. Maurice English (Chicago, 1963), pp. 146-47.

27. Sullivan, in English, p. 109.

28. Sullivan, *Kindergarten Chats,* pp. 139-41.

29. Frank Lloyd Wright, from 1930 Princeton Lectures, in *The Future of Architecture* (New York, 1970), p. 88.

30. Frank Lloyd Wright, *Autobiography* (New York, 1943), p. 140.

31. Wright, *Autobiography,* p. 142.

32. Wright, *Autobiography,* p. 81.

33. Norris Kelly Smith, *Frank Lloyd Wright: A Study in Architectural Content* (Englewood Cliffs, N. J., 1966), p. 166. The contradictions in Wright's philosophy have been examined by Smith, who connects them with the paradoxes of traditional Christianity, with the necessities for both "binding and loosing," and he finds in different periods in Wright's life emphases on one or the other. Smith, furthermore, sees a kind of harmonic resolution for Wright in his achievement of both the Kaufmann House, the framework for the family of individuals seen as "natural, growing, changing, dynamic, free," and the Johnson Wax Building, which shelters a voluntary community engaged in a mutual endeavor. These represent, respectively, the New Eden and the New Jerusalem, in Smith's terms, "heaven as a garden and heaven as a strong city." Smith, pp. 162-63.

34. Frank Lloyd Wright, "In the Cause of Architecture," *Architectural Record,* XXIII (1908), 156.

35. Frank Lloyd Wright, from *An Organic Architecture: The Architecture of Democracy* (1939); in Gutheim, p. 249.

36. Frank Lloyd Wright, "In the Cause of Architecture, II," *Architectural Record,* XXXV (1914), p. 142; in Gutheim, p. 56.

37. Wright, *Autobiography,* p. 80.

38. Frank Lloyd Wright, remarks for the opening of the Usonian House at the Exhibit: Sixty Years of Living Architecture, The Work of Frank Lloyd Wright, at the Guggenheim Museum, New York, 1953; in Frank Lloyd Wright, *The Natural House* (New York, 1970), p. 106.

39. Wright, *The Natural House,* p. 123.

40. Wright, *The Natural House,* p. 167.

41. Wright, *The Natural House,* p. 188.

42. Wright, *The Future of Architecture,* p. 181.

43. Wright, *The Natural House,* pp. 134, 136.

44. Wright, *Autobiography,* pp. 168-69.

45. Wright, *The Natural House,* p. 39.

46. Wright, *Autobiography,* p. 168.

47. Wright, *The Natural House,* p. 44.

48. Wright, *Autobiography,* p. 325.

49. Frank Lloyd Wright, *When Democracy Builds* (Chicago, 1945), p. 126.

50. Wright, *The Natural House,* p. 68.

51. Wright, *The Natural House,* pp. 68-73.

52. Wright, *The Natural House,* pp. 80-81.

53. Wright, *The Natural House*, pp. 199, 208.
54. Wright, *The Natural House*, p. 78.
55. Wright, *The Natural House*, p. 85.
56. Frank Lloyd Wright, an address to The Association of Federal Architects, Washington, D. C., 1938; in Gutheim, p. 244.
57. Wright, *When Democracy Builds*, p. 21.
58. Frank Lloyd Wright, "In the Cause of Architecture," *Architectural Review*, XXIII (1908), 156.
59. Frank Lloyd Wright, from *An Organic Architecture: The Architecture of Democracy* (1939); in Gutheim, p. 249.
60. Wright, *When Democracy Builds*, p. 126.
61. Joseph A. Barry, "Frank Lloyd Wright: the man who liberated architecture," *House Beautiful* (November, 1955), 234, 241, 243.

Chapter Five

1. See Chapter One and Chapter Three.
2. *A Brief Description of Phil-Ellena* (Philadelphia, 1844).
3. Edward Strahan [Earl Shinn], *Mr. Vanderbilt's House and Collection*, 10 vols. (New York, 1883-1884), II, 54; I, v, vi.
4. Andy Logan, "That was New York: Double Darkness and Worst of All," *New Yorker*, XXXIV (Feb., 22, 1958), 104; Nathan Silver, *Lost New York* (New York, 1972), p. 123.
5. Quoted in Logan, p. 104.
6. Quoted in Logan, p. 104.
7. Allen Churchill, *The Upper Crust* (Englewood Cliffs, N. J., 1970), p. 141; Wayne Andrews, *The Vanderbilt Legend* (New York, 1941), pp. 266-67, 281.
8. Anna Cora Mowatt, *Fashion*, in A. H. Quinn, *Representative American Plays* (New York, 1953), pp. 284, 290, 288, 311.
9. "New-York Daguerrotyped: Private Residences," *Putnam's*, III (1854), 232, 214, 241, 247, 246.
10. A. Forbes and J. W. Greene, *The Rich Men of Massachusetts* (Boston, 1851), pp. iii, 76.
11. Edward Chase Kirkland, *Dream and Thought in the Business Community* (Chicago, 1964), pp. 35-36.
12. Theodore Dreiser, *Sister Carrie* (Cambridge, Mass., 1953), p. 100.
13. F. Spencer Baldwin, "Some Aspects of Luxury," *North American Review*, CLXVIII (1899), 156, 162.
14. E. L. Godkin, "The Expenditure of Rich Men," *Scribner's Magazine*, XX, (1896), 495-60.
15. Andrew Carnegie, "Wealth," *North American Review* CXLVIII (1889), 653.
16. Mariana Van Rensselaer "Recent Architecture in America," *Century*, XXXI, n.s. IX (1885-1886), 550, 555.
17. Russel Sturgis, "The City House; The East and South," *Scribner's Magazine*, VII (1890), 711.
18. Ida M. Tarbell, "John D. Rockefeller: A Character Study," *McClure's*, XXV (1905), 387.
19. Gustavus Myers, *History of Great American Fortunes* (New York, 1936), pp. 288, 334.

20. Harry W. Desmond and Herbert Croly, *Stately Homes in America* (New York, 1903), pp. 3, 279, 317, 525.

21. Desmond and Croly, pp. 86, 92.

22. Desmond and Croly, pp. 279, 3.

23. Desmond and Croly, p. 36.

24. Desmond and Croly, pp. 12, 317, 327, 323.

25. Desmond and Croly, pp. 279-80.

26. Desmond and Croly, pp. 281, 448, 458.

27. Mark Twain, *The Gilded Age*, 2 vols. in 1 (New York, 1915), pp. 1-2, 48, 238.

28. Frank Norris, *The Pit* (New York, 1924), pp. 169, 189-90, 313.

29. Henry B. Fuller, *With the Procession* (Chicago, 1965), pp. 206, 267.

30. Fuller, pp. 59, 60.

31. Harold Frederick, *The Damnation of Theron Ware* (Cambridge, Mass., 1960), pp. 87, 92, 95.

32. Richard Grant White, "Old New York and its Houses," *Century*, XXVI, n.s. IV (1883), 845, 852, 859.

33. Edith Wharton, *The Age of Innocence* (New York, 1962), pp. 31, 20, 21.

34. F. Scott Fitzgerald, *The Great Gatsby* (New York, 1953), pp. 5, 89.

35. William Faulkner, *The Mansion* (New York, 1959), pp. 156, 153.

36. Herbert Croly, "Architectural Response to Social Change," *Architectural Record*, LVIII (1925), 186-87.

37. John P. Marquand, *Point of No Return* (Boston, 1949), pp. 554, 558.

Chapter Six

1. James Fenimore Cooper, *Notions of the Americans* (Philadelphia, 1828), p. 143.

2. Alice Carey, *Clovernook, or Recollections of our Neighborhood in the West* (1853); quoted in Henry Nash Smith, *The Virgin Land* (New York, 1950), p. 269.

3. William T. Elsing, "Life in New York Tenement-Houses as Seen by a City Missionary," in *The Poor in Great Cities*, Robert A. Woods, et. al. (New York, 1895), p. 68.

4. Wendell Phillips, *The Labor Question* (1884), quoted in Stephen Thernstrom, *Poverty and Progress* (Cambridge, Mass., 1964), pp. 33-34.

5. Jacob Riis, *The Battle with the Slums* [1902] (New York, 1970), p. 7.

6. Alfred T. White, *Improved Dwellings for the Laboring Classes*, 3 pamphlets bound as 1 (New York, 1879, 1885), p. 20.

7. Robert Treat Paine, "Homes for the People," *American Journal of Social Sciences*, XV (1882), 119-20.

8. William Henry Bishop, *The House of the Merchant Prince* (Boston, 1883), p. 235.

9. For detailed reviews of public and private action against slum housing see Robert W. de Forest and Lawrence Veiller, eds., *The*

Tenement House Problem (New York, 1903); Edith Elmer Wood, *The Housing of the Unskilled Wage Earner* (New York, 1919), and *Recent Trends in American Housing* (New York, 1939); James Ford, *Slums and Housing* (Cambridge, Mass., 1936); Roy Lubove, *The Progressives and the Slums* (Pittsburgh, Pa., 1962); Lawrence M. Friedman, *Government and Slum Housing* (Chicago, 1968).

10. White, *passim*.

11. Helen Campbell, *The Problem of the Poor* (New York, 1882), pp. 113, 116.

12. E. R. Gould, "The Economics of Improved Housing," *Yale Review*, V (1896-1897), 8.

13. Louise E. Dew, "Money-Making Model Tenements," *The World's Work*, XV (1908), 9998-10004.

14. Frank Chouteau Brown, "The Low-Rental Apartment—An Economic Fallacy," *Architectural Record*, LVI (1924), 65-67; "Low Rental Housing: Suburban Type," *Architectural Record*, LVI (1924), 206-17.

15. T. Thomas, *The Working-Man's Cottage Architecture* (New York, 1848), pp. 46 ff.

16. "A Hundred Thousand Homes: How they were Paid for," *Scribner's Monthly*, XI (1875-1876), 477-79.

17. W. A. Linn, "Co-operative Home-Winning: Some Practical Results of Building Associations," *Scribner's Magazine*, VII (1890), 570-71, 576.

18. Erastus Wyman, "Hope of a Home," *North American Review*, CLVI (1893), 228-35.

19. Joseph Kirkland, "Among the Poor in Chicago," in *The Poor in Great Cities*, p. 213.

20. White, p. 4.

21. W. H. Tolman, "Half a Century of Improved Housing Effort, by the New York Association for Improving the Condition of the Poor," *Yale Review*, V (1896-1897), 296-97.

22. Kirkland, p. 200.

23. William H. Rideing, "Squatter Life in New York," *Harper's*, LXI (1880), 562-69.

24. Allan Forman, in *The American Magazine*, IX (1888), 46-52; quoted in James Ford, *Slums and Housing* (Cambridge, Mass., 1936), p. 174.

25. Kirkland, p. 198.

26. Margaret Byington, "The Family in a Typical Mill Town," *American Journal of Sociology*, XIV (1909), 648-59.

27. "Homes for Working Men," *Lend a Hand*, XII (1894), 99-106.

28. Charles Loring Brace, *The Dangerous Classes of New York* (New York, 1880), pp. ii, 50, 29.

29. Jacob Riis, *How the Other Half Lives* (New York, 1890), pp. 142, 162, 118.

30. Jacob Riis, *The Battle with the Slums*, p.7.

31. Robert W. de Forest, "Foreword," in Lawrence Veiller, *Housing Reform* (New York, 1910), p. 6.

32. Tolman, p. 301.

33. Brace, p. 29.

34. Josiah Strong, *The Challenge of the City* (New York, 1907), pp. 156-57.

35. Riis, *How the Other Half Lives*, pp. 13, 174.
36. E. R. L. Gould, "The Only Cure for Slums," *Forum,* XIX (1895), 500; quoted in Ford, p. 199.
37. Edith Elmer Wood, *The Housing of the Unskilled Wage Earner, America's Next Problem* (New York, 1919), p. 23.
38. William Dean Howells, *A Hazard of New Fortunes* (New York, 1960), pp. 158, 160-61.
39. Rev. E. C. Guild, "Home Comforts and Amusements," *Unitarian Review and Religious Magazine,* VIII (1877), 527, 526.
40. Thomas, p. 41.
41. White, p. 7.
42. Gould, "The Economics of Improved Housing," p. 19.
43. Wood, pp. 28, 9.
44. Jane Addams, "The Housing Problem in Chicago," *The Annals of the American Academy of Political and Social Science,* XX (1902), 102, 106.
45. Riis, *How the Other Half Lives*, pp. 12-13.
46. Jacob Riis, *The Children of the Tenements* (New York, 1903), p. 57.
47. Riis, *Children of the Tenements*, pp. 68-69.
48. Edith Wharton, *The House of Mirth*, ed. R. W. B. Lewis (Boston, 1962), pp. 308, 313.
49. Jack London, *Martin Eden* (Baltimore, Md., 1969), pp. 178-79.
50. Michael Gold, *Jews without Money* (New York, 1966), pp. 120-21, 118.
51. Stephen Crane, "Maggie: A Girl of the Streets," in *The Red Badge of Courage and other Writings,* ed. Richard Chase (Boston, 1960), pp. 4-6.
52. Richard Wright, *Native Son* (New York, 1966), pp. 7-12.
53. Willard Motley, *Knock on Any Door* (New York, 1950), pp. 17, 19, 512.
54. Lawrence M. Friedman, *Government and Slum Housing* (Chicago, 1968), p. 15.
55. February number, *Architectural Record,* LXXIX (1936), *passim.*
56. Blair Bolles, "Resettling America: Mr. Tugwell's Dream Cities of Utopia," *American Mercury,* XXXIX (1936), 337.
57. Carol Aronovici, *Housing the Masses* (New York, 1939), pp. 120-121.
58. Edith Elmer Wood, *Recent Trends in American Housing* (New York, 1931), pp. 283-84.
59. James Ford, in collaboration with Catherine Morrow and George N. Thompson, *Slums and Housing,* 2 vols. (Cambridge, Mass., 1936), I, 240, 485.
60. Aronovici, pp. 120-21.

Chapter Seven

1. John Sergeant quoted in C. A. Weslager, *The Log Cabin* (New York, 1969), p. 269.
2. Russell Sturgis, *A Dictionary of Architecture and Building, Biographical, Historical, and Descriptive,* 3 vols. (New York, 1902; repr. Detroit, 1966).

3. See Chapter Two, "Domestic Architecture," *New England Magazine*, II (1832), 35.

4. Harold Robert Shurtleff, *The Log Cabin Myth*, ed. and introd. Samuel Eliot Morison (Cambridge, Mass., 1939), p. 186.

5. Shurtleff, pp. 188-89, 194.

6. C. P. Dwyer, *The Immigrant Builder, or Practical Hints to Handy-Men, showing clearly how to Plan and Construct Dwellings in the Bush, on the Prairie, or Elsewhere, Cheaply and Well* (Philadelphia, 1872), p. 16.

7. See Chapter Two; Alexis de Tocqueville, *Journey to America* (New Haven, Conn., 1960), p. 332.

8. Frances Trollope, *Domestic Manners of the Americans* [1832], ed. Donald Smalley (New York, 1941), pp. 48-49.

9. Catherine Stewart, *New Homes in the West*, [1843] (Ann Arbor, Michigan, 1966), pp. 12-13.

10. Stewart, pp. 2, 128-29, 104.

11. Biographical information about Mrs. Kirkland from John Nerber's introduction to his 1953 edition of *A New Home*, [1839] (New York).

12. Kirkland, pp. 69, 79-80.

13. Kirkland, pp. 300, 304, 303.

14. A. B. Longstreet, *Georgia Scenes*, [1825], (New York, 1957), p. 4.

15. Joseph G. Baldwin, *The Flush Times of Alabama and Mississippi*, [1853], (New York, 1957), pp. 104, 183-84.

16. Kirkland, p. 308.

17. William Gilmore Simms, *The Yemassee*, [1835], ed. C. Hugh Holman (Boston, 1961), pp. 10-11.

18. Simms, p. 46.

19. William Gilmore Simms, *The Wigwam and the Cabin*, [1845] (Ridgewood, N. J., 1968), pp. 191, 83.

20. John Pendleton Kennedy, *Swallow Barn*, [1832] (Hafner, N. Y. 1962), p. 449.

21. Kennedy, p. 469.

22. Constance Fenimore Woolson, "The Ancient City," *Harper's*, L(1874-1875), 169.

23. From the Baltimore *Republican*, December 11, 1839; quoted in Weslager, p. 262.

24. Weslager, pp. 268, 273.

25. See Chapter One.

26. Weslager, pp. 262-63; John Drury, *Historic Midwest Houses* (Minneapolis, Minn., 1947), p. 31.

27. Weslager, p. 304.

28. Chesla Sherlock, *Homes of Famous Americans* (Des Moines, Iowa, 1926), p. 72.

29. Sherlock, pp. 78, 69.

30. Frederick G. Mather, "The Vagaries of Western Architecture," *Lippincott's*, XXXI (1883), 529-44.

31. John Burroughs, "House-Building," *Scribner's Monthly*, XI (1875-1876), pp. 333-35.

32. John Burroughs, *Signs and Seasons* (Boston, 1886); quoted in Lewis Mumford, ed., *Roots of Contemporary American Architecture* (New York, 1952), p. 289.

33. John Burroughs, "The Vanity of Big Houses," *Cosmopolitan,* XLI (1906), 89.

34. William Dean Howells; quoted in Russell Lynes, *The Domesticated Americans* (New York, 1962), p. 28.

35. William Nowlin, *The Bark Covered House, or Back in the Woods Again,* [1876] (Ann Arbor, Michigan, 1966), pp. 29-30, 212-13.

36. Hamlin Garland, *A Daughter of the Middle Border* (New York, 1929), p. viii.

37. Garland, pp. 280-81, 35, 101.

38. Garland, pp. 103, 167, 320.

39. Garland, p. 330.

40. "Real Conversations IV: A Dialogue between James Whitcombe Riley and Hamlin Garland," recorded by Mr. Garland, *McClure's,* II (1893-1894), 219-222.

41. Willa Cather, *O Pioneers!* (Boston, 1937), pp. 3, 17, 13, 65, 106, 72.

42. Elbert Hubbard, *Little Journeys to the Homes of Great Men,* 14 vols. (New York, 1916), III, 191-92.

Chapter Eight

1. Karl Baedeker, ed., *The United States* [1893] (New York, 1971), pp. 84, 91, 263.

2. Booth Tarkington, *The Magnificent Ambersons* (New York, 1921), pp. 439-40.

3. Samuel Eliot Morison, *Harrison Gray Otis, 1765-1848: The Urbane Federalist* (Boston, 1969), p. 147.

4. Morison, p. 148.

5. Morison, p. 148.

6. James Fenimore Cooper, *Notions of the Americans,* 2 vols. (Philadelphia, 1828), II, 186-88, 193-94.

7. "*The Homes of American Authors,*" review, *Putnam's,* I (Jan., 1853), 23.

8. *Homes of American Authors* (New York, 1853), pp. 267, 269.

9. Mrs. Martha J. Lamb, *The Homes of America* (New York, 1879), pp. 133-37.

10. Lamb, pp. 64-67.

11. Lamb, pp. 2, 148.

12. Lamb, pp. 49, 199.

13. Lamb, pp. 177, 181, 222-23.

14. Lamb, p. 256.

15. William Cullen Bryant, ed., *Picturesque America; or The Land We Live In,* 2 vols. (New York, 1872), II, 438; I, 361.

16. Bryant, II, 244, 553-55.

17. Bryant, I, 498-99.

18. Bryant, I, 255.

19. T. B. Aldrich, "An Old Town by the Sea," *Harper's,* XLIX (1874), 643, 642.

20. John W. Chadwick, "Marblehead," *Harper's,* XLIX (1874), 187.

21. Frank Mayer, "Old Baltimore and its Merchants," *Harper's*, LX (1879-1880), 176.

22. Elbert Hubbard, *Little Journeys to the Homes of Great Men*, 14 vols. (New York, 1916), III, 110.

23. Hubbard, III, 9, 69, 218.

24. Hubbard, XI, 364, 401, 216, 62, 376.

25. Hubbard, XI, 428.

26. Hubbard, XI, 428.

27. Hubbard, XI, 428.

28. Chesla C. Sherlock, *Homes of Famous Americans*, 2 vols. (Des Moines, Iowa, 1926), I, 32, 37.

29. Sherlock, I, 40, 37.

30. Sherlock, I, 93-94, 104.

31. John Drury, *Old Chicago Homes* (Chicago, 1941), p. 97; John Drury, *Historic Midwest Houses* (Minneapolis, Minnesota, 1947), p. 197; Irvin Haas, *America's Historic Houses and Restorations* (New York, 1966), p. 20.

32. Quoted in *A Brief Historical Sketch of Port Townsend, Washington*, by William D. Walsh (Port Townsend, Washington, n.d.), p. 24.

33. Walsh, p. 3.

The House as Property and Home

1. Max Lerner, *America as Civilization* (New York, 1957), p. 557.

2. Charles Eliot Norton, "The Lack of Old Homes in America," *Scribner's Magazine*, V (1899), 636-40.

3. J. Elliot Cabot, "Notes on Domestic Architecture," *Atlantic*, I (1857), 258-60.

4. Wilson Flagg, "Rural Architecture," *Atlantic*, XXXVII (1876), 430-32.

5. William Dean Howells, *The Rise of Silas Lapham* [1885] (New York, 1957), pp. 20, 8, 38-39, 171, 283-84, 303, 331.

6. Mildred Howells, ed., *Life in the Letters of William Dean Howells*, 3 vols. (New York, 1929), I, 363-64 (August 10, 1884); I, 365 (August 10, 1884); I, 365-66 (August 22, 1884).

7. Hamlin Garland, *A Daughter of the Middle Border* (New York, 1929), p. 330.

8. *The Love Letters of Mark Twain*, ed. Dixon Wecter (New York, 1949), p. 312 (March 20, 1895).

9. J. F. W. W[are] "The New England Home," *The Monthly Religious Magazine*, XXVI (1861), 431, 356.

10. Christopher Crowfield [Harriet Beecher Stowe], "House and Home Papers," *Atlantic*, XIII (1864), 356.

11. Mariana van Rensselaer, "The Development of American Homes," *Forum*, XII (1891-1892), 669.

12. See Chapter Four.

13. Catherine Beecher and Harriet Beecher Stowe, *The American Woman's Home* (New York, 1869), dedication.

14. Charlotte Perkins Gilman, *The Home, its Work and Influence* (New York, 1903), pp. 38, 53, 58-59, 292, 302.

15. Mrs. L. H. Harris, "The Future of the Home," *Independent*, LXI (1906), 788-98.

16. Mrs. Frederick Scholff, "The Home at the Basis of Civic, Social, and Moral Uplift," *Pedagogical Seminary*, XVI (1909), 473, 481.

17. Mrs. A. M. F. Annan, "The Country Seat," *Godey's*, XXVII (1843), 206.

18. Crowfield [Stowe], pp. 40-47.

19. William Dean Howells, *Letters of an Altrurian Traveller* [1893-1894] (Gainesville, Fla., 1961), p. 85.

20. Price Collier, "Home Life, English and American," *Forum*, XVII (1894), 346, 347.

21. Edith Wharton and Ogden Codman, Jr., *The Decoration of Houses* (New York and London, 1898), p. 183.

22. Anna McClure Shell, "The House," *Atlantic*, XCVIII (1906), 693-97.

23. Emily Post, *The Personality of a House* (New York, 1930), pp. 3, 65-66, 196, 197.

24. R. T. H. Halsey and Elizabeth Tower, *The Homes of our Ancestors* (Garden City, N.J., 1925), p. xxii.

25. Chelsa Sherlock, *Homes of Famous Americans*, 2 vols. (Des Moines, Iowa, 1926), pp. 69-70, 183, 192.

26. Louis Bromfield, *The Farm* (New York, 1933), pp. 53, 75, 42-43, 108, 118, 296, 344, 341, 310, 345.

27. Mary Ellen Chase, *Silas Crockett* (New York, 1935), pp. 246, 248, 260-62, 358, 393.

28. *Home Ownership, Income and Types of Dwellings*, Vol. IV of *The Reports of the President's Conference on Home Building and Home Ownership* (Washington, D. C. 1932), p. 2.

29. *Home Ownership*, pp. 163, 2, 30.

30. Herbert J. Gans, *The Levittowners* (New York, 1967), pp. 277-78.

31. "Iconography," in relation to American domestic architecture, is brilliantly discussed in *Learning from Las Vegas* as well as in the unpublished *Learning from Levittown*, by Virginia Carroll, Denise Scott Brown, and Robert Venturi. Stephen Azenour, of Venturi's architectural firm, has been kind enough to show me a copy of their manuscript and to allow me to see the fine photographs to be incorporated in the book.

Index